DRIP, DRIP, SOLD

DRIP, DRIP, SOLD

ULTIMATE GUIDE TO REAL ESTATE DRIP CAMPAIGNS

Barry Thomas

Atlanta, GA
RISING STAR BOOKS

Drip, Drip, Sold: Ultimate Guide to Real Estate Drip Campaigns
Copyright © 2024 Barry Thomas

All rights reserved.

No part of this book may be reproduced or transmitted in any form or by any means, electronic or mechanical, including photocopying, recording or by any information storage and retrieval system, without written permission from the publisher, except for the inclusion of brief quotations in a review.

Address inquiries to the publisher:

Rising Star Books
1415 Hwy 85 N
Suite 310-299
Fayetteville, GA 30214

Learn more about the author at: **www.dripdripsold.com**

ISBN: 979-8-9921034-0-3 (paperback)
ISBN: 979-8-9921034-1-0 (ebook)

Library of Congress Control Number: 2024953120

Cover and Editorial Design: Annette Purkiss Johnson, Allwrite Publishing
Proofreading: Kimberly Seals

Printed in the United States of America

DEDICATION

To my wife and life partner

CONTENTS

Preface, xvii
How to Use This Book, xviii

Chapter 1: Introduction to Real Estate Drip Campaigns 1
What Is a Drip Campaign and How Does It Work? 2
Why Are Drip Campaigns Important to Real Estate Agents? 3
What Are the Benefits of Using Drip Campaigns to Nurture Leads and
Build Relationships? 4
Measuring the Success of Real Estate Drip Campaigns 4
Overview of the Different Types of Real Estate Drip Campaigns 6
Some of These Campaigns Aren't Directly Related to Buying and
Selling a House 8

**Chapter 2: Essential Software for Implementing Drip
Campaigns** 9
Overview of Drip Campaign Software and the Transition to Marketing
Automation Platforms 9
A Closer Look at Marketing Automation Platforms for
Drip Campaigns 11
Comparative Analysis of Marketing Software 13
Importing Your Lead List into CRM from Various
Common Sources 14

Chapter 3: Creating A Dynamic Market Trend Analysis 17
Example Campaigns Utilizing Market Trend Analysis 17
Market Trend Analysis Template 18
Instructions for Setting Up a Dynamic Market Trend Analysis 19
Instructions for Setting Up a Manual Market Trend Analysis 19

Chapter 4: New Subscriber/Lead Sign-Up Drip Campaign . . 21
User Scenario: New Subscriber/Lead Sign-Up Drip Campaign. . . . 21
New Subscriber/Lead Sign-Up Drip Campaign Use Cases 22
Step-By-Step Guide and Templates 22
Comprehensive Homebuyers Guide Template 29
Comprehensive Home Seller's Guide Template. 36
Sample Overview of Local Market Trends and Updates Report. . . . 41

Tracking the Success of the New Lead Sign-Up Campaign 42

Tips For Customizing the New Lead Sign-Up Campaign 43

Conclusion 44

Chapter 5: New Listings Drip Campaign **45**

User Scenario: New Listings Drip Campaign 45

New Listings Use Cases 46

Step-By-Step Guide and Templates 47

Tracking The Success of The New Listings Campaign 54

Tips For Customizing New Listings Drip Campaign 55

Conclusion 56

Chapter 6: Invalid Phone Number Recovery Drip Campaign . **57**

User Scenario: Invalid Phone Number Recovery Drip Campaign. . . 57

Invalid Phone Number Recovery Drip Campaign Use Cases 58

Step-By-Step Guide and Templates 59

Tracking The Success of The Invalid Phone Number Recovery Drip
Campaign 63

Tips for Customizing the Invalid Phone Number Recovery Drip
Campaign 64

Conclusion 65

Chapter 7: Invalid Email Recovery Drip Campaign **67**

User Scenario: Invalid Email Recovery Drip Campaign 67

Invalid Email Recovery Drip Campaign Use Cases 68

Step-By-Step Guide and Template 69

Tracking The Success of The Invalid Email Recovery Drip Campaign 71

Tips for Customizing Invalid Email Recovery Drip Campaign 72

Conclusion 73

Chapter 8: First-time Homebuyer Drip Campaign. **75**

User Scenario: First-time Homebuyer Drip Campaign. 76

First-time Homebuyer Use Cases 76

First-time Homebuyer Use Case Conclusion 77

Step-By-Step Guide and Templates 78

Tracking The Success of The First-time Homebuyer Campaign . . . 85

Tips for Customizing The First-time Homebuyer Drip Campaign . . 86

Conclusion 87

Chapter 9: Referral Request Drip Campaign **89**

User Scenario: Referral Request Drip Campaign. 89

Referral Request Drip Campaign Use Cases 90
Step-By-Step Guide and Templates 91
Tracking the Success of the Referral Request Drip Campaign 94
Tips for Customizing the Referral Request Drip Campaign 95
Conclusion 96

Chapter 10: Open House Drip Campaign 97
User Scenario 1: Open House Drip Campaign 97
User Scenario 2: Open House Invitation Drip Campaign 98
Open House Drip Campaign Use Cases 98
Step-By-Step Guide and Templates 99
Tracking the Success of the Open House Drip Campaign 104
Tips For Customizing the Open House Drip Campaign 105
Conclusion 106

Chapter 11: Just Sold Drip Campaign 107
User Scenario: Just Sold Drip Campaign 107
Just Sold Drip Campaign Use Cases 108
Step-By-Step Guide and Templates 109
Tracking the Success of the Just Sold Drip Campaign 115
Tips For Customizing the Just Sold Campaign 116
Conclusion 117

Chapter 12: Home Maintenance Drip Campaign. 115
User Scenario: Home Maintenance Drip Campaign 115
Home Maintenance Drip Campaign Use Cases 116
Step-By-Step Guide and Templates 117
Tracking the Success of the Home Maintenance Drip Campaign . .124
Tips for Customizing the Home Maintenance Drip Campaign 126
Conclusion 127

Chapter 13: Holiday Greetings Drip Campaign. 129
User Scenario: Holiday Greetings Drip Campaign 129
Holiday Greetings Drip Campaign Use Cases 130
Step-By-Step Guide and Templates 131
Tracking the Success of the Holiday Greetings Drip Campaign . . .136
Tips for Customizing the Holiday Greetings Drip Campaign 136
Conclusion 137

Chapter 14: Market Update Drip Campaign 139
User Scenario: Market Update Drip Campaign. 139

What Is A Market Update Report? 140

How to Create a Market Update Report 140

Outline of a Market Report 141

Sample Market Report 142

Step-By-Step Guide and Templates 144

Tracking the Success of the Market Update Drip Campaign 148

Tips for Customizing the Market Update Drip Campaign 149

Conclusion 150

Chapter 15: Buyer Education Drip Campaign. 151

User Scenario: Buyer Education Drip Campaign. 151

Buyer Education Drip Campaign Use Cases 152

Step-By-Step Guide and Templates 153

Tracking the Success of the Buyer Education Drip Campaign 162

Tips for Customizing the Buyer Education Drip Campaign 163

Conclusion 164

Chapter 16: Seller Education Drip Campaign. 165

User Scenario: Seller Education Drip Campaign 165

Seller Education Drip Campaign Use Cases 166

Step-By-Step Guide and Templates 167

Tracking the Success of the Seller Education Drip Campaign 173

Tips for Customizing the Buyer Education Drip Campaign 175

Conclusion 176

Chapter 17: Mortgage Education/Updates Drip Campaign . . 179

User Scenario: Mortgage Education/Updates Drip Campaign 179

Mortgage Education/Updates Drip Campaign Use Cases 180

Step-By-Step Guide and Templates 181

Tracking the Success of the Mortgage Updates Drip Campaign . . .192

Tips for Customizing Mortgage Updates Drip Campaign 192

Conclusion 193

Chapter 18: Client Testimonial Drip Campaign 195

User Scenario: Client Testimonials Drip Campaign 196

Client Testimonials Drip Campaign Use Cases 196

Step-By-Step Guide and Templates Step 1 197

Tracking the Success of the Client Testimonials Drip Campaign . . .203

Tips for Customizing the Client Testimonials Drip Campaign 204

Conclusion 204

Chapter 19: Birthday Wishes Drip Campaign. 207

User Scenario: Birthday Wishes Drip Campaign 207

Birthday Wishes Drip Campaign Use Cases 208

Step-By-Step Guide and Templates 208

Tracking the Success of the Birthday Wishes Drip Campaign 210

Tips for Customizing the Birthday Wishes Drip Campaign 210

Conclusion 211

Chapter 20: Home Improvement Tips Drip Campaign 213

User Scenario: Home Improvement Tips Drip Campaign. 213

Home Improvement Drip Campaign Use Cases 214

Step-By-Step Guide and Templates 214

Tracking the Success of the Home Improvement Drip Campaign . .222

Tips for Customizing the Home Improvement Drip Campaign 223

Conclusion 224

Chapter 21: Test Drive the Neighborhood 225

User Scenario: Test Drive the Neighborhood Drip Campaign. 226

Test Drive the Neighborhood Drip Campaign Use Cases 226

Step-By-Step Guide and Templates 227

Tracking the Success of the Test Drive the Neighborhood Drip
Campaign 232

Tips for Customizing the Test Drive the Neighborhood Drip
Campaign 233

Conclusion 234

Chapter 22: Continued Client Care Drip Campaign 235

User Scenario: Continued Client Care: Post-Transaction Drip
Campaign 235

Post-Transaction Follow-Up Drip Campaign Use Cases 236

Step-By-Step Guide and Templates 237

Tracking the Success of the Post-Transaction Follow-Up Drip
Campaign 241

Tips for Customizing the Post-Transaction Follow-Up Drip
Campaign 243

Conclusion 244

Chapter 23: New Construction Drip Campaign 247

User Scenario: New Construction Drip Campaign 248

New Construction Drip Campaign Use Cases 248

xi

Step-By-Step Guide and Templates 250
Tracking the Success of the New Construction Drip Campaign . . .251
Tips for Customizing the New Construction Drip Campaign 253
Conclusion 255

Chapter 24: Agent Introduction Drip Campaign 257
User Scenario: Agent Introduction Drip Campaign 257
Agent Introduction Drip Campaign Use Cases 258
Step-By-Step Guide and Templates 258
Tracking the Success of the Agent Introduction Drip Campaign . . .263
Tips for Customizing the Agent Introduction Drip Campaign 264
Conclusion 265

Chapter 25: Area Guides Drip Campaign 267
User Scenario: Area Guides Drip Campaign 267
Area Guides Drip Campaign Use Cases 268
Step-By-Step Guide and Templates 269
Tracking the Success of the Area Guides Drip Campaign 272
Tips for Customizing the Area Guides Drip Campaign 274
Conclusion 274

Chapter 26: Holiday Gift Drip Campaign 275
User Scenario: Holiday Gift Guide Drip Campaign 275
Holiday Gift Guide Drip Campaign Use Cases 276
Step-By-Step Guide and Templates 277
Tracking the Success of the Holiday Gift Guide Drip Campaign . . .285
Tips for Customizing the Holiday Gift Drip Campaign 286
Conclusion 287

Chapter 27: Moving Day Checklist Drip Campaign 289
User Scenario: Moving Day Checklist Drip Campaign. 289
Moving Day Checklist Drip Campaign Use Cases 290
Step-By-Step Guide and Templates 291
Tracking the Success of the Moving Day Checklist Drip Campaign .295
Tips for Customizing the Moving Day Checklist Drip Campaign . . .296
Conclusion 298

Chapter 28: Rekindling Cold Leads Drip Campaign 299
User Scenario: Rekindling Cold Leads Drip Campaign 299
Rekindling Cold Leads Drip Campaign Use Cases 300
Step-By-Step Guide and Templates 300

Tracking the Success of the Rekindling Cold Leads Drip Campaign . 307

Tips for Customizing the Rekindling Cold Leads Drip Campaign . . 308

Conclusion 309

Chapter 29: Best Practices for Real Estate Drip Campaign . 311

Tips for Creating Effective Real Estate Drip Campaigns 311

Choosing the Right Type of Drip Campaign for Your Audience . . .313

How to Analyze and Adjust Your Drip Campaigns for Maximum

Effectiveness 315

Conclusion 317

Chapter 30: Lead Conversions in Drip Campaign 319

Understanding Lead Conversion 319

Strategies for Enhancing Lead Conversion 319

Measuring and Optimizing Lead Conversion 320

Conclusion 320

Chapter 31: The Role of AI in Crafting "Drip Drip Sold" . . . 321

AI's Contribution to the Book 321

Expanding the Role of AI in Real Estate: Insights from

"Drip Drip Sold" 322

Conclusion 324

Chapter 32: Navigating Legal and Ethical Guidelines 327

Disclaimer 328

Conclusion 329

Chapter 33: Conclusion: Power of Real Estate Drip Campaigns . 331

How to Use Real Estate Drip Campaigns to Build Relationships and

Close More Deals 332

Importance of Selecting the Right Type of Drip Campaign for

Your Business 333

Closing 334

Chapter 34: Glossary 335

PREFACE

My wife, Shacara, is a real estate agent and my business partner in Rising Star Properties. I wrote this book because, like many agents, she doesn't focus on digital marketing or building an online presence. I wanted to create a step-by-step guide that she could use to maintain her success. During the process of documenting what I do, I realized this guide could be a valuable resource for any real estate agent, which inspired me to turn it into a book.

In my years as an IT professional managing the digital marketing and business operations for our company, I've learned that closing a sale is about much more than offering a great deal or showcasing a home's finest features. Yes, location and amenities are important—but the real secret to success lies in marketing. My wife and I have built our company on this principle, discovering that the art of real estate is in creating meaningful connections with buyers long before they're ready to sign a contract.

The journey that led to Drip, Drip, Sold has been one of trial, error, and growth. I've learned how to "drip" market, reaching potential clients in small, steady ways that nurture leads over time. These "drips" go beyond advertising properties; they're about building relationships and fostering trust.

In this book, I share the strategies, tips, and tools that can help agents guide buyers to the right homes—sometimes before they even know they're ready—while maintaining relationships that yield significant referrals. My hope is that these insights provide you with both practical knowledge and a fresh perspective on what it truly takes to succeed in real estate. For me, it's been a journey of passion, patience, and persistence—one drip at a time.

~Barry Thomas

HOW TO USE THIS BOOK

Are you tired of struggling to convert leads and close deals in the highly competitive real estate industry? Look no further than Drip, Drip, Sold: The Ultimate Guide to Real Estate Drip Campaigns.

This comprehensive guide provides step-by-step instructions for creating and optimizing all types of drip campaigns, from new listings to referral requests and beyond. By mastering the power of automated marketing, you can nurture your leads over time, build trust and credibility, and stay top-of-mind with potential clients until they're ready to take the next step.

Using this book is incredibly simple and straightforward. Each chapter is dedicated to a specific drip campaign topic and provides easy-to-follow instructions along with customizable email/SMS templates for each step.

The templates are provided as a starting point, and you can easily personalize them to fit your specific needs and market. Just copy and paste the templates into your email or SMS marketing CRM software and edit them as necessary to make them more personal and appealing to your target audience.

It's important to note that each chapter can be used independently of the others, allowing you to choose which drip campaign topics to focus on based on your business goals and the needs of your leads.

To make the most out of this book, it's recommended that you use a marketing CRM software with email and SMS capabilities to automate your drip campaigns. Automation of these campaigns is by for their most effective use. By automating the process, the sales manager, broker and/or agent will be able to focus time on following up with leads, showing and selling homes and/or monitoring the success of marketing efforts.

Overall, this book is designed to help you convert leads into clients and solicit referrals through effective drip marketing campaigns. By following the simple instructions and customizing the templates provided, you can create campaigns that resonate with your audience and drive results for your business.

1

INTRODUCTION TO REAL ESTATE DRIP CAMPAIGNS

Imagine two real estate agents, Sarah and Mike, both competing for clients in the same neighborhood. Mike uses traditional methods—sporadic phone calls and occasional mailers—to follow up with leads. He often loses track of conversations or forgets to follow up at the right time.

Sarah, on the other hand, implements a drip campaign. When a potential buyer signs up on her website, they automatically receive a series of emails tailored to their interests—tips for buying in the area, market updates, and even personalized property recommendations. Over weeks, Sarah's consistent, relevant communication builds trust and keeps her leads engaged.

When one of those leads is ready to buy, they call Sarah, saying, "I feel like you've been helping me all along." Meanwhile, Mike is left wondering why his leads keep going cold. Sarah's drip campaign made all the difference by nurturing her clients and positioning her as the go-to expert.

With drip campaigns, you can convert more leads with less effort and cost, freeing up your time to focus on other aspects of your business. In today's competitive real estate market, it's more important than ever for agents to establish strong relationships with leads and clients. Drip campaigns are a powerful and cost-effective tool for nurturing real estate leads by delivering targeted, personalized communication consistently over time to guide them toward a transaction.

In this chapter, we'll explore the basics of real estate drip campaigns, including:

- What drip campaigns are and how do they work
- Why drip campaigns are important for real estate agents

- The benefits of using drip campaigns to nurture leads and build relationships
- An overview of the types of drip campaigns that real estate agents can use
- How to measure the success of drip campaigns

By understanding the basics of drip campaigns and how they can benefit your real estate business, you can start building stronger relationships with your leads and closing more deals. So, let's dive in and discover the power of real estate drip campaigns.

What Is a Drip Campaign and How Does It Work?

A drip campaign in real estate is an automated marketing strategy that involves sending a series of targeted, personalized messages to leads or clients over time. These messages are designed to provide valuable information, build relationships, and keep the real estate agent top-of-mind with potential clients.

Drip campaigns typically involve a series of pre-written emails, SMS messages, or other forms of communication that are sent out at predetermined intervals. The content of these messages can vary depending on the goals of the campaign and the preferences of the target audience, but typically they will focus on providing information that is relevant and valuable to the lead or client.

The key to a successful drip campaign is providing personalized, relevant communication to the target audience. The messages should be tailored to the interests and needs of the leads or clients, providing information that is useful and valuable to them. By doing so, the real estate agent can build trust and establish credibility with the target audience, increasing the likelihood that they will ultimately choose to work with the agent.

Effectively managing and implementing drip campaigns requires the use of powerful software tools that automate and streamline the process. These tools not only save time and effort but also help you better organize your leads, personalize your messages, and monitor your campaign's performance. Once a drip campaign is set up, it can continue to send out regular messages to leads or clients without requiring ongoing effort from the agent. This saves time and resources while still providing valuable communication to the target audience.

Overall, drip campaigns are a powerful tool for real estate agents looking to build strong relationships with leads and clients and generate more business over time. By providing regular, targeted communication that is relevant and valuable to the target audience, drip campaigns can help agents stand out in a crowded market and win more business over time.

Why Are Drip Campaigns Important to Real Estate Agents?

Drip campaigns are an important tool for real estate agents looking to build relationships with leads and clients. By providing targeted, personalized communication over time, drip campaigns can establish trust, build credibility, and generate more business.

One key benefit of drip campaigns is the ability to nurture leads over time. By providing regular updates, valuable information, and personalized communication, real estate agents can keep potential clients engaged and interested in their services. This helps establish trust and build relationships, increasing the likelihood that leads will ultimately choose to work with the agent.

Another important benefit of drip campaigns is the ability to stay top-of-mind with leads and clients. By providing regular, relevant communication, agents can ensure that their brand is remembered when potential clients are ready to make a move. This can help agents stand out in a crowded market and win more business over time.

Drip campaigns are also a cost-effective way to generate leads and build relationships over time. Once a campaign is set up, it can continue to provide value to the target audience without requiring additional resources from the agent.

Overall, drip campaigns offer a powerful tool for real estate agents looking to build relationships, establish credibility, and generate more business over time. By providing targeted, personalized communication that is relevant and valuable to the target audience, drip campaigns can help agents stand out in a crowded market and win more business over time.

What Are the Benefits of Using Drip Campaigns to Nurture Leads And Build Relationships?

Drip campaigns are an essential marketing tool for real estate agents. By providing targeted and regular communication to leads and clients, drip campaigns can establish trust, build relationships, and generate more business over time.

One of the key advantages of drip campaigns is that they enable agents to nurture leads over time. By providing personalized communication, regular updates, and valuable information, agents can keep potential clients engaged and interested in their services. This can establish trust, build relationships, and increase the likelihood that leads will ultimately choose to work with the agent.

Drip campaigns also allow agents to save time and resources by automating communication. Once set up, campaigns can continue to provide regular communication to leads and clients without requiring ongoing effort from the agent. This can help agents focus on other important tasks while still staying top-of-mind with potential clients.

In addition, drip campaigns can be used to promote targeted events such as open houses, seminars, and community events. By providing personalized communication and invitations to these events, agents can generate interest and attendance from potential clients. This can help agents build relationships and establish themselves as experts in their local market.

Furthermore, drip campaigns can help agents re-engage paid leads and increase lead conversion. By providing personalized communication and valuable information to paid leads, agents can increase the likelihood of conversion and generate more business over time.

Overall, drip campaigns are a powerful tool for real estate agents looking to generate more business and build strong relationships with their leads and clients. By providing regular, targeted communication that is relevant and valuable to the target audience, drip campaigns can help agents stand out in a competitive market and win more business over time.

Measuring the Success of Real Estate Drip Campaigns

Understanding the effectiveness of your real estate drip campaigns is crucial in fine-tuning your strategies and achieving the best results. This

INTRODUCTION TO REAL ESTATE DRIP CAMPAIGNS

chapter will delve into the key metrics and performance indicators you should monitor to measure the success of your drip campaigns.

1. Open Rates are a primary metric. They indicate how many recipients are opening your emails. A high open rate generally suggests that your subject lines are compelling and your sender reputation is strong. In the real estate context, an open rate above the industry average (which varies but is often around 20-25%) is a good sign that your campaigns are resonating with your audience.

2. Another essential metric is Click-Through Rates (CTR). This measures the percentage of email recipients who clicked on one or more links contained in your email. CTR helps you understand how engaging your email content is. For real estate drip campaigns, a CTR higher than the industry average (typically around 2-3%) can indicate effective content that prompts action from your leads.

3. Conversion Rates are key to determining the actual effectiveness of your campaigns in driving your primary goal, whether it's property inquiries, appointment bookings, or actual sales. Tracking how many leads from your drip campaigns take the desired action can give you a clear picture of your ROI. An effective drip campaign should see a gradual increase in conversion rates over time.

4. Lead Growth Rate is also crucial. This metric tracks the growth in your leads over time, showing how well your drip campaigns are working in attracting new leads. A steady increase in leads suggests successful ongoing engagement and audience growth.

5. Monitoring the Bounce Rate is vital. It tells you the percentage of your emails that weren't delivered. A high bounce rate could indicate problems with your email list or issues with email deliverability.

6. Engagement Over Time measures how leads interact with your emails over a certain period. Are they losing interest, or is their engagement increasing? This long-term view can inform adjustments in campaign frequency and content to maintain or heighten interest.

By closely monitoring these metrics, you can gain valuable insights into your campaign's performance, allowing you to make data-driven decisions and continually refine your approach for maximum impact.

Overview of the Different Types of Real Estate Drip Campaigns

In this comprehensive guide, we present a variety of drip campaigns tailored for real estate agents, each designed to nurture leads, build lasting relationships, and offer valuable, targeted communication. Below is a list of 25 distinct drip campaigns, with each chapter in this book dedicated to providing detailed instructions on crafting and implementing these diverse campaigns effectively.

1. New Subscriber/Lead Sign-Up Drip Campaign: Engage and welcome new leads with tailored information and resources as they begin their real estate journey.

2. New Listings Drip Campaign: Regularly update subscribers with the latest property listings that match their search criteria.

3. Invalid Phone Number Recovery Drip Campaign: Reconnect with leads by rectifying and updating incorrect phone number details.

4. Invalid Email Recovery Drip Campaign: Address and correct inaccurate email information to maintain seamless communication.

5. First-time Homebuyer Drip Campaign: Offer guidance and support to first-time homebuyers navigating the property market.

6. Referral Request Drip Campaign: Encourage satisfied clients to refer friends and family, expanding your network.

7. Open House Drip Campaign: Promote upcoming open houses and engage potential attendees with compelling reasons to visit.

8. Just Sold Drip Campaign: Share recent successful sales to showcase your expertise and market knowledge.

9. Home Maintenance Drip Campaign: Provide valuable home maintenance tips and advice to homeowners.

10. Holiday Greetings Drip Campaign: Foster goodwill and stay connected with clients during festive seasons.

11. Market Update Drip Campaign: Keep clients informed with the latest market trends and insights.
12. Buyer Education Drip Campaign: Educate potential buyers about the nuances of purchasing property.
13. Seller Education Drip Campaign: Guide sellers through best practices for listing and selling their property.
14. Mortgage Education/Updates Drip Campaign: Share updates and essential information about mortgage options and market changes.
15. Client Testimonials Drip Campaign: Build credibility and trust by sharing positive experiences of past clients.
16. Birthday Wishes Drip Campaign: Personalize client relationships with celebratory messages on their birthdays.
17. Home Improvement Tips Drip Campaign: Offer creative and practical tips for home improvement and renovation.
18. Test Drive the Neighborhood Drip Campaign: Introduce potential buyers to neighborhoods with insights and local highlights.
19. Continued Client Care: Post-Transaction and Home Purchase Anniversary Drip Campaign: Maintain post-sale relationships with clients through regular check-ins and anniversary acknowledgments.
20. New Construction Drip Campaign: Update clients about new construction projects and developments in their area of interest.
21. Agent Introduction Drip Campaign: Introduce yourself to new leads and establish your professional background and services.
22. Area Guides Drip Campaign: Provide insightful guides about various neighborhoods, including amenities, lifestyle, and demographics.
23. Holiday Gift Guide Drip Campaign: Offer creative gift ideas during holiday seasons, enhancing client engagement.
24. Moving Day Checklist Drip Campaign: Assist clients with organized and stress-free moving through detailed checklists and tips.

25. Rekindling Cold Leads Drip Campaign: Revive interest and engagement from leads that have gone cold.

Each campaign chapter in this book will delve into the specific strategies, templates, and best practices necessary to execute these campaigns successfully, ensuring you have the tools to build trust, establish relationships, and drive business growth effectively. Let's explore the dynamic world of real estate drip campaigns and master the art of engaging communication.

Some of These Campaigns Aren't Directly Related to Buying and Selling a House

That's true! While some of the drip campaigns in this book may not be directly related to buying and selling a house, they are all designed to nurture relationships with potential clients and maintain connections with past clients. The ultimate goal of these campaigns is to establish your agency as a trusted and knowledgeable resource for all things related to real estate, which can lead to increased business in the long run.

For example, a home maintenance drip campaign may not directly result in a home sale, but it can help establish your agency as a helpful and informative resource for homeowners. By providing valuable tips and information on how to maintain a home, you can demonstrate your expertise in the field and build trust with your audience.

Similarly, a referral request drip campaign may not directly lead to a home sale, but it can help increase your agency's visibility and reputation within your community. By asking satisfied clients to refer their friends and family to your agency, you can tap into new potential clients who may not have otherwise heard of your agency.

Ultimately, the key to success with these types of drip campaigns is to provide value to your audience and establish yourself as a helpful and trustworthy resource in the real estate industry. While the campaigns may not always result in immediate sales, they can help build relationships and establish a strong foundation for future business opportunities.

2

ESSENTIAL SOFTWARE FOR IMPLEMENTING DRIP CAMPAIGNS

In this chapter, we delve into the various software tools that are crucial for implementing effective drip campaigns in the real estate industry. From email marketing and CRM systems to SMS marketing and analytics tools, we will explore the features and benefits of each category of software. Additionally, we will discuss the increasing role of marketing automation platforms, which offer comprehensive solutions by combining the functionality of individual software tools. By understanding the importance of these tools and learning how to leverage them in your drip campaigns, you will be better equipped to engage and nurture your leads, ultimately leading to increased conversions and business success.

Disclaimer: Please note that software tools and platforms mentioned in this chapter are subject to change over time. Some tools may be discontinued, rebranded, or replaced with new solutions. It is recommended to regularly review and update your software choices to ensure they meet your current needs and to stay informed about the latest developments in marketing technology.

Overview of Drip Campaign Software and the Transition to Marketing Automation Platforms

Drip campaigns play a crucial role in engaging and nurturing leads in the real estate industry. To implement these campaigns effectively, real estate professionals require various software tools, including email marketing, CRM, SMS marketing, and analytics solutions. As marketing strategies become more sophisticated, marketing automation platforms have emerged as comprehensive solutions that combine the functionality of these individual tools. In this section, we will provide a brief overview of the different software tools used in drip campaigns and discuss how marketing automation platforms have evolved to streamline marketing efforts.

- **Email Marketing Software**: Email marketing software enables real estate professionals to create, send, and track personalized emails as part of their drip campaigns. These tools offer features such as email templates, list segmentation, and automation capabilities. Popular email marketing software options include Mailchimp, Constant Contact, Sendinblue, and GetResponse.

- **Customer Relationship Management** (CRM) Software: CRM software helps manage and organize leads, tracking their preferences and interactions throughout the sales process. This is crucial for implementing targeted and personalized drip campaigns. Some widely used CRM platforms in the real estate industry include Salesforce, Zoho CRM, HubSpot CRM, and Pipedrive.

- **SMS Marketing Software**: SMS marketing software allows real estate professionals to send targeted text messages to leads as part of their drip campaigns. These tools automate message sending, track responses, and manage contact lists. Popular SMS marketing tools include Twilio, EZ Texting, SimpleTexting, and SlickText.

- **Analytics and Reporting Tools**: Monitoring the success of drip campaigns is essential for making data-driven adjustments and optimizing marketing strategies. Analytics and reporting tools provide insights into campaign performance, tracking key metrics, and identifying areas for improvement. Some popular analytics tools include Google Analytics, Kissmetrics, Mixpanel, and Tableau.

- **Marketing Automation Platforms**: As marketing efforts become more complex and interconnected, marketing automation platforms have emerged as comprehensive solutions that consolidate the functionality of email marketing, CRM, SMS marketing, and analytics tools. These platforms are designed to streamline marketing efforts, automate processes, and provide a unified view of lead management and campaign performance. Some well-known marketing automation platforms include HubSpot, Marketo, ActiveCampaign, and Keap (formerly Infusionsoft).

A Closer Look at Marketing Automation Platforms for Drip Campaigns

In the evolving landscape of digital marketing, real estate professionals require a diverse range of software tools to implement and manage their drip campaigns effectively. As marketing strategies become more sophisticated, marketing automation platforms have emerged as comprehensive solutions that consolidate the features of email marketing, CRM, SMS marketing, and analytics tools. Adopting a marketing automation platform can help real estate professionals streamline their marketing efforts, save time, and create more personalized and targeted campaigns, ultimately leading to higher conversion rates and business success.

Marketing automation platforms are powerful tools that enable real estate professionals to manage and implement drip campaigns effectively. By offering a comprehensive solution that combines email marketing, CRM, and SMS marketing capabilities, these platforms help streamline marketing efforts, save time, and ensure personalized communication with leads. In this section, we will explore some popular marketing automation platforms and discuss their features and benefits for real estate drip campaigns.

HubSpot:

HubSpot is an all-in-one inbound marketing, sales, and CRM platform that offers a wide range of tools for managing and automating your drip campaigns. Key features include:

- Email marketing with personalization, segmentation, and scheduling options
- Built-in CRM for managing leads and tracking interactions
- SMS marketing integration through third-party providers
- Marketing analytics and reporting for tracking campaign performance
- Landing page creation and lead capture forms
- Integration with various real estate software and tools

Marketo:

Marketo is a powerful marketing automation platform that provides a comprehensive suite of features for implementing and managing real estate drip campaigns. Key features include:

- Email marketing with advanced personalization, segmentation, and A/B testing capabilities
- Lead management and nurturing with integrated CRM functionality
- SMS marketing integration through third-party providers
- Customizable marketing analytics and reporting tools
- Landing page and form builders
- Integration with a wide range of software and tools for the real estate industry

ActiveCampaign:

ActiveCampaign is a marketing automation platform that focuses on email marketing, CRM, and marketing automation. It offers a variety of features to help real estate professionals run successful drip campaigns. Key features include:

- Email marketing with advanced personalization, segmentation, and automation options
- Built-in CRM for managing leads, deals, and sales pipelines
- SMS marketing integration through third-party providers
- Marketing analytics and reporting for tracking campaign performance
- Landing page and lead capture form builders
- Integration with various real estate tools and software

Keap (formerly Infusionsoft):

Keap is a marketing automation and CRM platform designed for small businesses, including real estate professionals. It offers a range of features to help you manage and automate your drip campaigns. Key features include:

- Email marketing with personalization, segmentation, and automation capabilities
- Integrated CRM for managing leads and tracking interactions
- SMS marketing integration through third-party providers

- Marketing analytics and reporting tools for measuring campaign success
- Landing page creation and lead capture forms
- Integration with a variety of real estate tools and software

Marketing automation platforms are essential tools for real estate professionals looking to implement effective and efficient drip campaigns. By combining email marketing, CRM, and SMS marketing capabilities, these platforms help streamline marketing efforts and ensure personalized communication with leads. Investing in a marketing automation platform that best suits your needs and integrates with your existing real estate tools will help you maximize the success of your drip campaigns and ultimately convert more cold leads into clients.

Comparative Analysis of Marketing Software

1. Email Marketing Software:
   - Examples: Mailchimp, Constant Contact, Sendinblue, GetResponse.
   - Features: Template designs, list segmentation, automation capabilities.
   - Pros and Cons: User-friendly for beginners, cost-effective; however, may have limitations in advanced automation and integration.
2. CRM Systems:
   - Examples: Salesforce, Zoho CRM, HubSpot.
   - Features: Lead management, interaction tracking, personalized drip campaign implementation.
   - Pros and Cons: Comprehensive client data management, enhances personalized marketing; can be expensive and require training.
3. SMS Marketing Tools:
   - Examples: Twilio, EZ Texting, SimpleTexting.
   - Features: Automated text message campaigns, response tracking, contact list management.

- Pros and Cons: Direct and immediate communication; however, limited content space and requires adherence to strict regulations.

4. Analytics and Reporting Tools:
- Examples: Google Analytics, Kissmetrics, Mixpanel.
- Features: Campaign performance tracking, key metrics analysis, insights into lead behavior.
- Pros and Cons: Invaluable for data-driven decisions; can be complex to understand and require analytical skills.

5. Marketing Automation Platforms:
- Examples: Marketo, ActiveCampaign, Keap.
- Features: Integration of email, CRM, SMS, analytics into a single platform.
- Pros and Cons: Streamlines marketing efforts, saves time; however, it can be expensive and may have more features than necessary for smaller businesses.
- Guidance for Real Estate Professionals: The choice of software should be aligned with the size of the business, budget, marketing goals, and technical expertise. For example, small agencies or individual agents may prefer cost-effective, easy-to-use email marketing software, while larger firms might benefit from comprehensive CRM and marketing automation platforms.

Understanding and selecting the right software tools is critical for the success of real estate drip campaigns. This comparative analysis aims to guide real estate professionals in making informed decisions to enhance their marketing strategies and achieve better lead engagement and conversion.

Importing Your Lead List into CRM from Various Common Sources

Before starting your drip campaigns, it is crucial to have an organized and up-to-date lead list. Many real estate professionals gather leads from various sources, such as website forms, open house sign-ins, and third-party lead providers. Importing your leads from these sources into your CRM system will help you manage and track your contacts more efficiently, allowing for targeted and personalized drip campaigns. In this section, we will discuss the process of importing leads from common sources into your CRM system.

Importing Leads from Website Forms:

Website forms are a popular method for capturing leads who express interest in your services or properties. Most CRM systems provide integration options with popular website form tools, such as Wufoo, JotForm, and Typeform. To import leads from these tools:

- Connect your form tool to your CRM using built-in integrations or third-party connectors like Zapier.
- Set up a workflow to automatically import new submissions into your CRM.
- Map form fields to corresponding CRM fields to ensure data consistency.

Importing Leads from Open House Sign-Ins:

Open house sign-ins can be an excellent source of leads. To import these leads into your CRM:

- Use a digital sign-in sheet app, such as Spacio or Open Home Pro, to collect visitor information.
- Export the list of attendees as a CSV or Excel file.
- Import the file into your CRM, mapping the columns to corresponding CRM fields.

Importing Leads from Third-Party Lead Providers:

Many real estate professionals purchase leads from third-party providers, such as Zillow, Trulia, and Realtor.com. To import these leads into your CRM:

- Export your leads from the provider's platform as a CSV or Excel file.
- Import the file into your CRM, mapping the columns to corresponding CRM fields.
- Apply appropriate tags or lead sources in your CRM to track the origin of your leads.

Importing Leads from Social Media:

Social media platforms, such as Facebook and LinkedIn, can also be valuable sources of leads. To import leads from social media into your CRM:

- Use built-in CRM integrations, if available, to connect your CRM with social media platforms.
- Alternatively, use third-party tools like Zapier to create automated workflows that import new leads from social media into your CRM.
- Ensure that appropriate tags or lead sources are applied in your CRM to track lead origin.

Importing your lead list into your CRM system is a crucial step in organizing and managing your contacts for effective drip campaigns. By consolidating leads from various sources and ensuring data consistency, you can create targeted and personalized campaigns that cater to each lead's unique needs and preferences. Taking the time to properly import and manage your leads will help you build stronger relationships and ultimately increase conversions and business success.

3

CREATING A DYNAMIC MARKET TREND ANALYSIS

Creating a Dynamic Market Trend Analysis is an essential strategy for real estate professionals looking to integrate real-time, relevant market data into their various drip campaigns. This chapter provides a comprehensive guide on developing an automated market analysis that dynamically updates with the latest trends, property values, and other critical market indicators. Such analysis is a powerful tool for agents to demonstrate their expertise, keep clients informed, and make data-driven decisions.

Example Campaigns Utilizing Market Trend Analysis

Drip campaigns leveraging market trend analysis keep leads engaged by delivering timely updates on local housing trends, price fluctuations, and buyer/seller activity. These insights position agents as knowledgeable experts while helping clients make informed decisions about entering or navigating the market.

- New Listing Alerts: Incorporate market trends to provide context on pricing and market conditions surrounding new listings.
- Monthly Market Updates: Send regular updates to clients about their local real estate market, including trends in prices, inventory levels, and buyer demand.
- Investment Opportunities: For clients interested in real estate investments, showing market trends can help them identify lucrative opportunities.
- Post-Transaction Follow-Up: Keep in touch with past clients by providing them with valuable insights into how their investment is performing in the current market.

When and Why to Use Market Trend Analysis

When:

- Launching a new property listing.
- During routine communication with potential buyers and sellers.
- When providing consultation to investors.

Why:

- To establish credibility and expertise in the real estate market.
- To provide clients with up-to-date information that can guide their decision-making process.
- To offer a personalized and value-added service that differentiates you from competitors.

Market Trend Analysis Template

Subject: [Your Area] Real Estate Market Trends Update

Dear [Client's Name],

As your dedicated real estate expert, I'm committed to keeping you informed about the latest trends in the [Your Area] market. Here's what's happening this month:

- Average Home Prices: [Auto-updated Figure]
- Recent Sales Trends: [Auto-updated Figure]
- Current Inventory Levels: [Auto-updated Figure]

These figures indicate [Brief Analysis Based on Data].

If you're considering buying, selling, or just curious about your property's value in the current market, let's connect to discuss how these trends can impact your real estate goals.

Best regards,

[Your Name]

[Contact Information]

CREATING A DYNAMIC MARKET TREND ANALYSIS

Instructions for Setting Up a Dynamic Market Trend Analysis

1. Choose the Right Platform: Select an email marketing platform or CRM software that supports API integrations with real estate databases like Zillow, Realtor.com, or local MLS systems.
2. Set Up API Integration: Connect your chosen platform with the real estate database. Configure the integration to pull in the latest market data (home prices, sales trends, etc.).
3. Create Your Email Template: Design an email template with placeholders for dynamic data. Ensure the template aligns with your branding and is visually appealing.
4. Automate Data Updates: Set up automation rules to update the market data in your email template regularly. Test the automation to ensure data is pulling correctly and updating as expected.
5. Launch and Monitor: Send out your first automated market trend analysis. Monitor open rates, click-through rates, and client feedback for further customization.

By following these steps, you'll be able to offer clients valuable, real-time insights into the real estate market, enhancing your reputation as a knowledgeable and tech-savvy real estate professional.

Instructions for Setting Up a Manual Market Trend Analysis

1. Collect Market Data: Regularly gather the latest market data manually from reliable sources such as Zillow, Realtor.com, local MLS systems, or real estate market reports. Focus on key metrics such as home prices, sales trends, inventory levels, and days on market.
2. Organize Data: Use a spreadsheet or database to organize the collected data. Ensure the data is accurately recorded and updated regularly to reflect the latest market trends.
3. Create Your Email Template: Design an email template in your email marketing platform. Insert placeholders where you will manually input the latest market data. Ensure the template aligns with your branding and is visually appealing.

4. Update Data in the Template: Manually input the latest market data into the email template at regular intervals (e.g., weekly or monthly). Double-check the accuracy of the data before sending.
5. Send and Monitor: Send out your manually updated market trend analysis emails to your clients. Monitor open rates, click-through rates, and client feedback to gauge the effectiveness of your communications and make adjustments as necessary.

By following these steps, you can provide clients with valuable, up-to-date market insights even without automation. This approach ensures you maintain regular communication with your clients, reinforcing your expertise and commitment to keeping them informed.

4

NEW SUBSCRIBER/LEAD SIGN-UP DRIP CAMPAIGN

Welcoming and nurturing new leads is crucial for real estate professionals, and an effective New Subscriber/Lead Sign-Up Drip Campaign can help you achieve this goal. In this chapter, we will provide a step-by-step guide for creating and executing a New Subscriber/Lead Sign-Up Drip Campaign that builds trust, shares valuable resources, and lays the groundwork for a long-term relationship with your audience. By following this guide, you can ensure your new leads receive a warm welcome and are well on their way to becoming clients.

User Scenario: New Subscriber/Lead Sign-Up Drip Campaign

Jennifer, a dedicated real estate agent, has been receiving a high volume of new leads on her website, but converting them into clients has been challenging. To tackle this, Jennifer implements a New Subscriber/Lead Sign-Up Drip Campaign designed to nurture these leads and build trust.

The campaign sends a series of well-timed communications, starting with a warm welcome email, followed by valuable resources like a Comprehensive Guide for Home Buyers and updates about new listings. Jennifer also offers personalized assistance and educational content, positioning herself as a knowledgeable and supportive resource.

By systematically engaging her leads, Jennifer keeps them interested, builds strong relationships, and demonstrates her commitment to their home-buying journey. This structured approach results in higher conversion rates, transforming more leads into satisfied clients. Implementing this drip campaign can help you achieve the same success in your real estate business.

New Subscriber/Lead Sign-Up Drip Campaign Use Cases

A New Subscriber/Lead Sign-Up Drip Campaign is essential for real estate professionals to welcome and nurture new leads who have expressed interest in their services. This type of campaign is designed to introduce your brand, share valuable resources, and establish trust with your new leads. By understanding the use cases for this campaign, you can better tailor your communications to meet the specific needs of your audience.

Use Cases for the New Subscriber/Lead Sign-Up Drip Campaign:

- When a new lead signs up for your newsletter or expresses interest in your services.
- When a new lead requests information or a consultation.
- When a new lead attends an open house or registers for a webinar.

Understanding the various use cases for a New Subscriber/Lead Sign-Up Drip Campaign will help you create more targeted and relevant communications. By addressing the specific needs of your audience, you can effectively build trust, share valuable resources, and ultimately convert new leads into clients.

Step-By-Step Guide and Templates

Step 1:

Send a welcome email on day 1 with a subject line "Welcome to [Agency Name] - Your Real Estate Journey Starts Here!"

Step 1 Email Template:

Subject: Welcome to [Agency Name] - Your Real Estate Journey Starts Here!

Dear [Subscriber],

Thank you for signing up with [Agency Name]! We're excited to help you with your real estate journey. As a dedicated team of real estate professionals, we're here to provide exceptional service and support to our clients.

NEW SUBSCRIBER/LEAD SIGN-UP DRIP CAMPAIGN

To get started, we've put together a series of valuable resources that can help you navigate the real estate market. In the coming days, you'll receive:

A comprehensive guide for home buyers.

A complete guide for home sellers.

An overview of local market trends and updates.

We'll also keep you informed about the latest news, market trends, and exclusive listings in the area. If you have any questions or would like to schedule a consultation, please don't hesitate to reply to this email.

Best regards,

[Agent Name]

[Agency Name]

Personalization:

Update the Subscriber Name and body with your agency name where appropriate.

Recommended Agent Action:

Monitor responses and follow up with leads who express interest in your services or request more information.

Step 2:

Send an SMS message on day 3 to check in with the new lead and see if they have any questions or concerns about the home buying process. Offer a helpful resource, such as the Comprehensive Guide for Home Buyers, to add value and build trust with the lead.

Step 2 SMS Template:

Hi [Subscriber], this is [Agent Name] with [Agency Name]. I hope you found the market trends update I sent you useful. If you have any questions or concerns about the home buying process, please don't hesitate to reach out. Here's a Comprehensive Guide for Home Buyers that I think you'll find helpful: [Link].

Have a great day!

Personalization:

Update the Subscriber Name and body with your links and phone numbers where appropriate.

Recommended Agent Action:

Monitor the engagement with the Comprehensive Guide for Home Buyers and follow up with a phone call or email for subscribers who show interest or have questions about the guide or the home buying process. Be prepared to offer personalized advice and support to help them navigate their journey.

Step 3:

Send an email on day 7 to share a link to an automatically updated list of new listings in the lead's desired area and price range. Encourage them to explore the listings and offer assistance in scheduling showings or answering questions about the properties.

Step 3 Email Template:

Subject: New Listings in [Your Area] - Find Your Dream Home Today!
Dear [Subscriber],

I hope you're finding the resources I've shared with you helpful in your home search. To keep you up-to date with the latest properties on the market, I've prepared a link to an automatically updated list of new listings in [Your Area] that match your criteria and budget:

[Link to Auto-Updated Property Listings]

Feel free to explore these properties at your convenience. If you're interested in scheduling a showing or have any questions about the properties, please don't hesitate to reach out. I'm here to help make your home search as seamless and enjoyable as possible.

Best regards,

[Agent Signature Block with Contact Information]

Personalization:

Update the Subscriber Name and body with your links and phone numbers where appropriate.

Recommended Agent Action:

Track the engagement with the auto-updated property listings and follow up with a phone call or email for subscribers who show interest or have questions about the properties. Be prepared to offer insights on the local market, schedule showings, and provide personalized support to help them find their dream home.

Step 4:

Send an SMS message on day 12 to touch base with the lead and offer personalized assistance in their home search. Use this opportunity to build rapport and gather more information about their specific needs and preferences.

Step 4 SMS Template:

Hi [Subscriber], this is [Agent Name] with [Agency Name]. I hope you've been finding the resources and listings I've shared helpful. If you have any questions or would like personalized assistance in your home search, please don't hesitate to reach out. I'm here to help you find your dream home. Have a great day!

Personalization:

Update the Subscriber Name and body with your links and phone numbers where appropriate.

Recommended Agent Action:

Follow up with a phone call or email for subscribers who respond to the SMS or express interest in receiving personalized assistance. Use the opportunity to learn more about their needs and preferences, and offer tailored solutions and property suggestions. Make sure to update their contact information and preferences in your CRM system to ensure you are reaching out to them in the most effective way possible.

Step 5:

Send an email on day 18 to offer helpful content about the home buying process. This could include a blog post or video on topics such as negotiating offers, understanding inspections, or preparing for closing. Providing valuable content will help establish you as a trusted resource and keep the lead engaged in their home search.

Step 5 Email Template:

Subject: Essential Tips for a Successful Home Buying Experience
Dear [Subscriber],

Buying a home can be an exciting and sometimes challenging process. As your real estate agent, my goal is to provide you with the knowledge and support you need to make informed decisions. I thought you might find this [Blog Post/Video] helpful, as it covers some essential tips for a successful home buying experience:

[Link to Blog Post/Video]

I hope you find this information useful! Remember, I'm always here to help you with any questions or concerns you may have during your home search journey. Please don't hesitate to reach out if you need assistance or guidance.

Best regards,

[Agent Signature Block with Contact Information]

Personalization:

Update the Subscriber Name and body with your links and phone numbers where appropriate.

Recommended Agent Action:

Monitor the engagement with the content provided and follow up with a phone call or email for subscribers who show interest or have questions about the home buying process. Offer personalized support and guidance to help them navigate the journey towards finding their dream home.

Step 6:

Send an SMS message on day 24 to check in with the lead and remind them that you're available to answer any questions or provide assistance. Offering your support can help strengthen your relationship with the lead and encourage them to reach out for help in their home search journey.

Step 6 SMS Template:

Hi [Subscriber], it's [Agent Name] from [Agency Name] checking in. I hope the resources and information I've shared have been helpful. Remember, I'm here to answer any questions you may have or assist you in your home search. If you need anything, just let me know. Have a great day!

Personalization:

Update the Subscriber Name and body with your links and phone numbers where appropriate.

Recommended Agent Action:

Follow up with a phone call or email for subscribers who respond to the SMS or express interest in receiving additional support. Offer personalized assistance based on their needs and preferences, and continue to provide valuable resources and information to help them in their home search journey. Make sure to update their contact information and preferences in your CRM system to ensure you are reaching out to them in the most effective way possible.

Step 7:

Send an email on day 30 to share a valuable resource that helps leads further understand the home buying process or provides tips on finding the right property. This demonstrates your commitment to helping your leads find the perfect home and keeps them engaged in their home search journey.

An example of a resource for this email could be a blog post or a downloadable PDF guide that provides tips and insights on finding the perfect home. The resource could cover topics such as:

1. How to determine your "must-haves" and "nice-to-haves" in a property
2. The importance of location and neighborhood research
3. Tips for attending open houses and property viewings
4. How to make the most of online property search tools
5. The role of a real estate agent in helping you find the right home

By sharing this type of resource, you are offering valuable information that can help leads make informed decisions during their home search process. It also demonstrates your expertise in the field and your commitment to providing support and guidance throughout their journey.

Step 7 Email Template:

Subject: Top Tips for Finding Your Perfect Home
Dear [Subscriber],

As your real estate agent, I want to make sure you have all the tools and information necessary to make your home search as seamless as possible. To help you in your journey, I'm sharing a resource that provides top tips for finding the perfect home:

[Link to Resource]

I hope you find this information helpful! Remember, I'm here to guide and support you throughout your home search process. If you have any questions or need assistance, please don't hesitate to reach out.

Best regards,
[Agent Signature Block with Contact Information]

Personalization:

Update the Subscriber Name and body with your links and phone numbers where appropriate.

Recommended Agent Action:

Monitor the engagement with the content provided and follow up with a phone call or email for subscribers who show interest or have questions about finding the perfect home. Offer personalized support and guidance to help them navigate their home search journey.

Comprehensive Homebuyers Guide Template

The Ultimate Home Buyer's Guide: From Dream to Reality

Welcome to the Ultimate Home Buyer's Guide! This comprehensive guide is designed to help you navigate the process of finding and purchasing your dream home. Our goal is to provide you with the knowledge, tools, and confidence to make informed decisions and turn your dreams into reality. We understand that buying a home is a significant milestone, and we're here to support you every step of the way.

Preparing for Your Home Search

These are the steps to preparing for your new or next home:

Assessing Your Needs and Wants

Before beginning your home search, it's important to identify your needs and wants in a new home. Make a list of essential features, such as the number of bedrooms, bathrooms, and desired location. Then, consider additional features that would be nice to have but not mandatory, such as a large backyard or updated kitchen. Having a clear understanding of your priorities will help you and your real estate agent focus your search on properties that truly meet your criteria.

Determining Your Budget

Establishing a realistic budget is crucial to avoid financial stress during the home buying process. To determine your budget, consider factors such as your monthly income, expenses, and any outstanding debts. It's also important to account for additional costs associated with buying a home, such as the down payment, closing costs, and moving expenses. A mortgage calculator can be a helpful tool to estimate your monthly mortgage payment based on your budget, down payment, and interest rate.

Importance of Pre-Approval

Obtaining a mortgage pre-approval is an essential step in the home buying process. A pre-approval is a written commitment from a lender, indicating the loan amount and terms they are willing to offer you based on your financial situation. Having a pre-approval in hand demonstrates to sellers that you are a serious and qualified buyer, giving you a competitive advantage in the market. Additionally, a pre-approval can help you stay within your budget and streamline the mortgage application process once you find your dream home.

Choosing the Right Real Estate Agent

A knowledgeable and experienced real estate agent can be an invaluable asset during your home search. They will help you navigate the market, identify suitable properties, and provide expert guidance throughout the entire process. When selecting an agent, consider factors such as their experience in your desired area, communication style, and availability. Don't hesitate to interview multiple agents to find the one that best aligns with your needs and preferences. Remember, your agent will be your advocate and partner in this journey, so it's important to choose someone you trust and feel comfortable working with.

The Home Search Process

Online Property Search Tools

The internet has revolutionized the way people search for homes. Online property search tools, such as Zillow, Trulia, and Realtor.com, allow you to browse available listings based on your criteria, view photos, and access detailed property information. Additionally, your real estate agent can provide you with access to the Multiple Listing Service (MLS), which contains the most up-to-date and accurate information on properties for sale. By utilizing these online resources, you can save time and effort in your home search while staying informed about new listings that meet your needs.

Open Houses and Private Showings

Attending open houses and scheduling private showings are essential for getting a true feel for a property. Open houses offer an opportunity to tour homes without the pressure of making an appointment, while private showings allow for a more in-depth, personalized experience. Your real estate agent can help you schedule showings and provide valuable insights during your visits. Be prepared to take notes, ask questions, and evaluate each property based on your needs and preferences.

Evaluating Potential Homes

As you tour properties, it's crucial to evaluate each home objectively. Consider factors such as the property's condition, layout, and potential for future growth. Additionally, take note of the neighborhood, local amenities, and any potential drawbacks, such as noise or traffic. While it's important to keep your emotional response in check, trust your instincts if a home feels right or wrong for you. Your real estate agent can also provide guidance on a property's potential value, market trends, and any concerns you may have.

The Role of Your Real Estate Agent

During the home search process, your real estate agent plays a vital role in helping you find the perfect property. They will use their knowledge of the local market and your preferences to identify suitable listings, schedule showings, and provide expert advice. Your agent will also be your advocate in the negotiation process, working to ensure you get the best possible deal on your new home. By maintaining open communication and a strong working relationship with your agent, you can streamline your home search and increase your chances of success.

Making an Offer and Negotiating

Understanding Market Value

Before making an offer on a property, it's important to understand its market value. This is the price at which similar homes in the same area have recently sold. Your real estate agent can provide you with a comparative market analysis (CMA) to help you determine a fair offer price based on comparable sales, current market conditions, and the specific features of the property. By basing your offer on market value, you increase your chances of being taken seriously by the seller and ultimately having your offer accepted.

Preparing a Competitive Offer

In a competitive real estate market, it's essential to make your offer stand out. To prepare a competitive offer, consider factors such as the seller's motivation, the property's condition, and any competing offers. Your real estate agent can provide guidance on how to structure your offer to appeal to the seller, which may include offering a higher price, providing a larger down payment, or minimizing contingencies. It's also a good idea to include a pre-approval letter from your lender to demonstrate your financial readiness to purchase the property.

Negotiation Strategies

The negotiation process can be complex and requires a combination of research, strategy, and effective communication. Your real estate agent will be your advocate during negotiations, working to ensure you get the best possible deal on your new home. Some negotiation strategies may include presenting a strong initial offer, being open to counteroffers, and being flexible on closing dates or other terms. It's important to maintain a level-headed and objective approach throughout the negotiation process to maximize your chances of success.

Contingencies and Conditions

Contingencies and conditions are clauses in your offer that protect you as the buyer by allowing you to cancel the contract under specific circumstances. Common contingencies include a satisfactory home inspection, obtaining financing, and the sale of your current home. It's essential to carefully consider the contingencies you include in your offer, as they can impact the strength of your offer and the likelihood of the seller accepting it. Your real estate agent can help you determine which contingencies are necessary and advise you on how to balance protecting your interests with presenting an appealing offer to the seller.

Navigating the Closing Process

The Role of Escrow, Title Companies, and Closing Attorneys

Escrow and title companies play a crucial role in the closing process by ensuring a smooth and secure transfer of property ownership. The escrow company acts as a neutral third party, holding funds and documents related to the transaction until all conditions have been met, including the collection of earnest money, which is a deposit made by the buyer to demonstrate their serious intent to purchase the property. The title company conducts a title search to confirm that the seller has a clear and marketable title to the property and provides title insurance to protect against potential claims or issues with the property's title. In some states, the closing attorney assumes the roles of both the escrow and title companies. The closing attorney collects and holds earnest money, oversees the legal aspects of the closing, ensures that all documents are properly prepared and executed, coordinates the final settlement, resolves any last-minute legal issues, and ensures that the property transfer adheres to all applicable laws and regulations. By conducting the title search, managing the disbursement of funds, and confirming that all contractual obligations are met, the closing attorney helps facilitate a smooth and legally sound transaction.

Home Inspections and Appraisals

A home inspection is an essential step in the home buying process, as it allows you to identify any potential issues or necessary repairs before closing. It's important to hire a qualified and experienced home inspector to conduct a thorough inspection of the property. If any issues are uncovered during the inspection, you can negotiate with the seller to address them or adjust the purchase price accordingly.

An appraisal is required by your lender to determine the fair market value of the property and ensure the loan amount is appropriate. If the appraisal comes in lower than the agreed-upon purchase price, you may need to renegotiate the terms of the sale or make up the difference with additional funds.

Securing Financing

Securing financing for your new home is a critical step in the closing process. It's important to work closely with your lender to provide any necessary documentation and ensure your loan is approved in a timely manner. Be prepared to provide financial statements, tax returns, and other documentation to support your loan application. Stay in close communication with your lender throughout the process, as delays in financing can impact your closing date and the overall success of your home purchase.

Closing Costs and Final Walk-Through

Closing costs are the fees and expenses associated with finalizing your home purchase, such as loan origination fees, title insurance, and escrow fees. These costs typically amount to 2-5% of the purchase price and are paid at closing. It's important to review your closing disclosure, a document provided by your lender, to ensure all costs are accurate and understand your financial responsibilities at closing.

Before the closing, you will have the opportunity to conduct a final walk-through of the property to confirm that all agreed-upon repairs have been made and the property is in the same condition as when you made the offer. If any issues are discovered during the final walk-through, address them with your real estate agent and the seller before closing.

By understanding the various aspects of the closing process and working closely with your real estate agent, lender, and other professionals involved, you can ensure a smooth and successful conclusion to your home buying journey.

Moving In and Beyond

Preparing for Your Move

Once you've successfully closed on your new home, it's time to prepare for the move. Start by creating a moving timeline and checklist to help you stay organized and on track. Sort through your belongings and decide what to keep, donate, or discard. Obtain packing supplies, such as boxes, packing paper, and bubble wrap, and begin packing non-essential items well in advance. Hiring a reputable moving company or enlisting the help of friends and family can make the moving process more manageable. Be sure to notify important parties, such as your employer, bank, and post office, of your change of address.

Setting Up Utilities and Services

Before moving into your new home, it's essential to set up utilities and services, including electricity, water, gas, internet, and cable. Research providers in your area and schedule appointments for installation or service transfers as needed. Additionally, consider setting up trash and recycling services and any other necessary home services, such as landscaping or pest control.

Home Maintenance Tips

Proper home maintenance is crucial for protecting your investment and ensuring your new home remains in good condition. Create a home maintenance schedule that includes tasks such as changing air filters, cleaning gutters, and checking smoke alarms. Stay vigilant for any signs of potential issues, such as leaks, pests, or structural problems, and address them promptly. Regular maintenance not only helps to prevent costly repairs but also keeps your home safe and comfortable.

Building a Long-Term Relationship with Your Agent

Your real estate agent can continue to be a valuable resource even after you've moved into your new home. Maintain a relationship with your agent, as they can provide guidance on home improvements, market trends, and potential future real estate transactions. Additionally, your agent can be a great source of referrals for local service providers, such as contractors, landscapers, and other professionals. A long-term relationship with your agent ensures that you have a trusted advisor to rely on for all your real estate needs.

By following these tips and working closely with your real estate agent, you can successfully navigate the entire home buying process, from searching for the perfect property to settling into your new home and beyond.

Conclusion

Thank you for choosing our Ultimate Home Buyer's Guide to help you on your journey to homeownership. We understand that the process can be complex, but with the right support and guidance, you can confidently move forward. Our team at [Agency Name] is dedicated to making your home buying experience as smooth and enjoyable as possible. If you have any questions or would like to discuss your home buying needs, please don't hesitate to reach out. We're here to help you make your dream home a reality!

Personalization of the Comprehensive Home Buyers Guide

Update the guide with your agency name where appropriate. Consider adding your logo, images, or graphics to make it more visually appealing and enhance your brand identity. You can also include links to relevant resources, blog posts, or articles that you or your agency have published.

Comprehensive Home Seller's Guide Template

The Ultimate Home Sellers's Guide: From Listing to Closing

Welcome to the Ultimate Home Seller's Guide! This comprehensive guide is designed to help you navigate the process of selling your home. Our goal is to provide you with the knowledge, tools, and confidence to make informed decisions and turn your selling experience into a successful and smooth process. We understand that selling a home is a significant milestone, and we're here to support you every step of the way.

Preparing to Sell Your Home

Assessing Your Selling Goals: Before listing your home, it's essential to clarify your selling goals. Determine your desired timeline for selling, your financial objectives, and any specific conditions you need to meet. Understanding your priorities will help you and your real estate agent develop a strategic plan for selling your home.

Pricing Your Home Correctly: Setting the right price is crucial for attracting buyers and achieving a successful sale. Conduct a comparative market analysis (CMA) to evaluate the prices of similar homes in your area.

Your real estate agent can provide valuable insights and help you determine a competitive and realistic listing price.

Enhancing Curb Appeal: First impressions matter, and enhancing your home's curb appeal can significantly impact potential buyers' perception. Consider simple improvements such as landscaping, fresh paint, and clean windows to make your home more inviting. Your real estate agent can offer specific recommendations tailored to your property.

Staging Your Home: Staging your home involves arranging furniture and decor to showcase the property's best features and create an inviting atmosphere. A well-staged home can help buyers visualize themselves living in the space. Consider hiring a professional stager or working with your real estate agent to stage your home effectively.

Making Necessary Repairs: Address any visible repairs or maintenance issues before listing your home. Fixing leaky faucets, repairing broken fixtures, and ensuring all systems are in working order can prevent potential buyers from being deterred by minor issues. A pre-listing home inspection can help identify areas that need attention.

Listing Your Home

Choosing the Right Real Estate Agent: A knowledgeable and experienced real estate agent is invaluable in the selling process. They will help you price your home, market it effectively, and navigate negotiations. When selecting an agent, consider their experience, track record, and familiarity with your local market. Interview multiple agents to find the best fit for your needs.

Professional Photography and Videography: High-quality photos and videos are essential for attracting buyers online. Professional photography can highlight your home's best features and create a strong first impression. Additionally, consider virtual tours or drone footage to provide a comprehensive view of your property.

Crafting a Compelling Listing Description: A well-written listing description can capture buyers' interest and provide essential information about your home. Highlight unique features, recent upgrades, and key selling points. Be honest and accurate in your description to set realistic expectations for potential buyers.

Marketing Your Home: Effective marketing is critical to reaching a wide audience of potential buyers. Your real estate agent will use various channels, including online listings, social media, email campaigns, and open houses, to promote your home. Additionally, consider traditional methods such as yard signs and print advertisements.

Showing Your Home

Preparing for Showings: Keep your home clean and clutter-free to make it appealing to buyers during showings. Consider temporarily storing personal items and excess furniture to create a spacious and neutral environment. Your real estate agent can provide tips on how to prepare your home for showings.

Open Houses and Private Showings: Open houses and private showings allow potential buyers to tour your home and envision themselves living there. Be flexible with scheduling and try to accommodate as many showings as possible. Your real estate agent will manage the logistics and provide valuable feedback after each showing.

Addressing Buyer Questions and Concerns: Be prepared to answer questions and address any concerns that buyers may have. Providing accurate information and being transparent about your home's condition can build trust and confidence. Your real estate agent can assist in handling inquiries and negotiations.

Receiving Offers and Negotiating

Reviewing Offers: When you receive offers, carefully review the terms and conditions with your real estate agent. Consider factors such as the offer price, contingencies, and closing timeline. Your agent will help you evaluate each offer and determine which one aligns best with your goals.

Negotiation Strategies: Negotiating the terms of the sale requires skill and strategy. Your real estate agent will represent your interests and work to achieve the best possible outcome. Be prepared to make counter-offers and consider various aspects of the deal beyond the price, such as contingencies and closing dates.

Contingencies and Conditions: Contingencies are clauses in the purchase agreement that must be met for the sale to proceed. Common contingencies include home inspections, financing, and appraisals. Understand the contingencies in each offer and how they may impact the sale. Your real estate agent can guide you through this process.

Accepting an Offer: Once you have evaluated and negotiated offers, it's time to accept the best one. Your real estate agent will help you finalize the terms and prepare the necessary paperwork. Accepting an offer marks the beginning of the closing process.

Navigating the Closing Process

The Role of Escrow, Title Companies, and Closing Attorneys: Escrow and title companies, along with closing attorneys, facilitate the closing process by handling funds, documents, and title transfers. In some states, closing attorneys assume the role of both escrow and title companies. They act as a neutral third party to ensure all conditions are met before releasing funds and conduct a title search to confirm that the seller has a clear and marketable title to the property. Additionally, closing attorneys provide title insurance to protect against potential claims. They oversee the legal aspects of the transaction, ensuring all documents are correctly prepared and executed, and addressing any legal issues that may arise during the closing process. Together, these professionals work to ensure a smooth and secure transfer of property ownership.

Home Inspections and Appraisals: Buyers will typically schedule a home inspection and appraisal as part of the closing process. Be prepared for these appointments and address any issues that arise. Your real estate agent can guide you on how to handle inspection findings and appraisal results.

Finalizing the Sale: As the closing date approaches, ensure all necessary paperwork is completed and any agreed-upon repairs or conditions are met. Your real estate agent and escrow officer will coordinate the final steps, including signing the closing documents and transferring ownership.

Closing Costs: Closing costs are the fees associated with finalizing the sale of your home. These may include escrow fees, title insurance, and agent commissions. Review the closing disclosure provided by the escrow company to understand your financial responsibilities at closing.

Moving Out

Planning Your Move: Once the sale is finalized, it's time to plan your move. Create a moving timeline and checklist to stay organized. Arrange for movers, packing supplies, and address changes. Consider donating or selling items you no longer need to streamline the moving process.

Canceling Utilities and Services: Notify utility companies and service providers of your move and schedule cancellations or transfers. Ensure all final bills are paid and services are disconnected or transferred to the new owner.

Final Walk-through: Before handing over the keys, conduct a final walk-through to ensure the property is in the agreed-upon condition. Address any last-minute issues and leave the home clean and ready for the new owners.

Post-Sale Considerations

Settling Outstanding Matters: After the sale, ensure all outstanding matters are settled, including paying any remaining bills and canceling homeowners' insurance. Keep records of the sale for tax purposes and future reference.

Reflecting on the Selling Experience: Take time to reflect on the selling experience and gather feedback from your real estate agent. Use this insight for any future real estate transactions and to improve your selling strategy.

Maintaining a Relationship with Your Real Estate Agent: Your real estate agent can continue to be a valuable resource even after the sale is complete. Maintain a relationship with your agent for future buying or selling needs, market updates, and referrals to local service providers.

Conclusion

Thank you for choosing our Ultimate Home Seller's Guide to assist you in your home selling journey. We understand that the process can be complex, but with the right support and guidance, you can confidently move forward. Our team at [Agency Name] is dedicated to making your home selling experience as smooth and successful as possible. If you have any questions or would like to discuss your home selling needs, please don't hesitate to reach out. We're here to help you achieve your selling goals!

Personalization of the Comprehensive Home Seller's Guide

Update the guide with your agency name where appropriate. Consider adding your logo, images, or graphics to make it more visually appealing and enhance your brand identity. You can also include links to relevant resources, blog posts, or articles that you or your agency have published.

Sample Overview of Local Market Trends and Updates Report

Local Market Trends and Updates in [Your Area] - Comprehensive Report

Introduction:

As a real estate expert in the [Your Area] community, I am pleased to provide you with this comprehensive report on the current market trends and updates that are shaping our local real estate landscape. This information will help you stay informed about the market conditions in our area and make more informed decisions regarding your real estate needs.

I. Home Prices

The average home price in [Your Area] has experienced [An increase/ Decrease] of [X%] over the past year, with the current median price standing at [$XXX,XXX]. This trend is driven by factors such as [Low Inventory Levels, Strong Buyer Demand, or Other Relevant Factors].

II. Sales Activity

The number of homes sold in [Your Area] in the past month has [Increased/Decreased] by [X%] compared to the same period last year. This change in sales activity can be attributed to [Seasonal Fluctuations, Economic Factors, or Other Relevant Reasons].

III. Days on Market

Homes in [Your Area] are currently spending an average of [XX] days on the market before being sold. This figure represents [An Increase/ Decrease] of [X%] compared to the same time last year, indicating [A Faster/Slower] pace of sales in our area.

IV. Inventory Levels

The inventory of available homes for sale in [Your Area] has [Increased/ Decreased] by [X%] over the past year. This change in inventory levels is primarily due to [Higher/Lower] levels of new construction, [Increased/Decreased] demand from buyers, or other relevant factors.

V. Mortgage Rates

Current mortgage rates remain near historic lows, with the average 30-year fixed-rate mortgage at [X.X%]. These low rates continue to make homeownership more affordable for many buyers and may be contributing to the [Increased/Decreased] sales activity in our local market.

Conclusion:

Understanding the local market trends and updates in [Your Area] is crucial for both buyers and sellers as they navigate the real estate process. If you have any questions or need assistance with your real estate needs, please don't hesitate to reach out. As an experienced real estate professional, I am here to help you achieve your goals.

Best regards,

[Your Name]

[Your Title]

[Your Contact Information]

Personalization of Local Market Trends and Updates Report

Update the guide with your agency name where appropriate. Consider adding your logo, images, or graphics to make it more visually appealing and enhance your brand identity. You can also include links to relevant resources, blog posts, or articles that you or your agency have published.

Tracking the Success of the New Lead Sign-Up Campaign

To effectively track the success of your New Lead Sign-Up Campaign, it's essential to monitor key metrics and engagement data throughout the campaign. By doing so, you can evaluate the performance of your campaign and make improvements as needed. Here are some critical aspects to consider when tracking the success of this campaign:

- Open rates and click-through rates (CTR): Keep an eye on the open rates and click-through rates of your emails. A high open rate indicates that your subject lines are capturing the attention of your leads, while a high CTR means your content is engaging and relevant. Comparing these metrics to industry benchmarks can help you assess the effectiveness of your campaign.

- SMS response rates: Monitor the response rates of your SMS messages to gauge how effectively they're engaging with your leads. High response rates indicate that your messages are resonating with your audience and encouraging them to take action.
- Leads converted to clients: Track the number of leads that convert into clients throughout the campaign. This is the ultimate measure of success, as it demonstrates the effectiveness of your drip campaign in guiding leads through the home buying process and converting them into clients.
- Engagement with provided resources: Monitor how leads are interacting with the resources you share throughout the campaign. Are they downloading the guides, visiting the blog posts, or clicking on the property listings? This information can help you determine which types of content are most effective at engaging your audience.
- Feedback from leads: Gather feedback from leads who have gone through the campaign, either by conducting surveys or engaging in direct conversations. This feedback can provide valuable insights into the effectiveness of your campaign and areas for improvement.

By tracking these metrics and analyzing the data, you can identify the strengths and weaknesses of your new lead sign-up campaign and make any necessary adjustments to improve its effectiveness.

Tips For Customizing the New Lead Sign-Up Campaign

To effectively customize your New Lead Sign-Up Campaign, you should consider the unique characteristics and preferences of your target audience. Here are some tips for customizing your campaign:

- Segment your leads: Segment your leads based on demographics, location, interests, and behaviors. This will enable you to create personalized content and messaging that is tailored to each group's specific needs and preferences.
- Use targeted subject lines: Craft subject lines that are specific and relevant to each lead segment. For example, if you are targeting first-time homebuyers, you could use subject lines such as

"Everything You Need to Know About Buying Your First Home" or "5 Tips for First-Time Homebuyers."

- Personalize your content: Use lead data to personalize your content, such as addressing leads by name or referencing their location or interests. This can help create a more personal connection with your leads and increase the likelihood of engagement.
- Provide local market insights: Customize your content to provide local market insights and updates specific to the geographic areas your leads are interested in. This can help position you as a local expert and increase the relevance of your content.
- Use a mix of content formats: Incorporate a mix of content formats, such as videos, infographics, and blog posts, to keep your leads engaged and interested. By providing a variety of content, you can appeal to different learning styles and preferences.
- Continuously evaluate and adjust: Continuously evaluate the performance of your campaign and adjust your content and messaging as needed. By regularly analyzing your data and insights, you can optimize your campaign and improve its effectiveness over time.

By customizing your New Lead Sign-Up Campaign to the unique needs and preferences of your target audience, you can increase engagement and drive more leads to convert into clients.

Conclusion

A well-designed New Lead Sign-Up Campaign can help real estate agents effectively engage with and convert new leads into clients. By providing valuable content, personalized messaging, and a streamlined user experience, agents can increase engagement and build stronger relationships with potential clients.

To maximize the effectiveness of your New Lead Sign-Up Campaign, it is important to follow best practices and continuously evaluate and adjust your approach based on performance metrics and feedback. By staying agile and responsive to your audience's needs and preferences, you can build a campaign that generates results and helps you grow your business.

5

NEW LISTINGS DRIP CAMPAIGN

In the competitive world of real estate, staying top-of-mind with potential buyers and investors is essential for success. A New Listings Drip Campaign is a type of automated email marketing campaign that alerts potential clients of the latest properties that meet their criteria. This campaign is especially effective for generating leads, nurturing relationships, and driving conversions. By sending out regular updates on new listings, you can attract new buyers, promote open houses, support your brand, and much more.

User Scenario: New Listings Drip Campaign

John, a real estate agent, struggles to stay top-of-mind with potential buyers and investors in a competitive market. To address this, he implements a New Listings Drip Campaign, which sends automated email updates about the latest properties that meet his clients' criteria.

This campaign helps John generate leads by providing valuable updates to potential buyers and investors, showcasing his expertise in the local market. By sending regular emails about new listings, he builds trust and keeps his clients informed, which enhances client retention. Additionally, the campaign promotes open houses and new listings, driving traffic and interest to his properties.

By systematically engaging his audience with relevant property updates, John establishes himself as a knowledgeable and helpful resource, leading to higher engagement and conversions. Implementing a New Listings Drip

Campaign can help you achieve similar success in keeping clients informed, nurturing relationships, and driving conversions.

New Listings Use Cases

A New Listings Drip Campaign can be a powerful way for real estate agents to keep their clients and leads informed about the latest properties that come onto the market. By sending regular updates on new listings that match their criteria, you can provide value to your audience and position yourself as a knowledgeable and helpful resource. In this section, we'll explore the key use cases for a New Listings Drip Campaign, including how to use it to build relationships with your audience, drive engagement, and ultimately, generate more business.

- Lead Generation: A New Listings Drip Campaign can help generate new leads by attracting potential buyers and investors interested in specific areas and property types. By providing them with regular updates on new listings, you can establish yourself as an expert in the local market and build trust with your clients.

- Client Retention: Staying top of mind with your clients is essential for building long-term relationships. By sending regular emails with new listings that meet their criteria, you can remind them of your services and showcase your expertise.

- Conversion: A New Listings Drip Campaign can help convert potential leads into clients by providing them with the information they need to make informed decisions. By sending them regular updates on new listings that meet their criteria, you can encourage them to take action and reach out to you for more information.

- Supporting a New Listing: If you have a new listing that you want to promote, a New Listings Drip Campaign can be an effective way to generate interest and drive traffic to the property. By sending out regular updates and highlighting the property's key features, you can encourage potential buyers to schedule a viewing or make an offer.

- Promoting Open Houses: If you are hosting an open house for a property, a New Listings Drip Campaign can be a great way to get the word out and attract potential buyers. By sending out an email blast to your contact list with details about the open house and a link to the property listing, you can encourage interested buyers to attend and learn more about the property.

- Supporting Your Brand: A New Listings Drip Campaign can be a great way to support your brand and establish yourself as an expert in the local real estate market. By sending out regular updates on the latest listings and providing valuable insights and advice, you can build trust with your clients and establish a reputation for excellence in the industry.

Overall, a New Listings Drip Campaign is an essential tool for real estate agents looking to generate new leads, retain clients, and drive conversions. In this chapter, we will provide you with a step-by-step guide on how to set up a successful New Listings Drip Campaign, including recommended email and SMS messages, time between each message, call-to-action recommendations, and more.

Step-By-Step Guide and Templates

Step 1:

Send an email to your subscriber list with the subject line "New Listing Alert: [Property Address]" announcing the new property listing. The email should be designed to capture the attention of the subscriber and entice them to learn more about the property.

Step 1 Email Template:

Subject: New Listing Alert: Beautiful 3 Bedroom Home in the Heart of the City
Dear [Subscriber Name],

We're excited to share our latest property listing with you! This beautiful 3 bedroom home is located in the heart of the city and features a spacious living room, modern kitchen, and stunning city views from the balcony.

To learn more about this amazing property, please click here to visit our website, or call us at [Phone Number] to book a tour. Our agents are available to answer any questions you may have and show you around the property at your convenience.

Thank you for subscribing to our newsletter and keeping up to date with our latest property listings. We look forward to hearing from you soon!

Best regards,

[Agent Signature Block with Contact Information]

Personalization:

Change the subject to reflect the property you are highlighting. Use descriptive language and be short and concise. Update the body with your links and phone numbers where appropriate.

Recommended Agent Actions:

Follow up with a phone call to subscribers who click the link or express interest in the property.

Step 2:

Send an SMS message on day 3 encouraging subscribers to check out the new property listing on your website. Monitor social media/website engagement and respond to any comments or questions.

Step 2 SMS Template:

Check out our latest property listing, [Property Address], on our website. Click <<here>> to view it now. Let us know if you have any questions or would like to book a tour!

Personalization:

Update the message with your links where appropriate.

Recommended Agent Actions:

Monitor social media and website engagement and respond to any comments or questions.

Step 3:

Send a follow-up email on day 7 after the initial email with the subject "Follow-up on [Property Address]." Provide additional details about the property, such as square footage, the number of bedrooms and bathrooms, and neighborhood information.

Encourage subscribers to call your agency or reply to the email to learn more or book a tour.

Step 3 Email Template:

Subject: Follow-up on Beautiful 3 Bedroom Home in the Heart of the City
Hello [Subscriber Name],

We wanted to follow up with you and provide more information about our latest property listing, located at [Property Address]. This beautiful 3 bedroom home features [Square Footage] of living space, [Number of Bedrooms] bedrooms, and [Number of Bathrooms] bathrooms.

Additionally, the property is located in a prime location in the heart of the city, with easy access to public transportation, shops, and restaurants.

If you're interested in learning more or booking a tour of the property, please call us at [Phone Number] or reply to this email. Our agents are available to answer any questions you may have and show you around the property at your convenience.

Thank you for your interest in our agency and our latest property listing. We look forward to hearing from you soon!

Best regards,

[Agent Signature Block with Contact Information]

Personalization:

Change the Subject to reflect the property you are highlighting. Use descriptive language and be short and concise. Update the body with your links and phone numbers where appropriate.

Recommended Agent Actions:

Monitor social media and website engagement and respond to any comments or questions. Follow up with a phone call to subscribers who reply to the email or express interest in the property.

Step 4:

On Day 14 send an SMS message checking in and seeing if the subscriber had any questions. It's important to follow up with a phone call to subscribers who reply to the SMS or express interest in the property to further nurture the lead and potentially convert them into a client.

Step 4 SMS Template:

Hello [Subscriber]. Just wanted to check in and see if you had any questions about our latest property listing, [Property Address]. Let us know how we can assist you.

Personalization:

Update the message with your links where appropriate.

Recommended Agent Actions:

Follow up with a phone call to subscribers who reply to the SMS or express interest in the property.

Step 5:

Send an email on day 17 after the initial email with the subject "Hear from a Satisfied Client." Include a testimonial from a satisfied client, highlighting the positive experience they had with your agency. Encourage subscribers to call your agency or reply to the email to learn more or book a tour.

Step 5 Email Template:

Subject: Hear from a Satisfied Client about [Property Address]
Hello [Subscriber Name],

We recently helped a client purchase a property with ease, and we wanted to share their testimonial with you. Here's what they had to say about their experience with our agency:

[Insert testimonial from a satisfied client, highlighting the positive experience they had with your agency]

We're proud to have helped our client find their dream home, and we're excited to help you do the same. If you're interested in learning more about this property or any of our other listings, please call us at

[Phone Number] or reply to this email. Our agents are available to answer any questions you may have and show you around the property at your convenience.

Thank you for your interest in our agency and our latest property listing. We look forward to hearing from you soon!

Best regards,

[Agent Signature Block with Contact Information]

Personalization:

Change the Subject to reflect the property you are highlighting. Use descriptive language and be short and concise. Update the body with your links and phone numbers where appropriate.

Recommended Agent Actions:

Follow up with a phone call to subscribers who reply to the email or express interest in the property.

Step 6:

Send an email on day 21 after the initial email with the subject "Frequently Asked Questions about [Property Address]." Address common questions about the property, such as its history, the neighborhood, the school district, and more. Encourage subscribers to call your agency or reply to the email to learn more or book a tour.

Step 6 Email Template:

Subject: Frequently Asked Questions about [Property Address]

Hello [Subscriber Name],

We've received some common questions about our latest property listing, located at [Property Address], and we wanted to provide some answers. Here are some of the most frequently asked questions we've received:

What is the history of the property?

[Answer]

What is the neighborhood like?

[Answer]

What school district is the property located in?

[Answer]
Are there any nearby parks or recreational areas?
[Answer]

We hope this information helps you in your decision-making process. If you have any additional questions or would like to schedule a tour, please call us at [Phone Number] or reply to this email. Our agents are available to answer any questions you may have and show you around the property at your convenience.

Thank you for your interest in our agency and our latest property listing. We look forward to hearing from you soon!

Best regards,

[Agent Signature Block with Contact Information]

Personalization:

Change the Subject to reflect the property you are highlighting. Use descriptive language and be short and concise. Update the body with your links and phone numbers where appropriate.

Recommended Agent Actions:

After sending this email, it's recommended to wait for 4 days and then follow up with a phone call to subscribers who reply to the email or express interest in the property. This will help to further nurture the lead and potentially convert them into a client.

Step 7:

Send an email on day 25 after the initial email with the subject "Exclusive Preview of [Property Address]." Offer subscribers an exclusive preview of the property on a specific date and time. Include details about the event, such as the location and how to RSVP. Encourage subscribers to call your agency or reply to the email to learn more or book a tour.

Step 7 Email Template:

Subject: Exclusive Preview of [Property Address]

Hello [Subscriber Name],

We're excited to offer you an exclusive preview of our latest property listing, located at [Property Address].

Join us on [Insert Date and Time] for a private showing of this beautiful [Insert Property Type].

During the preview, you'll have the opportunity to tour the property, ask questions, and learn more about what makes this property so special. Space is limited, so please RSVP by [Insert Deadline] to reserve your spot.

To RSVP or learn more about the property, please call us at [Phone Number] or reply to this email. Our agents are available to answer any questions you may have and show you around the property at your convenience.

Thank you for your interest in our agency and our latest property listing. We look forward to hearing from you soon!

Best regards,

[Agent Signature Block with Contact Information]

Personalization:

Change the Subject to reflect the property you are highlighting. Use descriptive language and be short and concise. Update the body with your links and phone numbers where appropriate.

Recommended Agent Actions:

Follow up with a phone call to subscribers who reply to the email or express interest in the property. This will help to further nurture the lead and potentially convert them into a client.

Step 8:

Send an email on day 30 after the initial email with the subject "Final Reminder: [Property Address] is still available!" Create a sense of urgency by letting subscribers know that the property is still available and encouraging them to act quickly. Encourage subscribers to call your agency or reply to the email to learn more or book a tour.

Step 8 Email Template:

Subject: Final Reminder: [Property Address] is still available!
Hello [Subscriber Name],

We wanted to send you a final reminder that our latest property listing, located at [Property Address], is still available. This is a rare opportunity to own a [Insert Property Type] in one of the most sought-after neighborhoods in town.

Don't miss out on this amazing opportunity. To learn more or schedule a tour, please call us at [Phone Number] or reply to this email. Our agents are available to answer any questions you may have and show you around the property at your convenience.

Thank you for your interest in our agency and our latest property listing. We look forward to hearing from you soon!

Best regards,

[Agent Signature Block with Contact Information]

Personalization:

Change the Subject to reflect the property you are highlighting. Use descriptive language and be short and concise. Update the body with your links and phone numbers where appropriate.

Recommended Agent Actions:

After sending this email, it's recommended to wait for 5 days and then follow up with a phone call to subscribers who reply to the email or express interest in the property. This will help to further nurture the lead and potentially convert them into a client.

Recommended Agent Actions:

After sending this SMS message, it's recommended to wait for subscribers to reply or express interest in the property. Once they do, it's important to follow up with a phone call to further nurture the lead and potentially convert them into a client.

Tracking The Success of The New Listings Campaign

Tracking the success of your New Listings Drip Campaign is critical to understanding what works and what doesn't, and how to improve your future campaigns. Here are some key metrics to track:

- Open rate: This is the percentage of subscribers who opened your emails. A low open rate may indicate that your subject line or email content needs improvement.
- Click-through rate (CTR): This is the percentage of subscribers who clicked on a link within your email. A low CTR may indicate that your call-to-action or content isn't compelling enough.
- Response rate: This is the percentage of subscribers who replied to your emails or SMS messages. A low response rate may indicate that your messaging or targeting needs improvement.
- Conversion rate: This is the percentage of subscribers who booked a tour or became a client. This is the ultimate goal of the campaign, so it's important to track this metric closely.

To track these metrics, you can use an email marketing platform like Mailchimp or Constant Contact, which provides detailed analytics on each email campaign you send. You can also use a CRM system like Salesforce or Hubspot to track leads and conversions.

Once you have this data, analyze it to understand what worked and what didn't. Identify areas for improvement and make changes to your future campaigns accordingly. With each iteration, you'll learn more about your audience and how to effectively nurture leads and convert them into clients.

Tips For Customizing New Listings Drip Campaign

Before diving into the tips for customizing your New Listings Drip Campaign, it's important to remember that one size does not fit all. To create a successful campaign, it's crucial to tailor your messaging and approach to your specific audience and their preferences.

By customizing your campaign, you can increase engagement, build trust, and ultimately convert more leads into clients. Here are some tips for customizing your New Listings Drip Campaign to help you get started.

- Personalize your messaging: Use your subscriber's name and any relevant information about their preferences or interests to make your messaging feel more personal and relevant.
- Segment your subscribers: Consider segmenting your subscribers based on their location, preferences, or behavior.

This can help you tailor your messaging to each group and increase engagement.

- Use high-quality visuals: Include high-quality images or videos of the property in your emails and SMS messages to make them more visually appealing and showcase the property's features.
- Leverage automation: Use an email marketing platform that offers automation to schedule your emails and SMS messages ahead of time, and to trigger follow-up messages based on subscriber behavior.
- Experiment with different messaging: Try different subject lines, calls-to-action, and content to see what resonates with your audience. Don't be afraid to test and iterate until you find the messaging that works best for your subscribers.

By customizing your New Listings Drip Campaign to your audience and their preferences, you can increase engagement, build trust, and ultimately convert more leads into clients.

Conclusion

The New Listings Drip Campaign is an effective way to nurture leads and promote your latest property listings. By sending a series of targeted emails and SMS messages, you can keep your subscribers engaged and interested in your agency's offerings.

To create a successful New Listings Drip Campaign, it is important to follow best practices such as personalizing your messaging, creating a clear call-to-action, and providing value to your subscribers. It's also critical to track your metrics and make adjustments based on what works and what doesn't.

By consistently executing this campaign, you can build a loyal subscriber base and ultimately convert more leads into clients. So why not try it and see how it can benefit your real estate business?

6

INVALID PHONE NUMBER RECOVERY DRIP CAMPAIGN

The Invalid Phone Number Recovery Drip Campaign is specifically designed to address the issue of leads providing incorrect or non-working phone numbers during the lead generation or collection process. This campaign aims to re-engage these leads by focusing on emails, to establish a connection and convert them into potential clients. While social media can also be utilized, our book concentrates on phone, SMS, and email as the primary forms of contact so we focus our attention on them alone.

By using a targeted approach to reach out to leads with incorrect phone numbers, you can demonstrate your persistence and adaptability as a real estate agent. This, in turn, helps to build trust and credibility with leads who may have initially provided incorrect contact information due to caution or hesitance.

The Invalid Phone Number Recovery Drip Campaign focuses on providing valuable content and resources, showcasing your expertise and understanding of the local real estate market, and offering personalized assistance to meet each lead's unique needs.

User Scenario: Invalid Phone Number Recovery Drip Campaign

Alex, a real estate agent, has been collecting leads through various online channels. However, he notices that many of these leads have provided invalid phone numbers, making follow-up difficult. To address this, Alex implements an Invalid Phone Number Recovery Drip Campaign, which sends a series of emails to re-engage these leads and request updated contact information.

This campaign allows Alex to reconnect with leads by highlighting his expertise and offering valuable real estate resources. By providing market insights and personalized assistance, he builds trust and encourages leads to update their contact information. Through this systematic approach, Alex not only recovers valuable leads but also strengthens his relationships with potential clients, ultimately increasing his chances of conversion. Implementing this campaign can help you ensure accurate contact information, improve engagement, and boost your conversion rates.

Invalid Phone Number Recovery Drip Campaign Use Cases

The Invalid Phone Number Recovery Drip Campaign is particularly helpful in situations where leads have provided incorrect or non-working phone numbers. By identifying these use cases and addressing the unique challenges they present, this campaign can effectively re-engage leads and increase the chances of conversion through email communication. The following use cases illustrate how the Invalid Phone Number Recovery Drip Campaign can be employed to address various scenarios.

- Incorrect Information Provided Intentionally: Some leads may intentionally provide incorrect phone numbers due to privacy concerns or a desire to avoid direct contact with a real estate agent. In these cases, the Invalid Phone Number Recovery Drip Campaign can help build trust and credibility with leads by providing valuable content and showcasing your expertise via email, thus increasing the likelihood that they will eventually share their correct contact information and engage with you.

- Genuine Mistake: In some instances, leads might provide an incorrect phone number by mistake. By implementing the Invalid Phone Number Recovery Drip Campaign, you can identify these leads and attempt to re-engage them through email, offering support and resources to help them with their real estate needs. This approach demonstrates your persistence and adaptability, increasing the chances that the lead will correct their contact information and continue their real estate journey with you.

- Disconnected or Changed Phone Numbers: Leads may provide a phone number that was once valid but has since been disconnected or changed. In these situations, the Invalid Phone Number

Recovery Drip Campaign can be used to reach out to leads via email, providing valuable information and resources related to the local real estate market. By demonstrating your commitment to supporting their real estate needs, you increase the likelihood that the lead will provide updated contact information and engage with you.

Understanding the various use cases for the Invalid Phone Number Recovery Drip Campaign allows you to effectively re-engage leads who have provided incorrect phone numbers. By addressing the unique challenges each scenario presents and focusing on email communication, you can build trust and credibility with leads, increasing the likelihood of converting them into potential clients. This campaign demonstrates your adaptability and commitment to meeting the diverse needs of your leads.

Step-By-Step Guide and Templates

Step 1:

In the first step, send an email to the lead informing them about the incorrect phone number they provided and offering assistance with their real estate needs. Make sure to include valuable content and highlight your expertise to build trust.

Step 1 Email Template:

Subject: [Agent Name] - Your Real Estate Expert: Let's Connect
Dear [Lead's Name],

I hope this email finds you well. My name is [Agent Name], and I'm a real estate agent with [Agency Name]. Recently, you provided your contact information in connection with your interest in the local real estate market. However, it seems that the phone number we have for you may be incorrect.

I wanted to reach out and offer my assistance with any questions or concerns you may have about buying, selling, or investing in real estate. As a knowledgeable and experienced agent in the area, I'm committed to helping clients like you navigate the market with confidence.

To help you get started, I've included some valuable resources and market insights below:

[Link to a Recent Market Report]

[Link to a Blog Post on the Home Buying Process]

[Link to a Neighborhood Guide]

If you'd like to discuss your real estate needs further, please don't hesitate to reply to this email with your correct phone number or an alternate method of communication. I look forward to the opportunity to assist you and help you achieve your real estate goals.

Best regards,

[Agent Signature Block with Contact Information]

Personalization:

Update the Lead's Name and include any relevant resources or links that may be helpful to them.

Recommended Agent Action:

Monitor your inbox for responses from leads who reply with their correct phone number or express interest in discussing their real estate needs. Promptly follow up with a phone call to those who provide their correct contact information, and engage with others via their preferred communication method to build rapport and better understand their needs.

Step 2:

On Day 6 send a follow-up email offering exclusive content to showcase your expertise and further build trust. This email should be sent 5 days after the initial email, allowing the lead time to review the resources you provided earlier.

Step 2 Email Template:

Subject: Exclusive Real Estate Insights from [Agent Name]

Dear [Lead's Name],

I hope you found the resources I shared in my previous email helpful. As a real estate expert, I strive to provide my clients with valuable insights and support to help them make informed decisions. Today, I wanted to share some exclusive content that I believe will be of great interest to you.

[Link to an In-Depth Market Analysis]
[Link to a Video Tour of a Popular Neighborhood]
[Link to a Guide on Property Investment Strategies]

I'm here to help you navigate the complex world of real estate, and I'd love to discuss your goals and needs in more detail. If you'd like to connect, please reply to this email with your correct phone number or an alternate method of communication.

Looking forward to hearing from you soon.

Best regards,
[Agent Signature Block with Contact Information]

Personalization:

Update the Lead's Name and include any exclusive content or links relevant to their interests.

Recommended Agent Action:

Monitor your inbox for responses from leads who reply with their correct phone number or express interest in discussing their real estate needs. Quickly follow up with a phone call to those who provide their correct contact information and engage with others via their preferred communication method. Focus on understanding their needs and providing personalized solutions.

Step 3:

On Day 12, send a personalized email that highlights local market trends and recent property listings further showcasing your expertise and dedication to helping the lead with their real estate needs.

Step 3 Email Template:

Subject: Local Market Trends and Property Listings from [Agent Name]
Dear [Lead's Name],

I hope you've found the exclusive content I've shared so far valuable. As a local real estate expert, I understand the importance of staying up to date with the latest market trends and property listings. Today, I wanted to provide you with a personalized snapshot of the current market situation in [Lead's Desired Area].

[Link to a General Market Trend Report]

[Link to a List of Featured Property Listings in the Area]

[Link to a Guide on Maximizing Property Value in the Local Market]

My goal is to help you make informed decisions and achieve your real estate objectives. I'd be more than happy to discuss these trends and listings with you, as well as answer any questions you may have. If you'd like to connect, please reply to this email with your correct phone number or your preferred method of communication.

Looking forward to hearing from you soon.

Best regards,

[Agent Signature Block with Contact Information]

Personalization:

Update the Lead's Name and customize the email with relevant market trends and property listings based on their interests.

Recommended Agent Action:

Monitor your inbox for responses from leads who reply with their correct phone number or express interest in discussing their real estate needs. Promptly follow up with a phone call to those who provide their correct contact information and engage with others via their preferred communication method. Use the opportunity to discuss local market trends and property listings, providing personalized guidance based on their needs.

Step 4:

On Day 22, send an email offering a free consultation to discuss the lead's real estate needs. This email demonstrates your commitment to helping them and provides a direct opportunity to connect.

Step 4 Email Template:

Subject: Free Real Estate Consultation from [Agent Name]

Dear [Lead's Name],

I hope the information I've shared with you over the past few weeks has been helpful in providing insights into the local real estate market. As a dedicated real estate professional, my top priority is assisting clients like you in achieving their real estate goals.

To further support you, I'd like to offer you a complimentary consultation to discuss your specific needs and answer any questions you may have. This can be conducted over the phone, via video call, or in person, depending on your preference.

If you're interested in taking advantage of this free consultation, please reply to this email with your correct phone number or preferred method of communication, and we can schedule a convenient time to connect.

Thank you for considering my services, and I look forward to the opportunity to help you with your real estate journey.

Best regards,

[Agent Signature Block with Contact Information]

Personalization:

Update the Lead's Name and ensure that the offer of a free consultation is clear and appealing.

Recommended Agent Action:

Monitor your inbox for responses from leads who reply with their correct phone number, express interest in the free consultation, or share their preferred method of communication. Promptly follow up with a phone call to those who provide their correct contact information and engage with others via their preferred communication method. Use the opportunity to schedule the consultation and provide personalized guidance based on their needs.

Tracking The Success of The Invalid Phone Number Recovery Drip Campaign

Tracking the effectiveness of your Invalid Phone Number Recovery Drip Campaign is essential to understand its impact and make necessary improvements. By evaluating certain key metrics, you can assess how well the campaign reconnects you with leads that previously had incorrect contact details. Here's how to effectively track the success of this campaign:

- Updated Contact Information Rate: The primary metric of success is how many leads update their phone numbers during the campaign. Use your CRM to track these updates and gauge the direct impact of your campaign.
- Response Rate to Alternate Contact Methods: If you're using email or direct mail as alternate methods, monitor the response rates. A high response rate signifies that your messages are engaging and that leads are interested in updating their contact details.
- Engagement with Follow-up Communications: Once you've obtained the correct phone numbers, track how these leads engage with your subsequent communications. Low engagement might indicate a need for more compelling content or follow-up strategies.
- Conversion Rate Post-Campaign: Measure how many leads, after updating their phone numbers, engage in meaningful actions such as inquiries, property viewings, or further consultations.
- Feedback and Suggestions: Solicit feedback from clients about the process of updating their phone numbers. This qualitative data can provide insights into the user experience and campaign perception.

Tips for Customizing the Invalid Phone Number Recovery Drip Campaign

Customizing your Invalid Phone Number Recovery Drip Campaign can significantly enhance its effectiveness and lead to better engagement and conversion rates. Here are some strategies to tailor your campaign:

- Personalization: Address subscribers by name in your communications. Customize the content based on any interactions or preferences known about the subscriber.
- Audience Segmentation: Group your audience based on demographics, interactions, or interests. Tailor your communications to these segments for more relevant messaging.
- Timing and Frequency: Experiment with the frequency of your messages. Determine the most effective timing based on when subscribers are likely to be responsive.
- Content Relevance: Provide information or insights related to real estate that is pertinent to the subscriber's interests. This might include market trends, property highlights, or investment tips.

- Incentivization: Motivate subscribers to update their contact details by offering incentives like exclusive reports, consultations, or access to unique listings.

Conclusion

The Invalid Phone Number Recovery Drip Campaign is a vital component in maintaining an effective communication line with potential clients in real estate. It addresses the challenge of incorrect contact details, ensuring that leads remain accessible and engaged. The campaign's success lies in its ability to adapt to each lead's needs and preferences, thereby enhancing the chances of re-establishing lost connections. When executed correctly, this campaign not only recovers valuable leads but also reinforces the reliability and attentiveness of your real estate services. Ultimately, this campaign plays a significant role in sustaining and growing your client base in the competitive real estate market.

7

INVALID EMAIL RECOVERY DRIP CAMPAIGN

An Invalid Email Recovery Drip Campaign is essential for reaching out to potential clients who provided non-working email addresses. This chapter delves into the strategic approach of using SMS messaging to establish communication, offering a second chance to connect and convert these leads into clients. Each step of the Invalid Email Recovery Drip Campaign is designed to gently nudge subscribers towards updating their contact information while simultaneously offering them value and maintaining engagement. This strategy ensures that leads stay connected and have every opportunity to benefit from your agency's services.

User Scenario: Invalid Email Recovery Drip Campaign

Rachel, a diligent real estate agent, notices that many of her leads have provided non-working email addresses, hindering her follow-up efforts. To address this, Rachel implements an Invalid Email Recovery Drip Campaign, focusing on SMS messaging to re-establish contact and request updated email information.

This campaign allows Rachel to reconnect with leads by sending personalized SMS messages, informing them of the email issue and requesting updated contact details. By using SMS, Rachel can efficiently reach multiple leads at once, saving significant time compared to making individual phone calls. Through this approach, Rachel provides value by sharing real estate insights and resources, building trust and credibility with her leads.

By maintaining engagement and offering a second chance to connect, Rachel ensures she doesn't lose potential clients due to incorrect email information. Implementing this campaign helps Rachel save time, recover lost leads, maintain accurate contact details, and improve her chances of converting leads into clients. This efficient method allows her to focus on other critical tasks, enhancing overall productivity.

Invalid Email Recovery Drip Campaign Use Cases

An Invalid Email Recovery Drip Campaign can be employed in various scenarios where email addresses provided by leads turn out to be incorrect or non-functional. By identifying and addressing these use cases, you can effectively re-engage leads and increase your chances of conversion through SMS communication. Below are the key use cases for the Invalid Email Recovery Drip Campaign:

- **Re-engagement with Non-Responsive Leads**: Leads often sign up through online forms, providing email addresses that turn out to be non-functional, leading to failed communication attempts. In such cases, the Invalid Email Recovery Drip Campaign comes into play. The strategy involves deploying SMS messages to these leads, notifying them about the email delivery issue. The SMS kindly requests an update of their contact details, aiming to recapture the lead's interest and re-establish a reliable communication channel.

- **Post-Event Follow-Up**: Events such as open houses or real estate seminars often result in a collection of email addresses that bounce back. To tackle this, the campaign initiates an SMS strategy targeting these attendees. The messages thank them for their participation and seek correct email information to forward detailed property information or event materials. This approach is designed to maintain the momentum generated from the event and ensure continuous engagement with the attendees who showed interest.

- **Database Cleansing and Updating**: Regular maintenance of the client database sometimes uncovers leads with outdated or incorrect email information. In addressing this, the campaign uses an SMS-based strategy to contact these leads. The messages emphasize the benefits of staying updated with the latest real estate listings and news, asking for an update of their email addresses. The goal here is to keep the client database accurate and up-to-date, thereby enhancing the effectiveness of future marketing campaigns.

- **Reviving Dormant Leads**: Over time, some leads become inactive or unresponsive, and there's a possibility that their contact details have changed. To revive these dormant leads, the campaign employs SMS messages, offering the latest market insights or property listings. The aim is to request updated contact information, thereby rekindling interest among these leads and reintegrating them into the active marketing funnel.
- **Client Feedback and Survey Participation**: When email requests for client feedback or survey participation meet with high bounce rates, the campaign leverages SMS as a solution. The strategy involves contacting these clients via SMS, providing a direct link to the survey or feedback form. This approach not only facilitates essential feedback but also prompts clients to update their contact information, ensuring future communications are successful.

Each of these use cases demonstrates the versatile application of the Invalid Email Recovery Drip Campaign in different scenarios, highlighting its role in enhancing client engagement, maintaining data accuracy, and ensuring the success of real estate marketing efforts.

Step-By-Step Guide and Template

Step 1:

Send an SMS message on day 1 after identifying a non-working email. This initial contact aims to inform the subscriber about the email issue and request an updated email address.

Recommended action: Monitor responses and be prepared to update the lead's contact information in your CRM system.

Step 1 SMS Template:

"Hello [Subscriber Name], this is [Agent Name] from [Agency Name]. We noticed an issue with the email you provided. Could you please update your email address for our records? Feel free to respond to this SMS or call us at [Phone Number]. Thanks!"

Personalization:

Update the message with your links where appropriate.

Recommended Agent Actions:

Assess the engagement with the content provided and follow up with subscribers who show interest or have questions.

Step 2:

Send an SMS message on day 3 to reiterate the request for an updated email and provide an opportunity for the subscriber to ask any real estate-related questions.

Step 2 SMS Template:

"Hi [Subscriber Name], it's [Agent Name] from [Agency Name] again. Just checking in to see if you had a chance to update your email. Also, if you have any real estate questions, feel free to ask. Here's our number again: [Phone Number]."

Personalization:

Update the message with your links where appropriate.

Recommended Agent Actions:

Assess the engagement with the content provided and follow up with subscribers who show interest or have questions.

Step 3:

Send a follow-up SMS message on day 7 to provide valuable real estate insights or tips, encouraging the subscriber to engage and update their email address.

Step 3 SMS Template:

"Hey [Subscriber Name], hope you're doing well! Here's a quick tip from [Agency Name] about [Real Estate Tip]. If you wish to receive more insights like this, please update your email with us. Looking forward to helping you with your real estate needs."

Personalization:

Update the message with your links where appropriate.

Recommended Agent Actions:

Assess the engagement with the content provided and follow up with subscribers who show interest or have questions.

Tracking The Success of The Invalid Email Recovery Drip Campaign

Tracking the success of your Invalid Email Recovery Drip Campaign is critical for understanding its performance and identifying areas for improvement. By analyzing specific metrics, you can gauge the campaign's effectiveness and make informed decisions to enhance its impact. Here are key metrics and methods to track the success of your campaign:

- **Updated Contact Information Rate**: This metric tracks the number of subscribers who update their email addresses during the campaign. It's a direct indicator of the campaign's effectiveness in resolving the issue of bad emails. Use your CRM software to monitor changes in contact details or maintain a manual record.
- **Response Rate to SMS Messages**: Monitor the number of subscribers who respond to your SMS messages. A high response rate indicates successful engagement and interest in maintaining contact. Track responses through your SMS platform and cross-reference with your CRM system for accuracy.
- **Conversion Rate Post-Campaign**: Assess how many subscribers, after updating their email addresses, take actions such as scheduling appointments, attending open houses, or engaging with property listings. Use conversion tracking in your CRM and analytics tools to measure the actions taken by subscribers after updating their information.
- **Engagement with Follow-Up Communications**: After updating their contact information, measure how engaged these subscribers are with subsequent email communications. Low open or click-through rates might indicate a need for

more compelling content. Analyze open and click-through rates using email marketing tools.

- **Client Feedback**: Gain insights from clients about the SMS outreach and update process. Feedback can provide valuable information on the effectiveness and perception of your campaign. Conduct surveys or direct conversations to collect feedback.

By monitoring these metrics, you can gain a comprehensive understanding of the Invalid Email Recovery Drip Campaign's effectiveness. This information is crucial for refining your approach, enhancing the campaign's efficiency, and ensuring that you are successfully re-engaging with leads that might have been lost due to incorrect email information. Regular analysis of these metrics allows for continuous improvement and optimization of the campaign.

Tips for Customizing Invalid Email Recovery Drip Campaign

By customizing the Invalid Email Recovery Drip Campaign, you can significantly enhance engagement and drive more successful outcomes. Tailoring the campaign to the specific needs and characteristics of your audience can lead to more effective communication and better conversion rates. Here are some tips for customizing the Invalid Email Recovery Drip Campaign:

- **Personalize the Messaging**: Use the subscriber's name in SMS messages to create a more personal touch. Customize the message content based on any known preferences or interactions the subscriber has had with your agency.
- **Segment Your Audience**: Group subscribers based on demographics, previous interactions, or property interests to ensure the messaging is relevant. Tailor SMS content according to these segments, addressing specific needs or interests.
- **Adjust the Timing**: Experiment with different intervals between SMS messages to determine the most effective frequency. Consider factors such as the time of day and days of the week when subscribers are most likely to respond.

- **Customize the Content**: Provide insights or information relevant to the subscriber's real estate interests or recent market trends in their area. Include local real estate statistics or news that might encourage subscribers to update their contact information.
- **Offer Incentives**: Encourage subscribers to update their email addresses by offering incentives like exclusive market reports, free consultations, or early access to new listings. Ensure these incentives are valuable and relevant to the audience's real estate goals.
- **Use Visual Aids in Follow-Up Emails**: Once the correct email is obtained, enhance your emails with images, videos, or infographics to make them more engaging. Visual aids can be particularly effective in showcasing properties, highlighting market trends, or explaining complex real estate concepts.
- **Monitor Engagement**: Track metrics such as response rates to SMS messages and subsequent email open and click-through rates. Use this data to refine the campaign, adjusting content, timing, and segmentation for better performance.

Customizing your Invalid Email Recovery Drip Campaign in these ways can make your outreach more effective and resonate more with your audience. A tailored approach not only improves the likelihood of recovering lost leads but also enhances the overall client experience, leading to more successful conversions and satisfied clients.

Conclusion

A Invalid Email Recovery Drip Campaign serves as an essential tool in the real estate sector, particularly for salvaging potential client relationships that might otherwise be lost due to incorrect email information. By employing strategic SMS messaging, this campaign effectively re-engages leads, ensuring the continuity of communication. It plays a crucial role in maintaining the integrity of your client database, thus enhancing the efficiency of your marketing efforts.

In implementing this campaign, it's vital to focus on personalizing your messaging, catering to the specific needs and preferences of each lead. This approach not only aids in recovering accurate contact details but also helps in building trust and rapport with potential clients. The success of this campaign hinges on your ability to track results meticulously and make data-driven adjustments for continuous improvement.

With the correct execution, the Invalid Email Recovery Drip Campaign can transform a technical hurdle into an opportunity for enhanced client engagement and business growth. It is a testament to the adaptability required in the dynamic world of real estate marketing and demonstrates the importance of having a robust strategy to manage and nurture leads effectively. Employed wisely, this campaign can be instrumental in expanding your client base and advancing the success of your real estate business.

8

FIRST-TIME HOMEBUYER DRIP CAMPAIGN

A First-time Homebuyer Drip Campaign is a series of targeted emails and SMS messages designed to educate and prepare clients who are new to the home buying process. The campaign typically begins with an introductory email welcoming the subscriber to the campaign and outlining what they can expect to learn. From there, the campaign will provide information about the home buying process, including topics such as:

- How to get pre-approved for a mortgage
- Understanding the different types of mortgages available
- Tips for finding the right home
- The importance of home inspections and how to choose a reputable inspector
- The closing process and what to expect on closing day
- How to make an offer on a home
- Negotiating with sellers
- The importance of a home appraisal and what to expect
- The home buying timeline
- Homeowner's insurance and why it's important
- How to choose a real estate agent and what to look for
- Understanding the costs of homeownership, including property taxes and utilities
- Tips for moving into a new home

Each email and SMS message in the campaign is designed to build trust and rapport with the client and provide them with the resources they need to make informed decisions throughout the home buying process. By the end of the campaign, the client should feel more confident and knowledgeable about the home buying process and ready to take the next steps towards finding their dream home.

User Scenario: First-time Homebuyer Drip Campaign

Chris, a real estate agent, notices that many of his new leads are first-time homebuyers who feel overwhelmed by the home buying process. To address this, Chris implements a First-time Homebuyer Drip Campaign, which sends a series of targeted emails and SMS messages to educate and guide these clients.

Through the campaign, Chris provides valuable information on topics such as getting pre-approved for a mortgage, understanding different types of mortgages, and tips for finding the right home. By systematically sharing insights on home inspections, making offers, negotiating with sellers, and understanding the costs of homeownership, Chris helps build trust and rapport with his clients.

This structured approach saves Chris time compared to individually educating each client, allowing him to focus on other critical tasks while ensuring his clients are well-informed and confident in their home buying journey. By the end of the campaign, Chris's clients feel more knowledgeable and ready to take the next steps toward finding their dream home. Implementing this campaign can help you build strong relationships with first-time homebuyers, position yourself as an expert, and ultimately increase your conversion rates.

First-time Homebuyer Use Cases

A First-time Homebuyer Drip Campaign can be an incredibly valuable tool for real estate agents looking to build relationships with new clients and guide them through the home buying process. By providing valuable information and resources, agents can establish themselves as trusted advisors and position themselves for long-term success. In this section, we'll explore some of the key use cases for a First-time Homebuyer Drip Campaign and provide tips for making the most of each one.

- Educating First-time Homebuyers: A primary use case for a First-time Homebuyer Drip Campaign is to educate new clients about the home buying process. Many first-time homebuyers may not know what to expect when buying a home, and this campaign can help guide them through each step of the process.

- Nurturing Leads: Another use case is to nurture leads who have expressed interest in buying a home but may not be ready to make a purchase yet. By providing valuable information and building trust with the client, this campaign can help keep them engaged and interested in your services.
- Positioning Yourself as an Expert: A well-designed First-time Homebuyer Drip Campaign can position you as an expert in your field. By providing valuable information and resources, clients will see you as a trusted advisor who can help guide them through the home buying process.
- Building Long-Term Relationships: A First-time Homebuyer Drip Campaign can also help you build long-term relationships with clients. By providing ongoing value and resources, clients are more likely to remember and recommend your services to others, even after they've completed their home purchase.
- Upselling Services: Finally, a First-time Homebuyer Drip Campaign can be used to upsell other services, such as home insurance, property management, or home improvement services. By positioning yourself as a trusted advisor, clients are more likely to turn to you for their future home-related needs.

First-time Homebuyer Use Case Conclusion

As you can see, a First-time Homebuyer Drip Campaign can be used in a variety of ways to help build relationships with clients and guide them through the home buying process. By focusing on providing value and building trust with your clients, you can position yourself as an expert in your field and set yourself up for long-term success. In the next section, we'll dive into the specifics of designing and implementing a successful First-time Homebuyer Drip Campaign.

Step-By-Step Guide and Templates

Step 1:

Send an initial email with the subject "Congratulations on Taking the First Step Toward Homeownership!" Provide a warm welcome and congratulations to the subscriber for taking the first step toward homeownership. Encourage them to reply to the email or call your agency to learn more about the home buying process.

Step 1 Email Template:

Subject: Congratulations on Taking the First Step Toward Homeownership!

Dear [Subscriber Name],

Congratulations on taking the first step toward homeownership! We understand that this is a big decision, and we're thrilled to be a part of your journey.

Our team at [Agency Name] is here to help you navigate the home buying process every step of the way. Whether you're a first-time homebuyer or a seasoned pro, we'll work with you to find the perfect home that fits your needs and budget.

Here is a copy of our comprehensive home buyer's guide "The Ultimate Home Buyer's Guide: From Dream to Reality". <<Link to Guide>>

Please feel free to reply to this email or call us at [Phone Number] to learn more about the home buying process or schedule a consultation with one of our agents.

Best regards,

[Agent Signature Block with Contact Information]

Personalization:

Update the Subscriber Name and body with your links and phone numbers where appropriate.

Recommended Agent Actions:

Follow up with a phone call to subscribers who reply to the email or express interest in the home buying process.

Step 2:

Send an SMS message on day 3 to check in with subscribers and see if they have any questions about the home buying process. Provide your agency's phone number for them to call with any questions.

Recommended action: Follow up with a phone call to subscribers who reply to the SMS or express interest in the home buying process.

Step 2 SMS Template:

Hi [Subscriber Name], it's [Agent Name] from [Agency Name]. Just wanted to check in and see if you had any questions about the home buying process. Let me know how I can help.

Personalization:

Update the message with your links where appropriate.

Recommended Agent Actions

Follow up with a phone call to subscribers who reply to the SMS or express interest in the home buying process.

Step 3:

Send an email on day 7 after the initial email with the subject "The Home Buying Process: Explained." Provide an overview of the home buying process and what to expect during each step. Encourage subscribers to call your agency or reply to the email to learn more.

Step 3 Email Template:

Subject: The Home Buying Process: Explained

Dear [Subscriber Name],

We hope this email finds you well! As a first-time homebuyer, the process of purchasing a home can seem daunting. That's why we've put together this email to help you understand what to expect during each step of the home buying process.

Step 1: Pre-Approval

Before you start searching for your dream home, it's important to get pre-approved for a mortgage. This will give you a better understanding of your budget and what you can afford. If you haven't already, we recommend reaching out to one of our trusted lenders to get pre-approved. If you need any recommendations, please don't hesitate to give us a call!

Step 2: Home Search

Once you've been pre-approved, it's time to start searching for your new home! We can help you create a list of must-haves and nice-to-haves to narrow down your search and find the perfect home for you.

Step 3: Offer and Negotiation

Once you've found a home you love, it's time to make an offer. We'll help you determine a fair price and negotiate with the seller to ensure you get the best deal possible.

Step 4: Home Inspection

Before finalizing the sale, it's important to have the home inspected by a professional. This will ensure there are no hidden surprises and you can make an informed decision about your purchase.

Step 5: Closing

Finally, it's time to close on your new home! We'll help you navigate the closing process and make sure everything goes smoothly.

We hope this email has been helpful in explaining the home buying process. If you have any questions or would like to learn more, please don't hesitate to give us a call at [Agent Phone Number] or reply to this email.

Best regards,

[Agent Signature Block with Contact Information]

Personalization:

Update the Subscriber Name and body with your links and phone numbers where appropriate.

Recommended Agent Actions:

Follow up with a phone call to subscribers who reply to the email or express interest in the home buying process.

Step 4:

Send an SMS message on day 10 with a reminder to subscribers to schedule a consultation with your agency to discuss their home buying goals and questions.

Step 4 SMS Template:

"Hi [Subscriber Name], just a friendly reminder to schedule your consultation with our agency to discuss your home buying goals and questions. Call us at [Phone Number] to schedule your appointment today!"

Personalization:

Update the message with your links where appropriate.

Recommended Agent Actions:

Follow up with a phone call to subscribers who reply to the SMS or express interest in the home buying process.

Step 5:

Send an email on day 14 after the initial email with the subject "Finding Your Dream Home." Provide tips and strategies for finding the perfect home, including how to work with a real estate agent and what to look for in a property.

Step 5 Email Template:

Subject: Finding Your Dream Home
Dear [Subscriber],

Congratulations on taking the first step towards homeownership! We hope that you have found our previous emails helpful in navigating the home buying process.

Now that you have a basic understanding of the process, it's time to focus on finding your dream home. Working with a knowledgeable real estate agent is crucial to finding the perfect property that meets your needs and fits within your budget.

Here are some tips and strategies to help you along the way:

Define your needs and wants: Make a list of your must-haves, such as the number of bedrooms, bathrooms, and square footage. Also, consider your lifestyle and what amenities and features are important to you.

Set a budget: Determine how much you can afford to spend on a home, including the down payment, closing costs, and monthly mortgage payments.

Work with a reputable agent: A good agent will listen to your needs, provide expert advice, and guide you through the home buying process.

Use online resources: There are many websites and apps available to help you search for properties and narrow down your options.

We encourage you to schedule a consultation with our agency to discuss your home buying goals and questions. Our experienced agents can help you find the perfect home that meets your needs and fits within your budget. If you need assistance in obtaining a pre-approval from a lender, we are happy to recommend a reputable lender in the area.

Thank you for considering our agency as your partner in the home buying process. We look forward to working with you to find your dream home.

Best regards,

[Agent Signature Block with Contact Information]

Personalization:

Update the Subscriber Name and body with your links and phone numbers where appropriate.

Recommended Agent Action:

Follow up with a phone call to subscribers who reply to the email or express interest in the home buying process.

Step 6:

Send an SMS message on day 17 with a reminder to subscribers to schedule a consultation with your agency if they have not yet done so.

Step 6 SMS Template:

"Hi [Subscriber Name], we wanted to remind you to schedule a consultation with our agency to discuss your home buying goals and questions.

Contact us at [Agent Phone Number] to schedule a meeting. We look forward to helping you find your dream home!"

Personalization:

Update the message with your links where appropriate.

Recommended Agent Action:

Follow up with a phone call to subscribers who reply to the SMS or express interest in the home buying process.

Step 7:

Send an email on day 21 after the initial email with the subject "Financing Your Home Purchase." Provide an overview of financing options for homebuyers, including mortgages, down payments, and closing costs. Encourage subscribers to call your agency or reply to the email to learn more.

Step 7 Email Template:

Subject: Financing Your Home Purchase
Dear [Subscriber],

We hope you're enjoying our First-Time Homebuyer Drip Campaign so far and finding the information helpful as you navigate the home buying process.

Today, we want to talk about financing your home purchase. For many first-time homebuyers, financing can be a confusing and daunting process. That's why we're here to help.

There are several financing options available for homebuyers, including mortgages, down payments, and closing costs. Our team of experts can help you understand the different types of financing available and guide you through the process to find the best option for your unique needs and budget.

If you have any questions or would like to learn more about financing options, please don't hesitate to call us at [Agency Phone Number] or reply to this email.

Best regards,
[Agent Signature Block with Contact Information]

Personalization:

Update the Subscriber Name and body with your links and phone numbers where appropriate.

Recommended Agent Action:

Follow up with a phone call to subscribers who reply to the email or express interest in the home buying process.

Step 8:

Send an SMS message on day 25 with a reminder to subscribers to schedule a consultation with your agency if they have not yet done so.

Step 8 SMS Template:

"Don't miss out on your dream home! Schedule a consultation with our agency today to discuss your home buying goals and questions. Reply to this message to schedule a call with us."

Personalization:

Update the message with your links where appropriate.

Recommended Agent Action:

Follow up with a phone call to subscribers who reply to the SMS or express interest in the home buying process.

Step 9:

Send an email on day 30 after the initial email with the subject "Making an Offer and Closing the Deal." Provide tips and strategies for making an offer on a property and closing the deal. Encourage subscribers to call your agency or reply to the email to learn more.

Step 9 Email Template:

Subject: Making an Offer and Closing the Deal
Dear [Subscriber],

Congratulations on taking the first step towards homeownership! We hope that our previous emails have been helpful in guiding you through the home buying process so far. In this email, we will be discussing how to make an offer on a property and close the deal.

Making an offer can be an exciting but also nerve-wracking experience. Our experienced agents will work with you to make sure that your offer is competitive and meets your needs. We will also guide you through the closing process and ensure that everything goes smoothly.

Here are a few tips to help you make an offer on a property:

Work with your real estate agent to determine a fair offer price based on the current market conditions and the property's value.

Include any contingencies in your offer, such as financing or inspection contingencies, to protect yourself during the buying process.

Be prepared to negotiate with the seller if necessary. Your agent will help you navigate this process and ensure that your needs are met.

Once your offer is accepted, the closing process begins. This includes finalizing your financing, getting a home inspection, and preparing for the closing itself. Our agents will be there to guide you every step of the way.

If you have any questions or would like to schedule a consultation with one of our agents, please don't hesitate to call us at [Agency Phone Number] or reply to this email. We would be happy to help you navigate the home buying process and find your dream home.

Best regards,

[Agent Signature Block with Contact Information]

Personalization:

Update the Subscriber Name and body with your links and phone numbers where appropriate.

Recommended action:

Follow up with a phone call to subscribers who reply to the email or express interest in the home buying process.

Tracking The Success of The First-time Homebuyer Campaign

As with any marketing campaign, it's important to track the success of your first-time homebuyer drip campaign to make sure it's meeting your goals and reaching your target audience. By monitoring your campaign's metrics, you can adjust your strategy and improve your results over time.

To track the success of the First Time Homebuyer Campaign, there are a few metrics to monitor:

- Email open rate: This is the percentage of subscribers who open your emails. A high open rate indicates that your subject lines are effective and that subscribers are interested in your content.
- Email click-through rate: This is the percentage of subscribers who click on links in your emails. A high click-through rate indicates that your content is engaging and that subscribers are taking action.
- SMS response rate: This is the percentage of subscribers who respond to your SMS messages. A high response rate indicates that your messages are effective and that subscribers are engaged.
- Phone call conversion rate: This is the percentage of subscribers who become clients after speaking with your agency on the phone. A high conversion rate indicates that your agents are effective at converting leads into clients.

By tracking the success of your first-time homebuyer drip campaign, you can gain valuable insights into what's working and what's not, and make data-driven decisions to optimize your strategy. With consistent monitoring and adjustment, you can ensure your campaign is effective in reaching and converting your target audience into satisfied homebuyers.

Tips for Customizing The First-time Homebuyer Drip Campaign

By personalizing the campaign, you can increase engagement and ultimately drive more successful outcomes for your business. Here are some tips for customizing the first-time homebuyer drip campaign:

- Personalize the messaging: Use the subscriber's name and include personalized recommendations based on their preferences.
- Segment your audience: Group subscribers by demographic, interests, and location to send more relevant messages.
- Adjust the timing: Test different waiting periods between messages to find the optimal cadence for your audience.

- Customize the content: Provide local real estate market insights, relevant statistics, and other resources that are specific to your audience's needs.
- Offer incentives: Consider offering incentives such as a free home inspection or consultation to encourage subscribers to take action.
- Use visual aids: Incorporate images, videos, and infographics to make your messages more engaging and informative.
- Monitor engagement: Keep track of email open rates, click-through rates, and other metrics to gauge the effectiveness of your campaign and make adjustments as needed.

By customizing your first-time homebuyer drip campaign, you can create a more personalized and effective experience for your audience, ultimately leading to more successful conversions and satisfied clients.

Conclusion

A first-time homebuyer drip campaign can be an effective way to guide potential clients through the complex process of buying a home. By providing helpful information, establishing trust, and staying in touch over time, you can build relationships with prospective buyers and position yourself as a knowledgeable and trustworthy agent. Remember to always personalize your messaging and track your results to continuously improve your campaign. With the right approach, a first-time homebuyer drip campaign can help you build a steady stream of new clients and grow your real estate business.

9

REFERRAL REQUEST DRIP CAMPAIGN

Referral requests are a critical component of any successful real estate business. A referral from a satisfied client can be one of the most effective ways to generate new business, but asking for referrals can be uncomfortable and challenging for many agents. A Referral Request Drip Campaign can help streamline the process by providing a systematic approach to asking for referrals over time. In this chapter, we'll explore how to create an effective Referral Request Drip Campaign, including the key components of a successful campaign, best practices for timing and messaging, and tips for optimizing your campaign to maximize your results. Whether you're a new agent just starting out or an experienced professional looking to grow your business, a Referral Request Drip Campaign can be an invaluable tool in your marketing arsenal.

User Scenario: Referral Request Drip Campaign

Alyssa, a meticulous real estate agent, knows the power of referrals in growing her business. To tap into this potential, Alyssa implements a Referral Request Drip Campaign. This campaign involves sending a series of emails and SMS messages to her satisfied clients, thanking them for their business and encouraging them to refer their friends and family who may be in the market for a new home.

By providing clear calls to action and offering incentives for referrals, Alyssa ensures that her clients feel appreciated and motivated to spread the word about her exceptional service. This approach not only generates a steady stream of new leads but also reinforces Alyssa's reputation as a trusted and reliable real estate professional.

Implementing this drip campaign can help you achieve similar success in leveraging your satisfied clients to expand your network and grow your business, ultimately leading to more referrals and successful transactions.

Referral Request Drip Campaign Use Cases

Referral marketing is a powerful way to grow your business, and a referral request drip campaign is a great way to turn your satisfied customers into brand ambassadors. By keeping your brand top of mind with your customers and reminding them to refer their friends and family to you, you can generate a steady stream of new business without spending a lot of money on marketing. Knowing who to target can make all the difference for a successful campaign. Below you will find a list of your target audience for this campaign:

- Existing clients: Send a referral request email to your existing clients, thanking them for their business and asking them to refer any friends or family who may be in the market for a new home.
- Previous clients: Reach out to previous clients who may have worked with you in the past, thanking them for their business and asking for any referrals they may have.
- Network contacts: Send an email to your network contacts, including other real estate agents, lenders, and industry professionals, asking for referrals.
- Social media followers: Utilize your social media channels to ask for referrals from your followers, providing them with a direct link to your website or contact information.
- Open house visitors: Follow up with visitors to your open houses, thanking them for their interest and asking for any referrals they may have.
- Local businesses: Partner with local businesses, such as home improvement stores or moving companies, to offer referral incentives and reach a wider audience.
- Personal connections: Reach out to your personal connections, such as friends and family, and ask for referrals.

A referral request drip campaign is a simple but effective way to generate new business through your existing customers. By reminding your customers to refer their friends and family to your business, you can tap into a powerful source of new leads and increase your revenue without spending a lot of money on advertising. By customizing your campaign to suit your business and your customers, you can make the most of this powerful marketing technique and turn your satisfied customers into brand ambassadors for your business.

Step-By-Step Guide and Templates

Step 1:

Send an initial email with the subject "Help Your Friends and Family Find Their Dream Home!" Thank the subscriber for their business and ask them to refer any friends or family who may be interested in buying or selling a home to your agency. Encourage them to call your agency or reply to the email with any referrals.

Step 1 Email Template:

Subject: Help Your Friends and Family Find Their Dream Home!
Dear [Subscriber Name],

Thank you for choosing our agency for your real estate needs. We appreciate your business and would like to ask for your help in referring anyone you know who may be interested in buying or selling a home. Our team of experienced agents will provide them with the best service possible.

If you have any friends or family members who are looking to buy or sell a home, please don't hesitate to refer them to our agency. You can either call us or reply to this email with their contact information.

Thank you for your continued support!

Best regards,

[Agent Signature Block with Contact Information]

Personalization:

Update the Subscriber Name and body with your links and phone numbers where appropriate.

Recommended Agent Action:

Follow up with a phone call to subscribers who reply to the email or express interest in referring someone to your agency.

Step 2:

Send an SMS message on day 7 after the initial email with a reminder to subscribers to refer anyone they know who may be interested in buying or selling a home to your agency.

Step 2 SMS Template:

"Don't forget to refer your friends and family who are interested in buying or selling a home to our agency. Call us or reply to this message with their contact information. Thank you!"

Personalization:

Update the message with your links where appropriate.

Recommended Agent Actions:

Follow up with a phone call to subscribers who reply to the SMS or express interest in referring someone to your agency.

Step 3:

Send an email on day 14 after the initial email with the subject "Why Choose Our Agency for Your Real Estate Needs?" Highlight your agency's unique selling points and why someone should choose your agency for their real estate needs. Encourage subscribers to refer anyone they know who may be interested in buying or selling a home to your agency.

Step 3 Email Template:

Subject: Why Choose Our Agency for Your Real Estate Needs?
Dear [Subscriber Name],

We hope this email finds you well. We would like to take this opportunity to highlight why our agency is the best choice for your real estate needs.

Our team of experienced agents has a proven track record of success and will work tirelessly to help you achieve your real estate goals.

We provide exceptional customer service and strive to make the home buying or selling process as stress-free as possible for our clients.

We are a local agency with extensive knowledge of the area and can provide you with valuable insights into the local real estate market.

If you know anyone who may be interested in buying or selling a home, please don't hesitate to refer them to our agency. You can either call us or reply to this email with their contact information.

Thank you for your continued support!

Best regards,

[Agent Signature Block with Contact Information]

Personalization:

Update the Subscriber Name and body with your links and phone numbers where appropriate.

Recommended action:

Follow up with a phone call to subscribers who reply to the email or express interest in referring someone to your agency.

Step 4:

Send an SMS message on day 21 with a reminder to subscribers to refer anyone they know who may be interested in buying or selling a home to your agency.

Step 4 SMS Template:

"Have you referred anyone to our agency yet? If not, now is the perfect time! Call us or reply to this message with their contact information. Thank you!"

Personalization:

Update the message with your links where appropriate.

Recommended action:

Follow up with a phone call to subscribers who reply to the SMS or express interest in referring someone to your agency.

Step 5:

Send an email on day 30 after the initial email with the subject "Thank You for Your Referrals!" Thank subscribers for any referrals they have provided and remind them to continue referring anyone they know who may be interested in buying or selling a home to your agency.

Step 5 Email Template:

Subject: Thank You for Your Referrals!

Dear [Subscriber Name],

We wanted to take a moment to thank you for referring your friends and family to our agency. We truly appreciate your trust and support.

If you know anyone else who may be interested in buying or selling a home, please don't hesitate to refer them to our agency. You can either call us or reply to this email with their contact information.

Thank you again for your referrals and for choosing our agency for your real estate needs.

Best regards,

[Agent Signature Block with Contact Information]

Personalization:

Update the Subscriber Name and body with your links and phone numbers where appropriate.

Recommended action:

Follow up with a phone call to subscribers who reply to the email or express interest in referring someone to your agency.

Tracking the Success of the Referral Request Drip Campaign

Tracking the success of your referral request drip campaign is essential to understanding how well it is performing and making adjustments to improve its effectiveness. Here are some metrics and methods to track the success of your campaign:

- Number of referrals received: This is the most obvious metric to track. Keep a record of the number of referrals you receive during the campaign period.

- Conversion rate: Track how many of the referrals you received turned into actual clients. This will give you an idea of how effective your campaign is at generating quality leads.
- Open and click-through rates: Measure the open and click-through rates of your emails to determine how engaged your subscribers are with your campaign. If the rates are low, it may be an indication that you need to improve the content or timing of your emails.
- Response rate: Keep track of the number of subscribers who respond to your emails or SMS messages. This will help you gauge how interested they are in referring someone to your agency.
- Feedback from clients: Ask your clients how they heard about your agency to get an idea of how effective your referral campaign is at generating leads.

To track these metrics, you can use email marketing tools or CRM software. You can also manually keep track of the number of referrals and conversions in a spreadsheet or document.

By tracking the success of your referral request drip campaign, you can make data-driven decisions to improve its effectiveness and generate more quality leads for your agency.

Tips for Customizing the Referral Request Drip Campaign

To make the most out of a Referral Request Drip Campaign, it is important to customize the campaign to fit your specific agency and audience. By making small tweaks and adjustments to the campaign, you can increase the effectiveness and success of the campaign. Here are some tips for customizing the Referral Request Drip Campaign:

- Personalize your emails and SMS messages: Use the subscriber's name and any other relevant information you have about them to make your communications feel more personalized and engaging.
- Use a clear call to action: Encourage subscribers to refer their friends and family to your agency with a clear call to action,

such as "Call us today to refer someone you know who may be interested in buying or selling a home."

- Offer incentives for referrals: While you cannot offer monetary rewards for referrals, you can offer incentives such as exclusive access to new listings or personalized home buying or selling consultations.
- Timing is key: Make sure to space out your messages appropriately and avoid bombarding subscribers with too many communications. Find a balance that works for your audience and your agency.
- Test and adjust: Continuously test and adjust your messaging to find what works best for your audience. Analyze metrics such as open rates and click-through rates to see what resonates with your subscribers and adjust accordingly.
- Make it easy to refer: Provide subscribers with easy-to-use tools and resources to refer their friends and family to your agency, such as a referral form on your website or social media.

By customizing your Referral Request Drip Campaign, you can increase the likelihood of receiving referrals from your subscribers and grow your client base.

Conclusion

The Referral Request Drip Campaign can be an effective way for real estate agents to generate new leads and expand their client base. By leveraging the power of referrals, agents can tap into the networks of their current clients and reach a wider audience. The key to success is to provide valuable content and incentives that encourage subscribers to refer their friends and family. By tracking the success of the campaign and making adjustments along the way, agents can ensure that they are maximizing their efforts and generating the best possible results.

10

OPEN HOUSE DRIP CAMPAIGN

The Open House Drip Campaign is a time-sensitive marketing strategy that aims to generate interest and attendance for your upcoming open house event. Typically, real estate open houses are scheduled two weeks in advance, which provides ample time to plan and execute a successful campaign. With a series of targeted emails and SMS messages, you can reach out to your subscriber list and encourage them to attend your open house event. By providing valuable information about the property and the event itself, you can generate a buzz around the property and increase the chances of finding potential buyers. In this chapter, we will walk you through the steps for creating an effective Open House Drip Campaign within the two-week timeframe.

User Scenario 1: Open House Drip Campaign

Dexter, a forward-thinking real estate agent, recognizes the importance of generating interest and driving attendance to his open house events. To achieve this, Dexter implements an Open House Drip Campaign. This campaign consists of a series of emails and SMS messages that provide detailed information about the property, the event schedule, and the benefits of attending.

By consistently engaging with potential buyers and keeping them informed about the open house, Dexter ensures a higher turnout and greater interest in the property. This approach not only builds excitement and anticipation but also positions Dexter as a proactive and detail-oriented real estate professional.

Implementing this drip campaign can help you achieve similar success in attracting potential buyers, engaging your audience, and driving attendance

97

at your open house events, ultimately leading to more successful transactions and satisfied clients.

User Scenario 2: Open House Invitation Drip Campaign

Emily, a real estate agent, has an upcoming open house for a beautiful property in a highly desirable neighborhood. To maximize attendance and generate interest, Emily decides to implement an Open House Invitation Drip Campaign. This campaign sends a series of well-timed communications to potential buyers, providing valuable information about the property, creating excitement, and ensuring they mark their calendars for the event.

By systematically engaging with prospective buyers, Emily can build anticipation and ensure a successful open house. This method not only helps in attracting more attendees but also increases the likelihood of receiving offers on the property.

Implementing this drip campaign can help you achieve similar success in organizing and promoting your open houses effectively.

Open House Drip Campaign Use Cases

The Open House Drip Campaign is an effective way to generate interest and attract potential buyers to a specific property. By providing valuable information and creating a sense of urgency, you can encourage subscribers to attend your open house and potentially make an offer on the property.

Here are some use cases for an Open House Drip Campaign:

- Generating Buzz for the Open House: The campaign can be used to generate excitement and interest for the upcoming open house event. It can include teasers about the property and the neighborhood to pique the interest of potential buyers.
- Attracting Attendees: The campaign can be used to attract potential buyers to the open house. It can include details about the property, the date and time of the open house, and any incentives for attending.
- Providing Information: The campaign can be used to provide attendees with more information about the property and the neighborhood. This can include information about nearby amenities, schools, and local attractions.

- Following Up with Attendees: The campaign can be used to follow up with attendees after the open house to gauge their level of interest in the property and answer any questions they may have.
- Building Relationships: The campaign can be used to build relationships with potential buyers who attend the open house. By providing value and staying in touch, agents can develop long-term relationships that lead to future business.

Step-By-Step Guide and Templates

Step 1:

Send an initial email with the subject "Join Us for an Open House at [Property Address]" to subscribers who have shown interest in the property or who fit the target buyer profile. Provide the date, time, and location of the open house and encourage subscribers to attend.

Step 1 Email Template:

Subject: Join Us for an Open House at [Property Address]
Dear [Subscriber],

We would like to invite you to our upcoming open house at [Property Address]. This is a fantastic opportunity for you to see the property in person and get a feel for the neighborhood.

The open house will be held on [Date] from [Time] at [Location]. We hope to see you there!

If you have any questions or would like to schedule a private showing, please don't hesitate to call our agency at [Agency Phone Number] or reply to this email.

Best regards,
[Agent Signature Block with Contact Information]

Personalization:

Update the Subscriber Name and body with your links and phone numbers where appropriate.

DRIP, DRIP, SOLD

Recommended Agent Actions:

Follow up with a phone call to subscribers who reply to the email or express interest in attending the open house.

Step 2:

Send an SMS message on day 3 after the initial email with a reminder to subscribers about the open house and the date and time.

Step 2 SMS Template:

"Hi [Subscriber Name], don't forget about our open house at [Property Address] on [Date] from [Time]. We hope to see you there! - [Your Agency Name]"

Personalization:

Update the message with your links and information where appropriate.

Recommended Agent Action:

Follow up with a phone call to subscribers who reply to the SMS or express interest in attending the open house.

Step 3:

Send an email on day 7 after the initial email with the subject "Get Ready for the Open House at [Property Address]" to provide subscribers with information about the property and what to expect at the open house. Include information about the home's features, the surrounding neighborhood, and any unique selling points. Encourage subscribers to attend the open house and ask them to RSVP if possible.

Step 2 Email Template:

Subject: Get Ready for the Open House at [Property Address]
Hello [Subscriber Name],

We hope this email finds you well. We wanted to remind you about the upcoming open house at [Property Address] on [Date] from [Time]. As a valued subscriber, we want to provide you with some additional information about the property to help you prepare for the event.

[Property Address] is a beautiful [Number of Bedrooms/Bathrooms] home located in the desirable [Neighborhood Name] neighborhood. Some of the home's features include [List some standout features such as an updated kitchen, outdoor entertaining space, etc.]. We believe that this home will be a perfect fit for someone who is looking for [Describe the type of buyer this home will appeal to].

In addition to the home itself, the surrounding neighborhood offers many amenities that are sure to impress. [Mention any nearby parks, restaurants, shopping centers, etc. that will make the area attractive to potential buyers.]

We encourage you to attend the open house and take a look for yourself. If possible, please RSVP so that we can ensure that we have enough staff on hand to answer any questions you may have.

Thank you for your continued interest in [Agency Name]. We look forward to seeing you at the open house!

Best regards,

[Agent Signature Block with Contact Information]

Personalization:

Update the Subscriber Name and body with your links and phone numbers where appropriate.

Recommended action:

Follow up with a phone call to subscribers who reply to the email or express interest in attending the open house.

Step 4:

Send an SMS message on day 10 with a reminder to subscribers about the open house and the date and time. Encourage them to RSVP if they haven't already done so.

Step 4 SMS Template:

"Hi [Subscriber Name], just a quick reminder about the open house at [Property Address] happening in 4 days. Have you RSVP'd yet? We'd love to see you there and show you around the property. Reply YES to confirm your attendance. - [Your Agency Name]"

DRIP, DRIP, SOLD

Personalization:

Update the message with your links and information where appropriate.

Recommended Agent Action:

Follow up with a phone call to subscribers who reply to the SMS or express interest in attending the open house.

Step 5:

Send an email on day 13 after the initial email with the subject "Don't Miss Out on [Property Address]!"

Provide subscribers with a sense of urgency by letting them know that the property is still available and encouraging them to attend the open house if they haven't already done so. Include any updates about the property or the open house, such as changes to the date or time.

Step 5 Email Template:

Subject: Don't Miss Out on [Property Address]!
Dear [Subscriber Name],

I wanted to follow up with you and remind you about the open house at [Property Address] tomorrow. This is a fantastic opportunity to tour the property and see if it could be your next dream home.

We still have spots available for the open house, so if you haven't already RSVP'd, please let us know if you plan to attend. You can simply reply to this email or call our office at [Phone Number].

I also wanted to let you know that there have been some updates to the property since our last email. [Include any updates here, such as recent renovations or price adjustments].

Don't miss out on this amazing opportunity. We look forward to seeing you at the open house!

Best regards,
[Agent Signature Block with Contact Information]

Personalization:

Update the Subscriber Name and body with your links and phone numbers where appropriate.

OPEN HOUSE DRIP CAMPAIGN

Recommended Agent Action:

Follow up with a phone call to subscribers who reply to the email or express interest in attending the open house.

Step 6:

Send an SMS message on day 14 (the day of the open house) with a final reminder about the open house. Be sure to send this email in the morning the day of to give the receiver time to adjust their schedule. Encourage subscribers to attend and provide any last-minute updates or information.

Step 6 SMS Template:

"Hi [Subscriber Name], just a friendly reminder that the open house at [Property Address] is happening today! Don't miss out on this amazing opportunity to see the property in person. We hope to see you there!"

Personalization:

Update the message with your links and information where appropriate.

Recommended Agent Actions:

Follow up with a phone call to subscribers who reply to the SMS or express interest in attending the open house.

Step 7:

Send an email on day 20 after the initial email with the subject "Thank You for Attending the Open House at [Property Address]!" Thank subscribers for attending the open house and provide them with any follow-up information they may need, such as how to schedule a showing or how to make an offer on the property.

Step 7 Email Template:

Subject: Thank You for Attending the Open House at [Property Address]!
Dear [Subscriber Name],

We wanted to take a moment to thank you for attending the open house at [Property Address]! We hope you enjoyed seeing the property and getting a sense of what makes it a truly special home.

As a reminder, if you have any questions about the property or would like to schedule a showing, please don't hesitate to reach out to our team. We're happy to answer any questions you may have and help you take the next steps in the home buying process.

Thank you again for your interest in this property and for attending the open house. We hope to see you again soon!

Best,

[Agent Signature Block with Contact Information]

Personalization:

Update the Subscriber Name and body with your links and phone numbers where appropriate.

Recommended Agent Action:

Follow up with a phone call to subscribers who reply to the email or express interest in scheduling a showing or making an offer on the property.

Tracking the Success of the Open House Drip Campaign

Tracking the success of an open house drip campaign can help you determine its effectiveness and make necessary adjustments to improve its performance. Here are some metrics you can track to measure the success of your campaign:

- Open house attendance: Keep track of how many people attended the open house to determine the effectiveness of your marketing efforts.
- RSVP rate: Track the number of people who RSVP'd to attend the open house to gauge the effectiveness of your messaging and targeting.
- Email open rates and click-through rates: Measure the open rates and click-through rates of your emails to determine the effectiveness of your messaging and calls to action.
- SMS response rates: Track the response rates of your SMS messages to determine how effective they are in driving attendance and engagement.

OPEN HOUSE DRIP CAMPAIGN

- Property inquiries and showings: Keep track of how many people inquired about the property or scheduled a showing to determine the effectiveness of your campaign in generating leads and interest.
- Offers and sales: Monitor how many offers and sales resulted from the open house to determine the ultimate success of your campaign in achieving your business goals.
- By tracking these metrics, you can gain valuable insights into the performance of your open house drip campaign and make necessary adjustments to improve its effectiveness in generating leads and driving sales.

Tips For Customizing the Open House Drip Campaign

The Open House Drip Campaign can be customized to meet the specific needs and goals of your real estate agency. By tailoring the campaign to your target audience and the unique features of each property, you can increase attendance at open houses and generate more leads and sales. Here are some tips for customizing the Open House Drip Campaign to make it more effective for your agency.

- Customize the messaging: Tailor the messaging to the specific property being showcased at the open house. Highlight the unique selling points of the property, such as its location, size, or amenities.
- Segment your list: Segment your email list by demographics, such as age or income, to ensure that your messaging resonates with each group. For example, you may want to highlight the family friendly features of a property to subscribers with children or emphasize the high-end finishes to those with higher incomes.
- Use eye-catching visuals: Use high-quality photos and videos of the property to grab subscribers' attention and showcase the property's features.
- Incorporate social media: Use social media to promote the open house and encourage subscribers to share the event with their friends and followers. You can create a Facebook event, post photos on Instagram, or even create a custom hashtag for the event.
- Personalize your follow-up: After the open house, personalize your follow-up communications based on each subscriber's level of interest. For example, you may want to send a more detailed follow

up email to subscribers who spent more time at the open house or expressed interest in making an offer.

By customizing the Open House Drip Campaign to your specific needs and audience, you can increase engagement and drive more traffic to your open house event.

Conclusion

The Open House Drip Campaign can be a valuable tool for real estate agents looking to attract potential buyers and showcase their properties. By following the step-by-step guide and customizing the campaign to fit your specific needs, you can effectively communicate with subscribers and encourage them to attend an open house event. By tracking the success of the campaign and making adjustments as necessary, you can improve your results and build lasting relationships with potential buyers. Don't be afraid to get creative and make the campaign your own – with the right strategy and execution, it can be a powerful way to grow your business and attract new clients.

11

JUST SOLD DRIP CAMPAIGN

The Just Sold Drip Campaign is designed to showcase your agency's recent successful real estate transactions and to remind subscribers that they too could experience similar success in either buying or selling their home. By highlighting recent sales, you can demonstrate your agency's expertise and track record of success, while also providing valuable insights into the current real estate market. This campaign can be customized for both buyers and sellers, allowing you to target specific segments of your subscriber list and provide them with relevant information and resources to help them achieve their real estate goals.

User Scenario: Just Sold Drip Campaign

Caleb, an ambitious real estate agent, wants to demonstrate his agency's success and attract new clients by showcasing recently sold properties. To achieve this, Caleb implements a Just Sold Drip Campaign. This campaign involves sending a series of emails and SMS messages that highlight his agency's recent successful transactions, including details about the sold properties, sale prices, and the short time they were on the market.

By sharing these success stories, Caleb not only showcases his agency's expertise and efficiency but also instills confidence in potential clients that they too can achieve similar results with his help. This approach builds trust and positions Caleb as a knowledgeable and results-driven real estate professional.

Implementing this drip campaign can help you achieve similar success in promoting your real estate expertise and attracting new clients, ultimately leading to increased referrals and successful transactions.

Just Sold Drip Campaign Use Cases

The Just Sold Drip Campaign is a powerful marketing tool that real estate agents can use to showcase their recent sales and generate new business. This campaign is ideal for agents who want to promote their expertise in the local market and demonstrate their ability to help clients buy or sell a property. Here are some use cases for the Just Sold Drip Campaign:

- Showcasing Your Success: By sharing your recent sales with your subscribers, you can demonstrate your expertise and establish yourself as a top agent in your market. This can help you attract new clients who are looking for an agent with a proven track record of success.

- Generating Referrals: When you share your recent sales with your subscribers, you can encourage them to refer their friends and family to you. People are more likely to refer someone they know if they have seen evidence of their success, so the Just Sold Drip Campaign can be a powerful tool for generating new business through referrals.

- Building Your Brand: By regularly sending out updates on your recent sales, you can help build your brand and establish yourself as a trusted authority in your local real estate market. This can help you attract more clients and grow your business over time.

- Educating Your Subscribers: The Just Sold Drip Campaign can also be a great way to educate your subscribers about the local real estate market. By sharing information about recent sales, you can help your subscribers understand current market conditions and make informed decisions about buying or selling a property.

- Building Relationships: Finally, the Just Sold Drip Campaign can be a powerful tool for building relationships with your subscribers. By sharing your recent sales and keeping them informed about the local real estate market, you can demonstrate that you care about their needs and are committed to helping them achieve their real estate goals.

No matter what your goals are as a real estate agent, the Just Sold Drip Campaign can be a valuable tool for promoting your recent sales and generating new business. By showcasing your success, building your brand, educating your subscribers, and building relationships, you can establish yourself as a top agent in your market and attract new clients for years to come.

Step-By-Step Guide and Templates

Step 1:

Send an initial email to subscribers who have shown interest in buying or selling a property with the subject "We Just Sold [Property Address]!" Highlight the details of the recently sold property, including the sale price, number of bedrooms and bathrooms, and any unique selling points. Encourage subscribers to contact your agency if they are interested in buying or selling a property.

Step 1 Email Template:

Subject: We Just Sold [Property Address]!

Dear [Subscriber],

We are excited to share that we have just sold [Property Address]! This stunning property boasts [Number of Bedrooms and Bathrooms], a [Unique Selling Point], and much more.

The property sold for [Sale Price], which is a testament to the quality of the property and our dedication to helping our clients achieve their real estate goals.

If you or anyone you know is interested in buying or selling a property, we would be happy to assist. Please don't hesitate to reach out to us at [Contact Information].

Thank you for your continued support.

Best regards,

[Agent Signature Block with Contact Information]

Personalization:

Update the Subscriber Name and body with your links and phone numbers where appropriate.

Recommended Agent Action:

Follow up with a phone call to subscribers who reply to the email or express interest in buying or selling a property.

Step 2:

Send an SMS message on day 7 after the initial email with a reminder of the recently sold property and a call-to-action to contact your agency for buying or selling a property.

Step 2 SMS Template:

Hi [Subscriber], we recently sold [Property Address]! Contact us today to learn how we can help you buy or sell a property. [Your Agency]

Personalization:

Update the message with your links and information where appropriate.

Recommended Agent Action:

Follow up with a phone call to subscribers who reply to the SMS or express interest in buying or selling a property.

Step 3:

Send an email on day 14 after the initial email with the subject "How We Helped Sell [Property Address]!" Provide subscribers with a detailed account of how your agency helped to sell the property, including your marketing strategy and negotiation techniques. Encourage subscribers to contact your agency if they are interested in buying or selling a property.

Step 3 Email Template:

Subject: How We Helped Sell [Property Address]!
Dear [Subscriber],

We wanted to take a moment to share with you how we helped sell [Property Address]. We know that selling a property can be a challenging process, but we were able to successfully close the sale thanks to our expertise and proven strategies.

Our marketing efforts helped to attract a wide range of potential buyers, and our negotiation techniques ensured that our client received the best possible price for their property. We are proud of our work and look forward to helping other clients achieve similar success.

If you or anyone you know is interested in buying or selling a property, we would be happy to assist. Please don't hesitate to reach out to us at [Contact Information].

Thank you for your continued support.

[Agent Signature Block with Contact Information]

Personalization:

Update the Subscriber Name and body with your links and phone numbers where appropriate.

Recommended Agent Action:

Follow up with a phone call to subscribers who reply to the email or express interest in buying or selling a property.

Step 4:

Send an SMS message on day 21 after the initial email with a reminder to subscribers of your agency's expertise in buying or selling a property.

Step 4 SMS Template:

Hi [Subscriber], our expertise helped us to sell [Property Address]. Contact us today to see how we can help you buy or sell a property. [Your Agency]

Personalization:

Update the message with your links and information where appropriate.

Recommended Agent Action:

Follow up with a phone call to subscribers who reply to the SMS or express interest in buying or selling a property.

Step 5:

Send an email on day 30 after the initial email with the subject "Thank You for Your Support!" Thank subscribers for their interest and support in your business and highlight the success of the property sale. Encourage subscribers to reach out to you for any real estate needs they may have in the future.

Step 5 Email Template:

Subject: Thank You for Your Support!
Dear [Subscriber],

I wanted to take a moment to thank you for your interest and support in our recent property sale. With your help, we were able to successfully close the deal and achieve our client's real estate goals.

I hope that you found the updates and information we provided throughout the process helpful and informative. We strive to provide the highest level of service to all of our clients and subscribers, and we appreciate your continued interest in our business.

If you have any real estate needs in the future, whether it be buying, selling, or investing, please do not hesitate to reach out to us. We would be happy to provide our expertise and assistance.

Thank you again for your support, and we look forward to staying in touch.

Best regards,
[Agent Signature Block with Contact Information]

Personalization:

Update the Subscriber Name and body with your links and phone numbers where appropriate.

Recommended Agent Action:

Follow up with a phone call to subscribers who reply to the email or express interest in buying or selling a property.

Step 6:

Send an SMS message on day 35 after the initial email with a reminder to subscribers about the recently sold property and to contact you for any real estate needs they may have.

Step 6 SMS Template

Hi [Subscriber Name], just a quick reminder that we recently sold the property at [Property Address], and we wanted to thank you for your support! If you have any real estate needs in the future, please don't hesitate to contact us. We'd be happy to help you out.

Personalization:

Update the message with your links and information where appropriate.

Recommended Agent Action:

Follow up with a phone call to subscribers who reply to the SMS or express interest in buying or selling a property.

Step 7:

Send an email on day 40 after the initial email with the subject "What's Next for [Neighborhood Name]?" Provide subscribers with an update on the local real estate market and any upcoming properties that may be of interest to them. Encourage subscribers to reach out to you for any real estate needs they may have.

Step 7 Email Template:

Subject: What's Next for [Neighborhood Name]?
Dear [Subscriber Name],

I hope this email finds you well. I wanted to provide you with an update on the local real estate market in [Neighborhood Name]. As you may know, the market has been very active lately, and there are several upcoming properties that may be of interest to you.

In addition to recently sold properties, there are also several new listings that have just hit the market. I would be happy to provide you with more information on these properties or any others that catch your eye.

Please feel free to reach out to me with any questions or concerns you may have. I am always available to help you with any real estate needs you may have, whether you are looking to buy or sell.

Thank you again for your support, and I look forward to hearing from you soon.

Best regards,
[Agent Signature Block with Contact Information]

Personalization:

Update the Subscriber Name and body with your links and phone numbers where appropriate.

Recommended Agent Action:

Follow up with a phone call to subscribers who reply to the email or express interest in buying or selling a property.

Step 8:

Send an SMS message on day 45 after the initial email with a reminder to subscribers about the local real estate market and to contact you for any real estate needs they may have.

Step 8 SMS Template:

Hi [Subscriber Name],
This is a reminder to keep your finger on the pulse of the local real estate market. If you have any real estate needs or questions, don't hesitate to reach out to us. We're always here to help. Thank you for your continued support. Best, [Your Agency Name]

Personalization:

Update the message with your links and information where appropriate.

Recommended Agent Action:

Follow up with a phone call to subscribers who reply to the SMS or express interest in buying or selling a property.

Step 9:

Send an email on day 50 after the initial email with the subject "Thank You for Your Continued Support!" Thank subscribers for their continued support and offer them any new information or updates about the real estate market. Encourage subscribers to reach out to you for any real estate needs they may have.

Step 9 Email Template:

Subject: Thank You for Your Continued Support!

Dear [Subscriber Name],

I wanted to take a moment to thank you for your continued interest and support in my real estate business. It's because of clients like you that I am able to provide exceptional service and achieve successful sales.

I am excited to share that the local real estate market is still going strong, and there are some great opportunities for both buyers and sellers. If you or anyone you know is interested in buying or selling a property, please don't hesitate to reach out to me. I would be happy to answer any questions you may have and provide you with the guidance you need.

Thank you again for your support, and I look forward to hearing from you soon.

Best regards,

[Agent Signature Block with Contact Information]

Personalization:

Update the Subscriber Name and body with your links and phone numbers where appropriate.

Recommended Agent Action:

Follow up with a phone call to subscribers who reply to the email or express interest in buying or selling a property.

Tracking the Success of the Just Sold Drip Campaign

Tracking the success of your Just Sold Drip Campaign is crucial to understanding the effectiveness of your marketing efforts and improving future campaigns. By monitoring metrics such as open rates, clickthrough rates, and conversions, you can gain valuable insights into subscriber engagement and adjust your approach accordingly.

To track the success of your Just Sold Drip Campaign, you can use email marketing software to monitor key metrics such as open rates, click-through rates, and conversions. By analyzing these metrics, you can gain insights into subscriber engagement and adjust your campaign accordingly. For example, if you notice a low open rate on a particular email, you can experiment with different subject lines to improve engagement. Similarly, if you notice a high click-through rate on a certain email, you can use that information to inform future campaigns.

In addition to monitoring email metrics, you can also track phone call and appointment activity generated by the campaign. By tracking these interactions, you can identify which subscribers are the most engaged and follow up with them directly to nurture the relationship.

Tracking the success of your Just Sold Drip Campaign is an ongoing process that requires consistent monitoring and adjustment. By analyzing metrics and tracking subscriber interactions, you can gain valuable insights into the effectiveness of your campaign and make improvements to achieve your marketing goals.

Tips For Customizing the Just Sold Campaign

While the Just Sold campaign is a great way to keep your subscribers engaged and informed about the success of your business, customizing it to fit your specific needs and goals can help you achieve even greater success. Here are some tips to help you personalize your Just Sold campaign and make the most of this powerful marketing tool.

- Tailor Your Content: Every real estate agency has a unique brand, and your Just Sold campaign should reflect that. Use language and imagery that aligns with your brand and appeals to your target audience. Consider showcasing your agency's values, expertise, and unique selling points in your messaging.
- Highlight Different Properties: While the Just Sold campaign is focused on one recently sold property, you can use it to promote other properties in your portfolio as well. Use your emails and SMS messages to highlight different properties that may be of interest to your subscribers and provide updates on their availability or price changes.
- Include a Call to Action: Encourage subscribers to take action by including a clear call to action in each message. Whether you want them to schedule a showing, request a market analysis, or simply reach out with any questions, make it easy for them to do so by providing clear instructions and contact information.

- Use Personalization: Personalizing your messages with your subscriber's name, location, or other relevant information can help increase engagement and make your communication feel more tailored to their needs.

By customizing your Just Sold campaign to fit your agency's unique needs and goals, you can maximize its effectiveness and build stronger relationships with your subscribers. Use these tips to help you create a campaign that resonates with your audience and drives real results for your business.

Conclusion

The Just Sold Drip Campaign is a powerful tool for real estate agents looking to stay in touch with their clients and stay top of mind. By highlighting recent sales and sharing insights about the local real estate market, you can keep your clients informed and engaged, while also positioning yourself as an expert in your field.

As with any drip campaign, it's important to track your results and make adjustments as needed. Pay close attention to open and click-through rates, as well as any replies or follow-up inquiries you receive. Use this information to refine your messaging and make sure you're providing value to your subscribers.

Remember that the ultimate goal of the Just Sold Drip Campaign is to build long-term relationships with your clients and to become their go-to resource for all things real estate. By consistently providing valuable information and staying top of mind, you'll be well-positioned to grow your business and build a loyal client base.

12

HOME MAINTENANCE DRIP CAMPAIGN

The Home Maintenance Drip Campaign is a powerful marketing tool for real estate agents and homeowners to keep their clients engaged with their properties. This campaign aims to educate and inform homeowners about the importance of home maintenance and to offer tips and advice on how to properly maintain their homes. The goal is to establish a long-term relationship with clients by providing them with valuable information that will help them take care of their homes and prevent any costly repairs or damage. By offering this value-added service, real estate agents and homeowners can build trust and credibility with their clients and position themselves as the go-to resource for all their home related needs.

User Scenario: Home Maintenance Drip Campaign

Jordan, a proactive real estate agent, wants to ensure that his clients are not only happy with their new homes but also well-equipped to maintain them. To achieve this, Jordan implements a Home Maintenance Drip Campaign. This campaign involves sending a series of emails and SMS messages that provide seasonal maintenance reminders, energy efficiency tips, DIY project ideas, and home safety advice.

By offering regular, valuable maintenance tips, Jordan helps his clients keep their homes in top condition and avoid costly repairs. This approach not only builds trust and rapport but also positions Jordan as a knowledgeable and caring real estate professional.

Implementing this drip campaign can help you achieve similar success in keeping your clients engaged and satisfied, ultimately leading to more referrals and successful transactions.

Home Maintenance Drip Campaign Use Cases

A Home Maintenance Drip Campaign is a powerful way to keep in touch with your clients and provide them with valuable information about how to maintain and care for their home. By providing tips and advice on home maintenance and repair, you can establish yourself as a trusted resource and keep your clients engaged with your business. In this chapter, we'll explore some of the most effective use cases for a Home Maintenance Drip Campaign, as well as provide you with a step-by-step guide for implementing your own campaign. Here are some examples of use cases:

- Seasonal Maintenance Reminders: Remind homeowners to perform routine maintenance tasks on their homes to prevent larger, more expensive problems down the road. This could include reminders to clean gutters, check smoke detectors, change HVAC filters, and perform other routine maintenance tasks.
- Energy Efficiency Tips: Provide homeowners with tips and tricks for making their homes more energy efficient. This could include suggestions for upgrading insulation, installing a programmable thermostat, and using energy-efficient appliances.
- DIY Project Ideas: Offer homeowners DIY project ideas that they can tackle to improve their homes. This could include ideas for repainting a room, building a garden bed, or installing a new light fixture.
- Home Safety Tips: Provide homeowners with tips for keeping their homes safe and secure. This could include suggestions for installing a security system, changing locks, and securing doors and windows.
- Home Improvement Ideas: Provide homeowners with inspiration and ideas for making improvements to their homes. This could include suggestions for updating kitchens and bathrooms, installing new flooring, or adding a deck or patio to their outdoor space.
- Seasonal Decorating Ideas: Offer homeowners tips and ideas for decorating their homes for different seasons and holidays. This

could include suggestions for decorating for Christmas, Halloween, and other holidays throughout the year.

- Homeowner Resources: Provide homeowners with access to resources and information that can help them navigate the challenges of home ownership. This could include information on local contractors and service providers, information on financing and mortgages, and other resources that homeowners may find helpful.

A Home Maintenance Drip Campaign is a valuable tool for any real estate professional looking to build lasting relationships with their clients. By providing regular, useful information about home maintenance and repair, you can establish yourself as a trusted resource and keep your clients engaged with your business. Whether you're looking to maintain your existing client relationships or attract new clients, a Home Maintenance Drip Campaign is a powerful way to build your reputation and grow your business.

Step-By-Step Guide and Templates

Step 1:

Send an initial email to subscribers with the subject "Home Maintenance Tips to Keep Your Property in Top Condition" providing helpful tips and advice for maintaining their property. Encourage subscribers to reach out to your agency for any questions or concerns they may have.

Step 1 Email Template:

Subject: Home Maintenance Tips to Keep Your Property in Top Condition
Dear [Subscriber],

We know that maintaining a property can be challenging, but it's important to keep it in top condition to ensure its longevity and value. That's why we're sharing some helpful home maintenance tips with you.

Here are a few tips to get you started:

- Regularly inspect and clean your gutters to prevent water damage
- Change your HVAC filters every 1-3 months to keep your system running efficiently

- Test your smoke detectors and carbon monoxide detectors regularly to ensure they are functioning properly
- Check for leaks in your plumbing system to prevent water damage and high water bills
- Inspect your roof for any damage or wear and tear

If you have any questions or concerns about maintaining your property, please don't hesitate to reach out to us at [Contact Information]. We're here to help you keep your property in top condition.

Best regards,

[Agent Signature Block with Contact Information]

Personalization:

Update the Subscriber Name and body with your links and phone numbers where appropriate.

Recommended Agent Action:

Follow up with a phone call to subscribers who reply to the email or express interest in any home maintenance concerns.

Step 2:

Send an SMS message on day 7 after the initial email with a reminder to subscribers to perform their home maintenance tasks and to reach out to your agency for any questions or concerns they may have.

Step 2 SMS Template:

Hi [Subscriber], just a friendly reminder to perform your home maintenance tasks to keep your property in top condition. If you have any questions or concerns, don't hesitate to reach out to us at [Contact Information]. - [Agent Name]

Personalization:

Update the Subscriber Name and body with your links and phone numbers where appropriate.

Recommended Agent Action:

Follow up with a phone call to subscribers who reply to the SMS or express interest in any home maintenance concerns.

Step 3:

Send an email on day 14 after the initial email with the subject "Preventing Costly Home Repairs" to provide subscribers with tips and advice on how to maintain their homes and prevent costly repairs. Include information on basic maintenance tasks such as changing air filters, cleaning gutters, and inspecting the roof. Encourage subscribers to contact your agency regarding any questions or concerns they may have.

Step 3 Email Template:

Subject: Preventing Costly Home Repairs

Dear [Subscriber],

At [Agency Name], we believe that one of the best ways to save money on your home is to take preventative measures against costly repairs. That's why we wanted to share with you some tips and advice on how to maintain your home and avoid unexpected expenses.

Some basic home maintenance tasks that can help prevent costly repairs include:

- Changing air filters regularly
- Cleaning gutters to prevent water damage
- Inspecting the roof for damage and leaks
- Checking the foundation for cracks or settling
- Maintaining appliances and systems such as HVAC, plumbing, and electrical

We hope these tips are helpful, and we encourage you to contact us with any questions or concerns you may have. Our team is here to help you protect your home and your investment.

Thank you for your continued support.

Best regards,

[Agent Signature Block with Contact Information]

Personalization:

Update the Subscriber Name and body with your links and phone numbers where appropriate.

Recommended Agent Action:

Follow up with a phone call to subscribers who reply to the email or express interest in home maintenance or repairs.

Step 4:

Send an SMS message on day 21 with a reminder to subscribers to perform their seasonal home maintenance tasks and to reach out to your agency for any questions or concerns they may have.

Step 4 SMS Template:

Hi [Subscriber], just a friendly reminder to perform your seasonal home maintenance tasks! Don't forget to change your air filters, clean your gutters, and check your smoke detectors. If you have any questions or concerns about your home maintenance, please don't hesitate to reach out to us at [Contact Information]. We're here to help.

Personalization:

Update the Subscriber Name and body with your links and phone numbers where appropriate.

Recommended Agent Action:

Follow up with a phone call to subscribers who reply to the SMS or express interest in any home maintenance concerns.

Step 5:

Send an email on day 30 after the initial email with the subject "Reminder: Schedule Your HVAC Maintenance Appointment Today!" Provide subscribers with a reminder to schedule their HVAC maintenance appointment and include any relevant information or promotions your agency may be offering. Encourage subscribers to schedule their appointment soon to ensure their HVAC system is ready for the upcoming season.

HOME MAINTENANCE DRIP CAMPAIGN

Step 5 Email Template:

Subject: Reminder: Schedule Your HVAC Maintenance Appointment Today!

Dear [Subscriber],

Just a friendly reminder to schedule your HVAC maintenance appointment before the upcoming season. Regular maintenance of your HVAC system ensures optimal performance and can prevent costly repairs down the line.

At [Agency Name], we are committed to providing our clients with the best possible service. That's why we are offering [Promotion/Discount] on HVAC maintenance appointments scheduled before [Date]. Don't miss out on this great opportunity to save!

To schedule your appointment or if you have any questions or concerns, please don't hesitate to reach out to us at [Contact Information].

Thank you for choosing [Agency Name].

Best regards,

[Agent Signature Block with Contact Information]

Personalization:

Update the Subscriber Name and body with your links and phone numbers where appropriate.

Recommended Agent Action:

Follow up with a phone call to subscribers who reply to the email or express interest in scheduling an HVAC maintenance appointment.

Step 6:

Send an SMS message on day 35 with a reminder to subscribers to schedule their seasonal plumbing maintenance and to contact your agency for any questions or concerns they may have.

Step 6 SMS Template:

Hi [Subscriber], just a friendly reminder to schedule your seasonal plumbing maintenance appointment to prevent any plumbing issues before they arise. If you have any questions or concerns, please don't hesitate to contact us at [Contact Information].

Personalization:

Update the Subscriber Name and links with phone numbers information where appropriate.

Recommended Agent Action:

Follow up with a phone call to subscribers who reply to the SMS or express interest in scheduling a plumbing maintenance appointment.

Step 7:

Send an email on day 45 after the initial email with the subject "Tips for Preparing Your Home for [Upcoming Season]" Provide subscribers with tips and advice on how to prepare their homes for the upcoming season, including any specific tasks or projects they should be aware of. Encourage subscribers to contact your agency for any questions or concerns they may have.

Step 7 Email Template:

Subject: Tips for Preparing Your Home for [Upcoming Season]
Dear [Subscriber],

As the [Upcoming Season] approaches, it's important to ensure your home is prepared for the changes in weather and temperature. To help you get started, we've compiled a list of tips and advice to make the transition as smooth as possible.

Some tips include:

[Tip 1]

[Tip 2]

[Tip 3]

If you have any questions or concerns, or if you need assistance with any home maintenance tasks, please do not hesitate to reach out to us at [Contact Information]. Our team of experts is here to help.

Thank you for choosing [Agency Name].

Best regards,

[Agent Signature Block with Contact Information]

Personalization:

Update the Subscriber Name and body with your links and phone numbers where appropriate. Add in tips based on the season.

Recommended Agent Action:

Follow up with a phone call to subscribers who reply to the email or express interest in scheduling a maintenance appointment.

Step 8:

Send an SMS message on day 50 with a reminder to subscribers to check their home's smoke detectors and carbon monoxide detectors and to contact your agency for any questions or concerns they may have.

Step 8 SMS Template:

Hi [Subscriber], it's time to check your home's smoke detectors and carbon monoxide detectors. Don't forget to replace the batteries if necessary. If you have any questions or concerns, please reach out to us at [Contact Information].

Personalization:

Update the Subscriber Name and links with phone numbers information where appropriate.

Recommended Agent Action:

Follow up with a phone call to subscribers who reply to the SMS or express interest in scheduling a plumbing maintenance appointment.

Step 9:

Send an email on day 60 after the initial email with the subject "The Importance of Regular Home Maintenance" to provide subscribers with tips and advice on how to keep their home in top condition. Offer a free consultation or inspection to subscribers who are interested in professional maintenance services.

Step 9 Email Template:

Subject: The Importance of Regular Home Maintenance

Dear [Subscriber],

As the seasons change, it's important to keep up with regular home maintenance tasks to ensure that your property stays in top condition. From cleaning gutters to checking smoke detectors, there are a number of tasks that should be performed regularly to keep your home safe and comfortable.

To help you stay on top of your home maintenance needs, we've put together a list of tips and advice on how to keep your property in great shape. Whether you're a first-time homeowner or an experienced property owner, these tips are sure to come in handy.

As a thank you for being a part of our community, we are also offering a free consultation or inspection to subscribers who are interested in professional maintenance services. Simply reply to this email or give us a call to schedule your appointment today.

Thank you for your continued support, and we look forward to helping you keep your home in top condition.

Best regards,

[Agent Signature Block with Contact Information]

Personalization:

Update the Subscriber Name and body with your links and phone numbers where appropriate.

Recommended Agent Action:

Follow up with a phone call to subscribers who reply to the email or express interest in professional maintenance services.

Tracking the Success of the Home Maintenance Drip Campaign

Tracking the success of your Home Maintenance Drip Campaign is essential to understanding how effective your emails and SMS messages are in engaging subscribers and promoting home maintenance. By monitoring key metrics such as open rates, click-through rates, and response rates, you can adjust your campaign strategy to ensure that you're providing valuable information and driving engagement. In this section, we'll outline some tips for tracking the success of your Home Maintenance Drip Campaign.

- Monitor email and SMS open rates: One of the most critical metrics to track for your Home Maintenance Drip Campaign is the open rate. The open rate measures the percentage of subscribers who opened your email or SMS message. By tracking open rates, you can gauge the effectiveness of your subject lines and adjust them to improve engagement.
- Track click-through rates: Another key metric to monitor is the click-through rate. This metric measures the percentage of subscribers who clicked on a link in your email or SMS message. By tracking click-through rates, you can understand which links are most popular with subscribers and adjust your content to align with their interests.
- Monitor response rates: Response rates measure the percentage of subscribers who respond to your emails or SMS messages. By tracking response rates, you can understand which subscribers are most engaged with your content and adjust your messaging to appeal to a wider audience.
- Use analytics tools: Most email marketing platforms and SMS providers offer analytics tools that can help you track key metrics for your Home Maintenance Drip Campaign. These tools can provide insights into subscriber behavior and help you identify opportunities for improving engagement.
- Follow-up engagement: Tracking how many subscribers reach out to you with questions or concerns will give you an idea of how engaged your audience is and if there are any specific areas where you can provide added support.

Tracking the success of your Home Maintenance Drip Campaign is essential to understanding how effective your messaging is in promoting home maintenance and engaging subscribers. By monitoring key metrics such as open rates, click-through rates, and response rates, you can adjust your campaign strategy to ensure that you're providing valuable information and driving engagement. Remember to use analytics tools and adjust your content to align with subscribers' interests to maximize your campaign's success.

Tips for Customizing the Home Maintenance Drip Campaign

The Home Maintenance Drip Campaign is an effective way to stay in touch with clients and help them stay on top of home maintenance tasks. Here are some tips for customizing this campaign to make it even more effective:

- Personalize your emails: Personalization is key to engaging your subscribers and keeping them interested in your content. Use their first name in the subject line and greeting, and tailor the content of your emails to their specific needs and interests.
- Provide value: Make sure your emails provide real value to your subscribers. Include useful tips and tricks for home maintenance tasks, as well as links to helpful resources and products. The more value you provide, the more likely your subscribers are to stay engaged with your campaign.
- Segment your list: Not all subscribers have the same needs or interests when it comes to home maintenance. Segment your list into different groups based on factors like home size, age, and location.
- This will allow you to send more targeted and relevant content to each group.
- Use a mix of media: Don't limit yourself to just emails and SMS messages. Consider using other forms of media, like videos and infographics, to provide information about home maintenance tasks. This can help break up the monotony of your campaign and keep subscribers engaged.
- Use a drip scheduling tool: To make sure your messages are sent at the right intervals, consider using a drip scheduling tool. This will allow you to set up your messages in advance and automate the sending process, so you can focus on other aspects of your business.

By customizing your Home Maintenance Drip Campaign in these ways, you can make it even more effective at engaging subscribers and keeping them informed about home maintenance tasks.

Remember to track your success and adjust your campaign as needed to ensure continued success.

Conclusion

A Home Maintenance Drip Campaign can be an incredibly effective way to stay top-of-mind with your clients and position yourself as a knowledgeable and helpful resource in the world of home ownership. By providing valuable information and reminders about home maintenance, you can help your clients keep their homes in top condition and avoid costly repairs down the road.

Through this campaign, you can also build stronger relationships with your clients, which can lead to repeat business and referrals. By tailoring the campaign to the needs of your audience and providing relevant and timely information, you can ensure that your clients view you as a trusted advisor and partner in their home ownership journey.

Remember to track the success of your campaign and make adjustments as needed to ensure that you are achieving your goals. With the right strategy and approach, a Home Maintenance Drip Campaign can be a powerful tool in your real estate marketing arsenal.

13

HOLIDAY GREETINGS DRIP CAMPAIGN

The Holiday Greetings Drip Campaign is a marketing strategy that uses a series of personalized emails and SMS messages to connect with clients and prospects during the holiday season. The goal of this campaign is to foster a relationship with your clients and keep your real estate business top of mind. By sending personalized holiday greetings, you can show your appreciation for your clients and create a lasting impression that will encourage them to work with you in the future. This chapter will provide you with a Step-By-Step Guide and Templates for creating an effective Holiday Greetings Drip Campaign.

User Scenario: Holiday Greetings Drip Campaign
Scenario: Spreading Holiday Cheer to Clients and Prospects

Anthony, a dedicated real estate agent, understands the value of maintaining strong relationships with his clients and prospects throughout the year. To stay connected and show his appreciation, Anthony implements a Holiday Greetings Drip Campaign. This campaign consists of a series of personalized emails and SMS messages sent during the holiday season, aiming to spread cheer and express gratitude.

By sending warm holiday greetings, John reinforces his connection with current clients, rekindles relationships with past clients, and keeps his business top-of-mind for prospects. This thoughtful approach not only enhances client loyalty but also positions John as a caring and attentive real estate professional.

Implementing this drip campaign can help you achieve similar success in nurturing client relationships and maintaining a strong presence in the minds of your clients and prospects during the holiday season, ultimately leading to more referrals and successful transactions.

Holiday Greetings Drip Campaign Use Cases

In this chapter, we will be focusing on the electronic side of the Holiday Greetings Drip Campaign. This type of campaign can be used to show your appreciation to your clients and contacts during the holiday season, while also keeping your business top-of-mind. Below are some use cases for the Holiday Greetings Drip Campaign:

- Express gratitude to current clients: Sending a holiday greeting to your current clients is a great way to show your appreciation for their business and loyalty. It's also an opportunity to remind them of the services you offer and encourage them to refer friends and family to your business.
- Reconnect with past clients: The holiday season is a perfect time to reach out to past clients and let them know that you appreciate their business and hope to work with them again in the future.
- Strengthen relationships with referral sources: If you have referral sources who have sent business your way throughout the year, sending them a holiday greeting is a thoughtful way to acknowledge their contributions to your business.
- Reach out to leads and prospects: For leads and prospects who have shown interest in your services but haven't yet made a purchase, sending a holiday greeting can keep your business top-of-mind and encourage them to consider your services when they're ready to make a move.
- In addition to the above use cases which are focused solely on electronic communication by email and SMS, you can incorporate the following into your plan:
- Send personalized holiday greeting cards: Sending physical greeting cards is a great way to show your clients that you appreciate their business and value their relationship. Be sure to include a personalized message and your agency's contact information.

- Create a holiday-themed video: Creating a video message for your clients is another great way to connect with them during the holiday season. Share your agency's holiday traditions or your favorite things about the season and be sure to include a call-to-action at the end.
- Host a holiday party or event: Hosting a holiday party or event for your clients is a great way to show your appreciation and strengthen your relationships. This could be a virtual event or an in-person gathering, depending on local regulations.

In the following sections, we will provide you with templates for email and SMS messages that you can use to execute a successful Holiday Greetings Drip Campaign.

When to Launch Your Holiday Greetings Drip Campaign

The holiday season is a busy time for many people, and as a real estate agent, it's important to time your holiday greetings drip campaign appropriately. To make the most of your campaign, consider launching it on the first day of the holiday season. The timing can vary depending on the holiday you're targeting, but generally, the holiday season begins in late November with Thanksgiving in the United States, and ends in early January after New Year's Day.

Launching your campaign on the first day of the holiday season gives you plenty of time to spread cheer and keep in touch with your clients throughout the holidays. It's also a great way to remind your clients of your services and expertise in the real estate market, which can help generate business in the new year.

Now that you know when to launch your holiday greetings drip campaign, let's dive into the templates and steps you can use to make it a success.

Step-By-Step Guide and Templates

Step 1:

Send an email on the first day of the holiday season with a subject line "Happy Holidays from [Agency Name]!" Use this email as an opportunity to wish your subscribers happy holidays and express gratitude for their business. This initial email should be light and festive, without a sales pitch.

Step 1 Email Template:

Subject: Happy Holidays from [Agency Name]!

Dear [Subscriber],

As we enter the holiday season, we wanted to take a moment to wish you and your loved ones a joyous and peaceful holiday season. We are so grateful for your business and the trust you have placed in us to help you with your real estate needs.

We hope this holiday season is filled with warmth, love, and happy memories. From all of us at [Agency Name], happy holidays!

Best regards,

[Agent Signature Block with Contact Information]

Personalization:

Update the Subscriber Name and body with your links and phone numbers where appropriate.

Recommended Agent Action:

None

Step 2:

Send an SMS message on day 7 with a holiday greeting and an invitation to reach out to your agency for any real estate needs they may have.

Step 2 SMS Template:

Hi [Subscriber], just wanted to wish you a happy holiday season! If you have any real estate needs or questions, don't hesitate to contact us at [Contact Information].

Personalization:

Update the Subscriber Name and body with your links and phone numbers where appropriate.

Recommended Agent Action:

Follow up with a phone call to subscribers who reply to the SMS or express interest in buying or selling a property.

Step 3:

Send an email on day 14 with a subject line "Holiday Home Tips from [Agency Name]" providing your subscribers with holiday-themed home maintenance tips or decorating ideas. This email should be informative and helpful without being sales-focused.

Step 3 Email Template:

Subject: Holiday Home Tips from [Agency Name]

Dear [Subscriber],

As the holiday season is in full swing, we wanted to share some tips to help you keep your home safe and festive during this special time of year. Here are some holiday-themed home maintenance tips and decorating ideas to keep in mind:

- Decorate safely: Use non-flammable decorations, avoid overloading electrical outlets, and never leave candles unattended.
- Be energy-efficient: Use LED lights, turn off holiday lights during the day, and adjust your thermostat to save energy.
- Host guests comfortably: Prepare guest rooms with fresh linens and towels, and consider providing extra toiletries and blankets.
- Manage holiday stress: Take breaks, practice self-care, and prioritize your tasks to avoid feeling overwhelmed.

We hope you find these tips helpful and that they add to your holiday spirit. If you have any real estate questions or concerns, don't hesitate to reach out to us at [Contact Information].

Happy Holidays!

Best regards,

[Agent Signature Block with Contact Information]

Personalization:

Update the Subscriber Name and body with your links and phone numbers where appropriate.

Recommended Agent Action:

Follow up with a phone call to subscribers who reply to the email or express interest in buying or selling a property.

DRIP, DRIP, SOLD

Step 4:

Send an SMS message on day 21 with a holiday greeting and a reminder to subscribers to reach out to your agency for any real estate needs they may have.

Step 4 SMS Template:

Hi [Subscriber], just a friendly reminder to reach out to us at [Contact Information] for any real estate needs you may have this holiday season. Happy holidays!

Personalization:

Update the Subscriber Name and body with your links and phone numbers where appropriate.

Recommended Agent Action:

Follow up with a phone call to subscribers who reply to the SMS or express interest in buying or selling a property.

Step 5:

Send an email on day 28 with a subject line "Thank You for a Great Year!" Thank subscribers for their business throughout the year and express gratitude for their loyalty. You can also include any updates about your agency or the real estate market during the holiday season. Encourage subscribers to reach out to you for any real estate needs they may have in the coming year.

Step 5 Email Template:

Subject: Thank You for a Great Year!

Dear [Subscriber],

As the year comes to a close, we want to take a moment to thank you for your business and loyalty to our agency. We appreciate your trust in us and are grateful for the opportunity to help you achieve your real estate goals.

We hope that this holiday season is filled with joy, laughter, and good health for you and your loved ones. As always, we are here to help you with any real estate needs you may have in the coming year.

If you're interested in learning more about the real estate market during the holiday season, be sure to check out our latest blog post [Link to Blog Post].

Thank you again for your continued support. We wish you a happy and healthy new year!

Best regards,

[Agent Signature Block with Contact Information]

Personalization:

Update the Subscriber Name and body with your links and phone numbers where appropriate.

Recommended Agent Action:

Follow up with a phone call to subscribers who reply to the email or express interest in buying or selling a property.

Step 6:

Send an SMS message on day 30 with the message "Thank you for your business this year! Wishing you happy holidays and a great new year! Contact us for any of your real estate needs."

Step 6 SMS Template:

Hi [Subscriber], just wanted to thank you for your business this year and wish you happy holidays! Looking forward to working with you in the new year. Don't hesitate to contact us for any of your real estate needs.

Personalization:

Update the Subscriber Name and body with your links and phone numbers where appropriate.

Recommended Agent Action:

Follow up with a phone call to subscribers who reply to the email or express interest in buying or selling a property.

Tracking the Success of the Holiday Greetings Drip Campaign

Tracking the success of your Holiday Greetings Drip Campaign can help you measure the effectiveness of your outreach efforts and make any necessary adjustments to optimize your future campaigns. Here are some ways you can track the success of your Holiday Greetings Drip Campaign:

- Open rates: Keep an eye on the open rates of your emails and SMS messages. This metric can help you determine the level of engagement your subscribers have with your content. A higher open rate means that more subscribers are interested in your message, while a lower open rate may indicate that your content needs improvement.
- Click-through rates: Track the click-through rates of your emails and SMS messages to see how many subscribers are engaging with your content and taking action. A high click-through rate indicates that your message resonated with your audience and inspired them to take the next step.
- Responses: Monitor the responses you receive from subscribers to gauge their level of interest in your services. Responding to these messages promptly can help you build stronger relationships with your clients and potentially lead to new business opportunities.
- Sales: Keep track of any new business that comes in as a direct result of your Holiday Greetings Drip Campaign. This can help you determine the return on investment (ROI) of your campaign and justify the time and resources spent on it.

By tracking these metrics, you can gain valuable insights into the success of your Holiday Greetings Drip Campaign and make data-driven decisions to improve future campaigns.

Tips for Customizing the Holiday Greetings Drip Campaign

The Holiday Greetings Drip Campaign is a great way to show your appreciation for your clients and stay top-of-mind during the holiday season. Here are some tips to help you customize this campaign for your agency and your clients:

- Personalize your messages: Use your clients' names and any relevant information to make your messages more personal and engaging. Mention specific properties or transactions you have worked on together, or any other details that show you remember and value your clients.
- Use holiday-themed graphics and colors: Add some festive touches to your emails and SMS messages with holiday-themed graphics, such as snowflakes, ornaments, or a seasonal color scheme. Be sure to keep your branding consistent and professional.
- Focus on Personalization: The holiday season is a great opportunity to connect with your clients on a more personal level. Use this campaign to show your appreciation for their business and build stronger relationships. One way to do this is by using Personalization in your emails and SMS messages. Address clients by name and include personalized messages that are relevant to their specific needs and interests. This will help your clients feel valued and appreciated, and can lead to increased engagement and loyalty.
- Additionally, you can consider sending physical greeting cards that are handwritten and personalized for each client. This shows an extra level of effort and care that can be appreciated by the client.
- Keep your messages short and sweet: During the busy holiday season, your clients are likely receiving lots of messages from various sources. Make sure your messages are concise, to-the-point, and easy to read on any device.
- Follow up with personalized messages: After sending your holiday greetings, follow up with personalized messages to your clients to show you care about their needs and are ready to assist them with any real estate questions or concerns.

By customizing your Holiday Greetings Drip Campaign with these tips, you can create a memorable and effective campaign that helps you build and maintain strong relationships with your clients.

Conclusion

As we wrap up this chapter on the Holiday Greetings Drip Campaign, we hope that you have gained valuable insights into how to connect with your clients during the holiday season. By sending personalized emails, SMS messages, and holiday cards, hosting events, and creating videos, you can show your clients how much you appreciate their business and build stronger relationships with them.

Remember, the key to success with this campaign is to stay genuine, authentic, and focused on building relationships, rather than just making sales. By keeping the holiday season in mind and focusing on showing gratitude and appreciation, you can make a lasting impact on your clients and create a loyal customer base that will continue to support your business in the years to come.

14

MARKET UPDATE DRIP CAMPAIGN

A market update drip campaign is a powerful tool to keep your clients informed about the real estate market trends and how it can affect their buying or selling decisions. As a real estate agent, you must stay on top of the latest trends and statistics to provide your clients with the most accurate information possible. This is where a market update drip campaign comes in.

Through a series of carefully crafted emails and SMS messages, you can provide your clients with the most up-to-date information on the market trends in their area. You can keep them informed about the latest changes in interest rates, property values, and more. By doing so, you position yourself as an expert in your field and build trust with your clients.

In this chapter, we will discuss the different use cases, step-by-step guide, and templates for creating an effective market update drip campaign. You will learn how to keep your clients engaged and informed, build stronger relationships, and ultimately, grow your business.

User Scenario: Market Update Drip Campaign

Lena, a seasoned real estate agent, understands the importance of keeping her clients well-informed about the ever-changing real estate market. To ensure her clients have the latest market insights, Lena implements a Market Update Drip Campaign. This campaign involves sending a series of emails and SMS messages that provide regular updates on local market trends, including average home prices, inventory levels, and recent sales data.

By consistently delivering timely and relevant market information, Lena helps her clients stay informed and make better decisions regarding their real estate investments. This approach not only builds trust and rapport but also positions Lena as a knowledgeable and proactive real estate professional.

Implementing this drip campaign can help you achieve similar success in keeping your clients engaged and informed, ultimately leading to more satisfied clients and successful transactions.

What Is A Market Update Report?

A market update report is a type of communication that provides information and insights about the real estate market to clients and potential clients. It can include data on recent home sales, trends in home prices and inventory, changes in mortgage rates, and any other relevant information about the real estate market in a particular area.

Market update reports are important for both buyers and sellers because they provide valuable insights into the current state of the market. For buyers, market updates can help them understand the current market conditions and make more informed decisions about when and where to buy a home. For sellers, market updates can help them understand how to price their home and what to expect during the selling process.

In the context of a drip campaign, a market update can be a powerful tool for staying top-of-mind with clients and potential clients. By providing regular updates on the market, you can position yourself as a trusted advisor and build stronger relationships with your audience.

How to Create a Market Update Report

- Determine your target audience: Before creating your report, it's important to define who your target audience is. Consider their knowledge level of the real estate market, their preferences for data visualization, and any other factors that may influence how you present your information.
- Collect relevant data: Gather information on the local real estate market, including sales data, housing inventory, pricing trends, and any other data points that are relevant to your target audience.

- Organize your data: Organize the data you collected into categories and sections that are easy to read and understand. Consider using charts, graphs, and other visual aids to make the data more accessible.
- Analyze the data: Once you have organized your data, take a step back and analyze what it means for the local real estate market. Identify any trends, patterns, or outliers that may be noteworthy.
- Write your report: Use your analysis to write a report that summarizes the state of the local real estate market. Be sure to include any insights or predictions based on your analysis.
- Design your report: Choose a visually appealing design for your report that reflects your brand and is easy to read. Consider using a mix of text, images, and graphics to make the report more engaging.
- Review and edit: Before sharing your report with your target audience, review it for accuracy and clarity. Make any necessary edits to ensure that the report is informative, engaging, and easy to understand.
- Share your report: Once your report is complete, share it with your target audience through email, social media, or any other channels that are relevant to your marketing strategy.

By following these steps, you can create a market update report that is informative, engaging, and useful for your target audience.

Outline of a Market Report

1. Introduction
- Brief overview of the purpose of the report
- Explanation of what a market update is and why it's important for people interested in buying or selling a home

2. State of the Market
- An overview of the current state of the real estate market in your area, including recent trends in home prices, inventory levels, and interest rates
- Use charts, graphs, and other visual aids to help explain the data in a clear and easy-to understand way

3. Factors Affecting the Market

- Identify and explain the key factors that are currently impacting the local real estate market, such as changes in the economy, demographics, and government policies
- Use real-world examples and anecdotes to help readers understand how these factors are influencing the market

4. Advice for Buyers and Sellers
- Provide practical tips and advice for people who are looking to buy or sell a home in the current market
- This could include things like advice on timing your purchase or sale, strategies for negotiating offers, and guidance on selecting the right real estate agent

5. Conclusion
- Summarize the key points of the report and provide a call-to-action for readers, such as encouraging them to contact your agency for more personalized advice or to sign up for your mailing list to receive future market updates

Remember to use plain language and avoid jargon as much as possible to make the report as accessible as possible to a wide range of readers.

Sample Market Report

Fulton County, Georgia Market Update
Current as of March 2023

Overview:

The real estate market in Fulton County, Georgia remains strong. Prices have increased slightly over the past year, and homes are selling quickly. Inventory is still low, but new listings are coming on the market every day.

Key Metrics:
Median Sales Price: $350,000
Average Days on Market: 45
Months of Supply: 2.5
Number of Active Listings: 1,500

MARKET UPDATE DRIP CAMPAIGN

Market Trends:

Over the past year, the median sales price in Fulton County has increased by 3%. Homes priced between $250,000 and $500,000 are in high demand and are selling quickly. The number of active listings is down slightly from last year, which is contributing to the low inventory levels. However, new listings are coming on the market every day, and there is still plenty of opportunity for buyers and sellers.

Advice for Buyers:

If you are looking to buy a home in Fulton County, it is important to act quickly. Homes are selling fast, so be prepared to make an offer as soon as you find a property you like. Work with a knowledgeable real estate agent who can help you navigate the competitive market and find the right home for your needs.

Advice for Sellers:

If you are thinking about selling your home in Fulton County, now is a great time to do so. With low inventory levels and high demand, homes are selling quickly and often for above asking price. Work with a skilled real estate agent who can help you price your home appropriately and market it effectively to attract interested buyers.

Sources:

Fulton County Board of Realtors
Georgia MLS

This market report is intended to provide general information and should not be construed as legal or financial advice. Please consult with a qualified professional for personalized advice related to your specific situation.

Market Update Drip Campaign Use Cases

A Market Update Drip Campaign is an excellent way to keep your clients and prospects informed about the latest trends and changes in the real estate market. By providing valuable information, you establish yourself as a trusted authority in the industry and keep your clients engaged with your business. Here are some Market Update Drip Campaign Use Cases that you can implement to stay top of mind with your clients and prospects.

- Monthly Market Reports: Send monthly market reports to your clients and prospects, breaking down the current state of the real estate market in your area. Include information such as the average home price, days on market, and inventory levels. This type of update allows your clients and prospects to keep up with the real estate market and potentially make informed decisions about buying or selling a home.

- Quarterly Market Update Emails: In addition to the monthly market reports, send quarterly market update emails to your clients and prospects. In these emails, provide a more comprehensive look at the market, including any notable trends, changes in inventory levels, and projections for the upcoming quarter. This type of update allows your clients and prospects to stay informed about the real estate market and make decisions based on the latest information.

- Annual Real Estate Forecast: At the beginning of each year, send out an annual real estate forecast to your clients and prospects. This report should provide an overview of the previous year's real estate market and what to expect in the upcoming year. This type of update shows your clients and prospects that you are on top of the latest trends and that you are committed to providing them with valuable information.

By implementing a Market Update Drip Campaign, you can keep your clients and prospects informed and engaged with your business. By providing valuable information, you can establish yourself as a trusted authority in the industry and keep your clients coming back for more. Try out these Market Update Drip Campaign Use Cases and see how they work for you!

Step-By-Step Guide and Templates

Market reports can be sent on varying recurring basis. Because of this we can approach this campaign in various ways. We can create a campaign that is sent out to our subscribers monthly that will contain a "Monthly

Market Report". Additionally we can send out "Quarterly" and "Yearly" Market Reports. There are really no "Steps" required. So only a few templates will follow:

Monthly Template:

Send an initial email to subscribers who have shown interest in the local real estate market with the subject "Monthly Market Update - [Month/Year]." Provide subscribers with an overview of the current real estate market in their area, including any recent changes in housing prices, inventory, and sales activity. Include any relevant statistics, graphs, or charts to make the information easily understandable. Create and send this report at the beginning of every month.

Email Template:

Subject: Monthly Market Update - [Month/Year]
Dear [Subscriber],

We are pleased to share with you the latest market update for [City/County/State]. The real estate market has been [Strong/Steady/Slow] in recent months, with [Increase/Decrease] in housing prices and [High/Low] inventory levels.

[Include relevant statistics, graphs, or charts to illustrate the information]

As always, if you have any questions or are interested in buying or selling a property in the area, please don't hesitate to reach out to us at [Contact Information].

Thank you for your continued interest in the local real estate market.
Best regards,
[Agent Signature Block with Contact Information]

Personalization:

Update the Subscriber Name and body with your links and phone numbers where appropriate. Make the information specific to the city, county and or state your report is about.

Recommended Agent Action:

Follow up with a phone call to subscribers who reply to the email or express interest in buying or selling a property.

Quarterly Template:

Send an initial email to subscribers who have shown interest in the local real estate market with the subject "Quarter Market Update - [Quarter/Year]." Provide subscribers with an overview of the current real estate market in their area, including any recent changes in housing prices, inventory, and sales activity. Include any relevant statistics, graphs, or charts to make the information easily understandable. Create and send this report at the beginning of every Quarter.

Email Template:

Subject: Monthly Market Update - [Month/Year]
Dear [Subscriber],

We are pleased to share with you the latest market update for [City/County/State]. The real estate market has been [Strong/Steady/Slow] in recent months, with [Increase/Decrease] in housing prices and [High/Low] inventory levels.

[Include relevant statistics, graphs, or charts to illustrate the information]

As always, if you have any questions or are interested in buying or selling a property in the area, please don't hesitate to reach out to us at [Contact Information].

Thank you for your continued interest in the local real estate market.
Best regards,
[Agent Signature Block with Contact Information]

Personalization:

Update the Subscriber Name and body with your links and phone numbers where appropriate. Make the information specific to the city, county and or state your report is about.

Recommended Agent Action:

Follow up with a phone call to subscribers who reply to the email or express interest in buying or selling a property.

Yearly Template:

Send an initial email to subscribers who have shown interest in the local real estate market with the subject "Yearly Market Update - [Year]." Provide subscribers with an overview of the current real estate market in their area, including any recent changes in housing prices, inventory, and sales activity. Include any relevant statistics, graphs, or charts to make the information easily understandable. Create and send this report every Year on the same day.

Email Template:

Subject: Yearly Market Update - [Year]
Dear [Subscriber],

We are pleased to share with you the latest market update for [City/County/State]. The real estate market has been [Strong/Steady/Slow] in recent months, with [Increase/Decrease] in housing prices and [High/Low] inventory levels.

[Include relevant statistics, graphs, or charts to illustrate the information]

As always, if you have any questions or are interested in buying or selling a property in the area, please don't hesitate to reach out to us at [Contact Information].

Thank you for your continued interest in the local real estate market.
Best regards,
[Agent Signature Block with Contact Information]

Personalization:

Update the Subscriber Name and body with your links and phone numbers where appropriate. Make the information specific to the city, county and or state your report is about.

Recommended Agent Action:

Follow up with a phone call to subscribers who reply to the email or express interest in buying or selling a property.

Tracking the Success of the Market Update Drip Campaign

Tracking the success of a market update drip campaign is essential to determine whether the campaign is achieving its objectives. By tracking the metrics of the campaign, you can identify areas that need improvement and make adjustments to improve the effectiveness of the campaign. Here are some ways to track its effectiveness:

- Email Open Rates: The email open rate is the percentage of subscribers who opened your email. Tracking email open rates is crucial to determine the success of your campaign. A low email open rate can be an indication that the email's subject line was not compelling or relevant to your subscribers.
- Click-Through Rates: Click-through rates are the percentage of subscribers who clicked on a link within your email. This metric helps you determine the relevance of the content you are sharing with your subscribers. If your click-through rate is low, it may be an indication that your content is not relevant or valuable to your subscribers.
- Unsubscribe Rates: The unsubscribe rate is the percentage of subscribers who have opted out of receiving further communication from your agency. Tracking unsubscribe rates is essential to understand why subscribers are leaving your list. If the unsubscribe rate is high, it may be an indication that the content is not relevant, or the frequency of communication is too high.
- Response Rates: Tracking response rates can help you identify subscribers who are interested in your content and may have real estate needs. You can follow up with these subscribers to convert them into potential clients.
- Conversion Rates: Conversion rates refer to the percentage of subscribers who took action, such as contacting your agency, scheduling a consultation, or visiting your website. This metric helps

you determine the effectiveness of your campaign in generating leads and converting them into potential clients.

Tracking the success of a market update drip campaign is essential to measure the effectiveness of the campaign in achieving its objectives. By tracking the metrics mentioned above, you can make adjustments to your campaign and improve its effectiveness. It is crucial to monitor these metrics regularly to identify areas that need improvement and make adjustments to ensure the success of your campaign.

Tips for Customizing the Market Update Drip Campaign

Creating a successful market update campaign depends on providing relevant and timely information to your subscribers. Here are some tips for customizing your market update campaign to your specific region and area of operation:

- Research Your Local Market: Stay up-to-date on your local real estate market by reviewing recent sales data, analyzing market trends, and keeping tabs on new developments or zoning changes. This will help you provide valuable and accurate information to your subscribers.
- Segment Your Subscribers: Segmenting your subscribers based on their location and interests can help you provide more relevant and personalized market updates. Use your CRM or email marketing software to segment your list based on factors such as location, property type, or buying/selling status.
- Provide Context and Analysis: Don't just share data - provide context and analysis to help subscribers understand what it means for them. This could include insights on market trends, comparisons to previous months or years, and forecasts for the future.
- Use Visuals: Use charts, graphs, and other visual aids to help subscribers better understand the data you are sharing. Visuals can also make your emails more engaging and increase the likelihood that your subscribers will read and share them.
- Include Calls-to-Action: Encourage subscribers to take action based on the information you provide. This could include scheduling a

consultation with your agency, signing up for a property search portal, or attending an upcoming open house or event.

By customizing your market update campaign to your specific region and area of operation, you can provide valuable and engaging content to your subscribers and strengthen your relationships with them over time.

Remember to monitor your campaign's success by tracking key metrics such as open and click-through rates, subscriber engagement, and lead generation. This will help you refine your approach and make data-driven decisions to improve your campaign's effectiveness.

Conclusion

A market update drip campaign is an effective way for real estate agents to keep their clients informed about the latest trends and developments in the local real estate market. By providing valuable information on a regular basis, you can establish yourself as a trusted source of information and position yourself as an expert in your field.

When creating a market update drip campaign, it's important to keep your audience in mind and tailor your content to their specific interests and needs. By providing relevant and useful information, you can keep your clients engaged and interested in what you have to say.

Additionally, tracking the success of your campaign is crucial to ensuring that it's meeting your goals and providing value to your clients. By regularly reviewing your analytics and making adjustments as needed, you can continue to improve your campaign and deliver the best possible results.

Overall, a well-executed market update drip campaign can be a valuable tool for real estate agents looking to build their brand and attract new clients. By following the tips and strategies outlined in this chapter, you can create a successful campaign that will help you achieve your goals and grow your business.

15

BUYER EDUCATION DRIP CAMPAIGN

One of the most important aspects of being a real estate agent is educating your clients about the home buying process. Buyers may feel overwhelmed or unsure of where to start, and it's up to you to guide them through the journey. That's where a buyer education drip campaign comes in. By providing valuable information and resources through a series of targeted emails and messages, you can help buyers feel confident and informed throughout the process.

The buyer education drip campaign is designed to provide prospective homebuyers with the information they need to navigate the home buying process. From understanding the pre-approval process to making an offer, and everything in between, this campaign aims to equip buyers with the knowledge and tools they need to make informed decisions. The campaign can be tailored to the specific needs of your clients and can be customized to reflect your agency's branding and messaging. Whether your clients are first time homebuyers or seasoned veterans, a buyer education drip campaign can help them feel prepared and confident throughout the process.

User Scenario: Buyer Education Drip Campaign

Ethan, a dedicated real estate agent, wants to help his clients feel confident and informed throughout the home-buying process. To achieve this, Ethan implements a Buyer Education Drip Campaign. This campaign involves sending a series of emails and SMS messages that provide valuable insights on various aspects of buying a home, from getting pre-approved for a mortgage to understanding the closing process.

By offering consistent, clear, and helpful information, Ethan ensures that his clients are well-prepared to make informed decisions. This approach not only builds trust and rapport but also positions Ethan as a knowledgeable and supportive real estate professional.

Implementing this drip campaign can help you achieve similar success in educating your clients and enhancing their home-buying experience, ultimately leading to more satisfied clients and successful transactions.

Buyer Education Drip Campaign Use Cases

A buyer education drip campaign is an excellent way to provide valuable information to potential homebuyers and establish your agency as a trusted resource. By providing educational content through a series of emails or messages, you can help your clients feel more confident and informed about the homebuying process. Here are some use cases for a buyer education drip campaign.

- First-time homebuyers: For many first-time homebuyers, the homebuying process can be overwhelming and confusing. A buyer education drip campaign can help educate first-time homebuyers on the basics of the process, including how to get pre-approved for a mortgage, how to find a real estate agent, and what to expect during the closing process.
- Niche markets: If your agency specializes in a particular niche market, such as luxury homes or vacation properties, a buyer education drip campaign can be an effective way to educate potential buyers on the unique aspects of that market. For example, you could provide information on the specific features and amenities that are desirable in luxury homes or the rental potential of vacation properties.
- Homebuying trends: A buyer education drip campaign can also be a great way to keep potential homebuyers up-to-date on the latest homebuying trends and market conditions. By providing regular updates on things like interest rates and home prices, you can help your clients make informed decisions about when and how to buy a home.
- Homebuying mistakes to avoid: Another effective use case for a buyer education drip campaign is to educate potential homebuyers

on common mistakes to avoid during the homebuying process. By providing information on things like how to avoid overpaying for a home or how to recognize red flags during a home inspection, you can help your clients make more informed decisions and avoid costly mistakes.

By providing valuable information and resources to potential homebuyers, a buyer education drip campaign can help establish your agency as a trusted and knowledgeable resource. Whether you're targeting first-time homebuyers or a specific niche market, a well-executed buyer education drip campaign can help you build relationships with potential clients and ultimately drive more business to your agency.

Step-By-Step Guide and Templates

Step 1:

Send an initial email to subscribers who have shown interest in buying a property with the subject.

"Welcome to Our Buyer Education Program!" Introduce the program and explain that it is designed to provide them with valuable information about the home buying process. Encourage subscribers to reach out to your agency with any questions they may have.

Step 1 Email Template:

Subject: Welcome to Our Buyer Education Program!
Dear [Subscriber],

We are thrilled to welcome you to our Buyer Education Program! This program is designed to provide you with valuable information about the home buying process and help you make informed decisions along the way.

Here are the steps involved with buying a home:
1. Find a real estate agent
2. Get pre-approved for a mortgage
3. Start your search
4. Make an offer
5. Get a home inspection

6. Close the sale!

7. Move in!

Our team of experienced agents is here to assist you throughout the home buying journey. Please don't hesitate to reach out to us with any questions or concerns you may have. We're always here to help.

Thank you for entrusting us with your real estate needs. We look forward to working with you.

Best regards,

[Agent Signature Block with Contact Information]

Personalization:

Update the Subscriber Name and body with your links and phone numbers where appropriate.

Recommended Agent Action:

Follow up with a phone call to subscribers who reply to the email or express interest in buying a property.

Step 2:

Send an email on day 7 with the subject line "Working with a Real Estate Agent." Provide subscribers with an overview of how working with a real estate agent can benefit them and encourage them to reach out to your agency for any questions or concerns they may have.

Step 2 Email Template:

Subject: Working with a Real Estate Agent

Dear [Subscriber],

We know that buying a home can be a complex and overwhelming process, but you don't have to go through it alone. Working with a real estate agent can benefit you in many ways. Firstly, real estate agents have a wealth of knowledge and experience in the local market, which can help you find the right property at the right price. They can also help you navigate the often-complex buying process, including negotiating contracts and closing deals.

In addition, real estate agents have access to a wide range of resources and tools that can make your home buying experience smoother and more efficient. They can provide you with market data and analysis, property listings, and insights into local trends and conditions.

Furthermore, working with a real estate agent can save you time and energy. Agents can schedule property viewings and handle administrative tasks on your behalf, freeing you up to focus on other aspects of your life.

Ultimately, the benefits of working with a real estate agent extend beyond just finding and buying a property. Agents can become trusted advisors and partners in your real estate journey, helping you achieve your goals and navigate any challenges along the way. Feel free to reach out to one of our excellent real estate agents today at [Agent Phone Number] to help you find your home.

Thanks again for your continued support!

Best regards,

[Agent Signature Block with Contact Information]

Personalization:

Update the Subscriber Name and body with your links and phone numbers where appropriate.

Recommended Agent Action:

Follow up with a phone call to subscribers who reply to the email or express interest in buying a property.

Step 3:

Send an email on day 10 after the initial email with the subject "The Importance of Pre-Approval." Explain the importance of getting pre-approved for a mortgage before beginning the home search process. Provide tips for getting pre-approved and offer your agency's assistance in the process.

Step 3

Email Template:

Subject: The Importance of Pre-Approval

Dear [Subscriber],

As you begin your home buying journey, we want to stress the importance of getting pre-approved for a mortgage. Pre-approval is a vital step in the home buying process, as it helps you determine your budget and ensures that you are shopping for homes within your price range.

Our team is here to assist you with the pre-approval process. We can provide you with recommendations for trusted mortgage lenders and guide you through the application process. Don't hesitate to reach out to us with any questions you may have.

Thank you for allowing us to assist you in your home buying journey.

Best regards,

[Agent Signature Block with Contact Information]

Personalization:

Update the Subscriber Name and body with your links and phone numbers where appropriate.

Recommended Agent Action:

Follow up with a phone call to subscribers who reply to the email or express interest in buying a property.

Step 4:

Send an SMS message on day 14 after the initial email with a reminder to subscribers to start looking for homes within their pre-approved budget and to contact your agency with any questions or concerns they may have.

Step 4 SMS Template:

Hi [Subscriber], just a friendly reminder to start looking for homes within your pre-approved budget. We're here to assist you throughout the home buying journey, so don't hesitate to reach out to us with any questions or concerns you may have.

Personalization:

Update the Subscriber Name and body with your links and phone numbers where appropriate.

Recommended Agent Action:

Follow up with a phone call to subscribers who reply to the SMS or express interest in buying a property. Step 5:

Send an email on day 21 after the initial email with the subject "How to Find the Perfect Home." Provide tips for finding the perfect home, including determining must-haves and deal-breakers and working with a knowledgeable agent. Offer your agency's assistance in the home search process.

Step 5 Email Template:

Subject: How to Find the Perfect Home
Dear [Subscriber],

Finding the perfect home can be a daunting task, especially if you're a first-time homebuyer. That's why we've put together a guide to help you navigate the process and find the home of your dreams. Here are some tips to get you started:

- Determine your budget: Before you start looking at homes, it's important to determine how much you can afford. Work with a lender to get pre-approved for a mortgage and set a budget for your home search.
- Identify your must-haves: Make a list of your must-haves and deal breakers. This will help you narrow down your search and save time.
- Work with a trusted agent: Working with a trusted agent can make all the difference in your home search. Our team has years of experience helping buyers find their dream homes and we would love to help you too.

If you're ready to start your home search, give us a call at [Agent Contact Information]. We're here to help every step of the way.

Best regards,

[Agent Signature Block with Contact Information]

Personalization:

Update the Subscriber Name and body with your links and phone n umbers where appropriate.

Recommended Agent Action:

Follow up with a phone call to subscribers who reply to the email or express interest in buying a property.

Step 6:

Send an email on day 30 with a subject line "Financing Your Dream Home" providing information on different financing options and how to get pre-approved for a mortgage. Include a call-to-action for subscribers to reach out to your agency for any financing questions or concerns they may have.

Step 6 Email Template:

Subject: Financing Your Dream Home
Dear [Subscriber],

Congratulations on taking the first step towards finding your dream home! Now that you have an idea of what you're looking for, it's important to consider how you will finance your purchase.

Our agency has compiled a list of different financing options, including mortgages and loans, that may be available to you. We can also help you get pre-approved for a mortgage so that you know exactly how much you can afford.

Don't hesitate to reach out to us for any financing questions or concerns you may have. We're here to help you make your dream home a reality.

Best regards,
[Agent Signature Block with Contact Information]

Personalization:

Update the Subscriber Name and body with your links and phone numbers where appropriate.

Recommended Agent Action:

Follow up with a phone call to subscribers who reply to the email or express interest in financing options.

Step 7:

Send an email on day 35 with the subject line "Negotiating for Your Dream Home." Provide subscribers with tips on how to negotiate for the best price on a home and encourage them to reach out to your agency for any questions or concerns they may have.

Step 7 Email Template:

Subject: Negotiating for Your Dream Home
Dear [Subscriber],

We know that finding and buying your dream home can be a stressful process, but it doesn't have to be.

In today's market, it's more important than ever to know how to negotiate for the best price on a home.

Here are some tips and tricks for negotiating the price of your dream home:

- Hire a real estate agent: A knowledgeable and experienced real estate agent can help you navigate the negotiation process and ensure you get the best deal on your dream home.
- Research the market: Before making an offer, do your research to determine the market value of the property. Look at similar homes in the area that have recently sold or are currently on the market. This will give you a better idea of what the home is actually worth and what you should offer.
- Know your budget: Determine your budget before making an offer. Consider all of your monthly expenses, including your mortgage payment, property taxes, insurance, and any potential repairs or renovations. Make sure you're comfortable with the amount you're willing to spend on a home.
- Be prepared to walk away: Don't be afraid to walk away if the seller is not willing to negotiate. Remember, there are other homes on the market and you don't want to overpay for a property.
- Offer a fair price: Make a fair offer based on your research and budget. Consider any repairs or renovations that need to be made and adjust your offer accordingly.

DRIP, DRIP, SOLD

- Be flexible: If the seller is not willing to negotiate on price, consider other factors that can make the deal more attractive, such as a faster closing date or a shorter inspection period.

We hope you find them useful and feel free to contact us with any questions or concerns you may have.

Thanks again for your continued support!

Best regards,

[Agent Signature Block with Contact Information]

Personalization:

Update the Subscriber Name and body with your links and phone numbers where appropriate.

Recommended Agent Action:

Follow up with a phone call to subscribers who reply to the email or express interest in financing options.

Step 8:

Send an SMS message on day 42 with a reminder to subscribers about the importance of pre-approval before house hunting and to reach out to your agency for any questions or concerns they may have.

Step 8 SMS Template:

Hi [Subscriber], just a friendly reminder that getting pre-approved for a mortgage before house hunting can save you time, money, and stress. Contact us to learn more and get started!

Personalization:

Update the Subscriber Name and body with your links and phone numbers where appropriate.

Recommended Agent Action:

Follow up with a phone call to subscribers who reply to the SMS or express interest in buying a property.

Step 9:

Send an SMS message on day 56 with a reminder to subscribers about the importance of having a home inspection and to reach out to your agency for any questions or concerns they may have.

Step 9 SMS Template:

Hi [Subscriber], just a friendly reminder that having a home inspection can help you avoid costly surprises after buying a home. Contact us to learn more and get started!

Personalization:

Update the Subscriber Name and body with your links and phone numbers where appropriate.

Recommended Agent Action:

Follow up with a phone call to subscribers who reply to the email or express interest in buying a property.

Step 10:

Send an email on day 63 with the subject line "It's Time to Buy Your Dream Home!" Provide subscribers with a call-to-action to reach out to your agency to start the home buying process and to schedule a consultation with one of your agents.

Step 10 Email Template:

Subject: It's Time to Buy Your Dream Home!
Dear [Subscriber],

Congratulations! You've made it through our buyer education program and we hope you've found the information helpful. Now, it's time to take the next step and start the home buying process.

We encourage you to reach out to our agency to schedule a consultation with one of our agents. They'll work with you to understand your unique needs and find the perfect home for you. Don't hesitate to contact us at [Contact Information] to get started.

Thank you for choosing our agency as your partner in the home buying journey. We look forward to working with you!

Best regards,
[Agent Signature Block with Contact Information]

Personalization:

Update the Subscriber Name and body with your links and phone numbers where appropriate.

Recommended Agent Action:

Follow up with a phone call to subscribers who reply to the email or express interest in scheduling a consultation.

Tracking the Success of the Buyer Education Drip Campaign

Tracking the success of your buyer education drip campaign can provide valuable insights into the effectiveness of your marketing efforts and help you make informed decisions about future campaigns. Here are some key metrics to track:

- Email open rates: Track the percentage of subscribers who open your emails. This can give you an idea of how engaged your audience is and whether your subject lines are effective.
- Click-through rates: Track the percentage of subscribers who click on links in your emails. This can help you understand which content is most engaging and which calls-to-action are most effective.
- Conversion rates: Track the percentage of subscribers who take a specific action, such as contacting your agency or scheduling a consultation with an agent. This can help you measure the overall effectiveness of your campaign in generating leads and closing deals.
- Subscriber engagement: Monitor how frequently subscribers interact with your emails or other content, such as social media posts or blog articles. This can help you identify which subscribers are most engaged and likely to convert into clients.
- Return on investment (ROI): Calculate the return on investment for your campaign by comparing the cost of the campaign to the revenue generated from new clients or closed deals. This can help you determine whether your marketing efforts are worth the investment.

By tracking these metrics and analyzing the data, you can gain valuable insights into the effectiveness of your buyer education drip campaign and make data-driven decisions about how to optimize your future marketing efforts.

Tips for Customizing the Buyer Education Drip Campaign

Customizing your buyer education drip campaign is essential to make it stand out from your competitors and appeal to your target audience. By tailoring your messaging to your specific market and audience, you can increase engagement and ultimately close more deals. In this section, we'll provide some tips and best practices for customizing your buyer education drip campaign. Understand your audience: Before creating your campaign, take the time to understand your target audience. Consider their age, income, and lifestyle to create content that resonates with them.

- Customize content: Tailor your content to match the needs and preferences of your audience. For example, if you are targeting first-time homebuyers, provide them with step-by-step guides, whereas if you are targeting seasoned homebuyers, provide them with more advanced tips.
- Use visuals: Use visuals such as images, videos, or infographics to make your content more engaging and easier to understand.
- Keep it simple: Avoid using jargon or technical terms that your audience may not understand. Keep your content simple and easy to digest.
- Provide value: Offer valuable information and resources to your subscribers. This can include market trends, home buying tips, and advice on negotiating prices.
- Be consistent: Consistency is key in any drip campaign. Make sure you have a regular schedule for sending out emails and other content.
- Personalize your communication: Use Personalization tokens in your emails to address your subscribers by their first name. This will make your communication more personal and engaging.
- Monitor your campaign: Monitor your campaign's performance regularly to see what is working and what is not. Use this information to tweak your campaign for better results.

By customizing your buyer education drip campaign to your specific market and audience, you can establish yourself as a trusted resource for home buyers and increase your chances of closing more deals. Keep in mind that the key to success is providing valuable, relevant content that resonates with your audience and addresses their specific pain points and concerns. Use the tips and best practices outlined in this section to create a buyer education drip campaign that sets you apart from your competitors and helps you build long-lasting relationships with your clients.

Conclusion

The Buyer Education Drip Campaign is an effective way for real estate agents to educate their subscribers and guide them through the home buying process. By providing valuable information, helpful tips, and personalized assistance, agents can establish themselves as trusted advisors and help their clients achieve their dream of homeownership.

Throughout this chapter, we've covered the key components of a successful Buyer Education Drip Campaign, including use cases, step-by-step templates, and tips for customizing the campaign to your specific market and audience. We've also discussed the importance of tracking the success of your campaign to ensure it's reaching and engaging your subscribers.

By implementing the strategies outlined in this chapter, agents can build stronger relationships with their clients, increase their brand awareness, and ultimately close more deals. We hope that the information provided here has been helpful and wish you success in your future real estate endeavors.

16

SELLER EDUCATION DRIP CAMPAIGN

Selling a home can be a daunting task, especially for those who are doing it for the first time. The seller education drip campaign is designed to help guide potential home sellers through the process and provide them with valuable information and resources to make informed decisions. This campaign will help educate potential home sellers on topics such as pricing their home, preparing their home for sale, and choosing the right real estate agent. By providing sellers with the knowledge and tools they need, they can feel confident and empowered when it comes time to sell their home.

User Scenario: Seller Education Drip Campaign

Janelle, an experienced real estate agent, aims to educate her clients about the home-selling process, helping them feel more confident and informed. To achieve this, Janelle implements a Seller Education Drip Campaign. This campaign involves sending a series of emails and SMS messages that provide valuable insights on various aspects of selling a home, including pricing strategies, home staging, marketing techniques, and negotiation tips.

By consistently providing useful information, Janelle can guide her clients through the complexities of selling their homes, ensuring they are well-prepared and making informed decisions. This approach not only builds trust and rapport with her clients but also positions Janelle as a knowledgeable and reliable real estate professional.

Implementing this drip campaign can help you achieve similar success by educating your clients and enhancing their home-selling experience, ultimately leading to more successful transactions and satisfied clients.

Seller Education Drip Campaign Use Cases

The Seller Education Drip Campaign is a powerful tool that can help real estate agents educate their clients about the home selling process. By providing valuable information to potential sellers, you can position your agency as a trusted resource and increase the likelihood of securing new listings. Let's dive into some of the most effective use cases for a seller education drip campaign.

- Preparing to Sell: Before a homeowner decides to list their property, they need to be aware of the various steps and considerations involved in the home selling process. Agents can create drip campaigns that provide valuable information on topics such as preparing the home for sale, pricing strategies, and working with a real estate agent.
- Home Staging: Home staging is a critical part of the home selling process. Agents can use drip campaigns to educate their clients on the importance of staging their home, as well as provide tips and resources for effective staging.
- Pricing Strategies: Pricing a home correctly is key to a successful home sale. Agents can use drip campaigns to educate their clients on various pricing strategies, including comparative market analysis, appraisals, and online tools.
- Marketing Strategies: A successful home sale requires effective marketing strategies. Agents can create drip campaigns that provide information on effective marketing techniques, such as online advertising, social media, and open houses.
- Negotiation: Negotiation is a critical part of the home selling process. Agents can use drip campaigns to educate their clients on negotiation techniques and strategies, as well as provide resources for working with potential buyers.
- Closing the Sale: Closing the sale can be a complex process, and homeowners need to be aware of the various steps involved. Agents can create drip campaigns that provide information on the closing process, including title searches, home inspections, and closing costs.
- Post-Sale Considerations: After the sale is complete, there are still important considerations for homeowners. Agents can use drip

campaigns to educate their clients on post-sale considerations, such as tax implications and moving tips.

The Seller Education Drip Campaign is a powerful tool that can help real estate agents educate their clients on the home selling process. By providing valuable information and resources, agents can build trust with their clients and position themselves as experts in the industry. Use the above use cases to craft a drip campaign that will help your clients navigate the home selling process with confidence.

Step-By-Step Guide and Templates

Step 1:

Send an email on day 1 with a subject line "Preparing Your Home for Sale." In this email, provide tips and strategies for preparing a home for sale, including decluttering, making repairs, and staging. You can also include your agency's contact information for any questions or concerns.

Step 1 Email Template:

Subject: Preparing Your Home for Sale
Dear [Subscriber],

If you're planning to sell your home, it's important to take the necessary steps to prepare it for the market. In this email, we'll provide you with tips and strategies for preparing your home for sale.

Here are some key points to keep in mind:

- Declutter your home: Removing clutter can make your home appear more spacious and help potential buyers envision themselves living there.
- Make necessary repairs: Fixing any visible issues can make your home more appealing and help increase its value.
- Stage your home: Staging can help your home stand out and attract more potential buyers.

We understand that preparing your home for sale can be overwhelming, and that's why we're here to help. If you have any questions or concerns about the home selling process, don't hesitate to reach out to us.

DRIP, DRIP, SOLD

Best regards,
[Agent Signature Block with Contact Information]

Personalization:

Update the Subscriber Name and body with your links and phone numbers where appropriate.

Recommended Agent Action:

Follow up with a phone call to subscribers who reply to the email or express interest in buying or selling a property.

Step 2:

Send an email on day 7 with a subject line "Determining the Value of Your Home." Provide information on how to determine the value of a home, including researching comparable homes and working with a real estate agent. You can also include your agency's contact information for any questions or concerns.

Step 2 Email Template:

Subject: Determining the Value of Your Home
Dear [Subscriber],

One of the most important steps in selling your home is determining its value. In this email, we'll provide you with tips and strategies for determining the value of your home.

Here are some key points to keep in mind:

Research comparable homes: Looking at homes in your area that are similar to yours can give you an idea of what your home is worth.

Work with a real estate agent: A real estate agent can provide you with a more accurate valuation of your home based on current market conditions and comparable homes in your area.

We understand that determining the value of your home can be overwhelming, and that's why we're here to help. If you have any questions or concerns about the home selling process, don't hesitate to reach out to us.

Best regards,

[Agent Signature Block with Contact Information]

Personalization:

Update the Subscriber Name and body with your links and phone numbers where appropriate.

Recommended Agent Action:

Follow up with a phone call to subscribers who reply to the email or express interest in buying or selling a property.

Step 3:

Send an email on day 14 with a subject line "Listing Your Home for Sale." Provide information on how to create a listing for a home, including writing a compelling description and taking high-quality photos. You can also include your agency's contact information for any questions or concerns.

Step 3 Email Template:

Subject: Listing Your Home for Sale
Dear [Subscriber],

Now that your home is ready to sell and you've determined its value, it's time to create a listing. In this email, we'll provide you with tips and strategies for creating a compelling listing for your home.

Here are some key points to keep in mind:

Write a compelling description: Your home's description should be engaging and highlight its best features.

Take high-quality photos: Photos are often the first thing potential buyers see, so it's important to take high-quality photos that showcase your home's best features.

We understand that creating a listing can be overwhelming, but we're here to help. Our agency specializes in helping sellers navigate the home selling process and getting their homes sold quickly and at the right price. If you have any questions or concerns about creating a listing, don't hesitate to reach out to us.

Best regards,
[Agent Signature Block with Contact Information]

Personalization:

Update the Subscriber Name and body with your links and phone numbers where appropriate.

Recommended Agent Action:

Follow up with a phone call to subscribers who reply to the email or express interest in buying or selling a property.

Step 4:

Send an email on day 21 with a subject line "Negotiating the Sale of Your Home". Provide information on how to negotiate effectively and close a deal, and include your contact information for any questions or concerns.

Step 4 Email Template:

Subject: Negotiating the Sale of Your Home
Dear [Subscriber],

Selling a home can be a complex process, and negotiating the sale can be especially challenging. In this email, we'll provide you with tips and strategies for negotiating the sale of your home effectively.

Here are some key points to keep in mind:

Price your home appropriately: Setting the right price from the beginning can attract more buyers and increase your chances of a successful sale.

Be prepared for offers: Understand what offers may be reasonable and what to expect during the negotiation process.

Consider all offers: Don't reject an offer outright. Instead, negotiate and work with the buyer to come to an agreement that works for both parties.

We understand that selling your home can be overwhelming, and that's why we're here to help. If you have any questions or concerns about the home selling process, don't hesitate to reach out to us.

Best regards,
[Agent Signature Block with Contact Information]

Personalization:

Update the Subscriber Name and body with your links and phone numbers where appropriate.

Recommended Agent Action:

Follow up with a phone call to subscribers who reply to the email or express interest in buying or selling a property.

Step 5:

Send an email on day 21 with a subject line "Negotiating the Sale of Your Home". Provide information on how to negotiate effectively and close a deal, and include your contact information for any questions or concerns.

Step 5 Email Template:

Subject: Preparing for the Home Inspection
Dear [Subscriber],

Congratulations on making it this far in the home selling process! As we move forward, it's important to start preparing for the home inspection.

In this email, we'll provide you with information on what to expect during a home inspection and how to prepare for it.

Here are some key points to keep in mind:

What to expect: The home inspector will evaluate the condition of the home and identify any potential issues. They will inspect the roof, foundation, electrical and plumbing systems, and more.

How to prepare: Make sure the home is clean and tidy, and ensure all systems are in working order. It's also a good idea to compile a list of any recent repairs or upgrades.

Tips for success: Be present during the inspection, and don't be afraid to ask questions or provide additional information.

We understand that the home inspection can be nerve-wracking, but we're here to help. If you have any questions or concerns, don't hesitate to reach out to us.

Best regards,

[Agent Signature Block with Contact Information]

Personalization:

Update the Subscriber Name and body with your links and phone numbers where appropriate.

Recommended Agent Action:

Follow up with a phone call to subscribers who reply to the email or express interest in buying or selling a property.

Step 6:

Send an email on day 35 with a subject line "Preparing for Closing Day". This email should provide information on what to expect on closing day, how to prepare for it, and what to bring. It's also a good time to remind the seller to notify their utility companies and change their address with the post office.

Step 6 Email Template:

Subject: Preparing for Closing Day
Dear [Subscriber],

Congratulations! Your home sale is nearing the finish line. In this email, we'll provide you with some important information on how to prepare for closing day.

Here are some key points to keep in mind:

Review the closing documents: Review the closing documents in advance to ensure that everything is in order.

Prepare the necessary documents: Gather all of the necessary documents, such as your driver's license and any paperwork related to the sale.

Bring certified funds: You may need to bring certified funds to cover the closing costs and any other fees.

Notify your utility companies: Be sure to notify your utility companies of your move-out date and arrange for final billing.

Change your address: Don't forget to change your address with the post office to ensure that your mail is forwarded to your new home.

If you have any questions or concerns about the closing process, don't hesitate to reach out to us. We're here to help you every step of the way.
Best regards,
[Agent Signature Block with Contact Information]

Personalization:

Update the Subscriber Name and body with your links and phone numbers where appropriate.

Recommended Agent Action:

Follow up with a phone call to subscribers who reply to the email or express interest in buying or selling a property.

Step 7:

Send an email on day 35 with a subject line "Preparing for Closing Day". This email should provide information on what to expect on closing day, how to prepare for it, and what to bring. It's also a good time to remind the seller to notify their utility companies and change their address with the post office.

Tracking the Success of the Seller Education Drip Campaign

Tracking the success of your seller education drip campaign is essential for understanding how well your marketing efforts are resonating with your audience. By measuring key performance indicators (KPIs), you can gain insights into the effectiveness of your campaign and make data-driven decisions to optimize it.

Specific things to track:

- Open rates: This metric measures the percentage of subscribers who opened your emails. A high open rate indicates that your subject lines and email content are compelling and relevant to your audience.
- Click-through rates (CTRs): CTRs measure the percentage of subscribers who clicked on links within your emails. This metric helps you understand how engaged your audience is with your content.

- Conversion rates: This metric measures the percentage of subscribers who take a desired action, such as filling out a contact form or scheduling a consultation. This metric is a direct reflection of how effective your campaign is at converting leads into customers.
- Unsubscribe rates: This metric measures the percentage of subscribers who opt-out of your campaign. While it's normal to have some unsubscribes, high unsubscribe rates may indicate that your content is not meeting your audience's expectations.

Ways To Track

Email marketing software: Most email marketing platforms, such as Mailchimp and Constant Contact, offer built-in tracking features that allow you to track KPIs, such as open rates and CTRs.

- Google Analytics: You can use Google Analytics to track website traffic and user behavior, including the number of conversions that result from your seller education campaign.
- CRM software: If you're using a customer relationship management (CRM) platform, such as Salesforce or Hubspot, you can track the progress of individual leads and see how your seller education campaign is impacting your overall sales pipeline.

Once you have identified the key metrics to track the success of your Seller Education Drip Campaign, you can use this information to make adjustments and optimize your campaign for better results. Here are some tips on how to adjust your campaign based on the things you are tracking:

- Open Rates: If you notice that your open rates are low, it may be time to revisit your subject lines and email content. Try using more attention-grabbing subject lines and make sure your email content is engaging and informative. You could also try sending your emails at different times of the day to see if that improves open rates.
- Click-Through Rates: Low click-through rates could indicate that your content is not relevant or compelling enough. Consider tweaking your messaging or offering more valuable information to your subscribers. You could also experiment with different calls-to-action and see if that improves clickthrough rates.

- Conversion Rates: If your conversion rates are low, it may be time to re-evaluate your lead magnet or offer. Make sure your offer is relevant to your subscribers and provides value to them. You could also consider adding more urgency to your messaging or offering a limited-time discount or promotion to encourage conversions.
- Unsubscribe Rates: High unsubscribe rates may indicate that your content is not resonating with your subscribers. Consider surveying your audience to better understand their needs and preferences, and adjust your content accordingly. You could also consider segmenting your list and sending more targeted messages to specific groups of subscribers.

By tracking these metrics and making adjustments as needed, you can ensure that your Seller Education Drip Campaign is delivering the results you want and helping you connect with potential sellers more effectively.

Tips for Customizing the Buyer Education Drip Campaign

Customizing your seller education drip campaign is essential to stand out from competitors and appeal to your target audience. By tailoring your messaging to your specific market and audience, you can increase engagement and ultimately close more deals. In this section, we'll provide some tips and best practices for customizing your seller education drip campaign.

- Understand your audience: Before creating your campaign, take the time to understand your target audience. Consider their age, income, and lifestyle to create content that resonates with them.
- Customize content: Tailor your content to match the needs and preferences of your audience. For example, if you are targeting homeowners in a specific neighborhood, provide them with market trends and data specific to their area.
- Use visuals: Use visuals such as images, videos, or infographics to make your content more engaging and easier to understand.
- Keep it simple: Avoid using jargon or technical terms that your audience may not understand. Keep your content simple and easy to digest.

- Provide value: Offer valuable information and resources to your subscribers. This can include tips on home staging, preparing for open houses, and how to choose the right agent.
- Be consistent: Consistency is key in any drip campaign. Make sure you have a regular schedule for sending out emails and other content.
- Personalize your communication: Use Personalization tokens in your emails to address your subscribers by their first name. This will make your communication more personal and engaging.
- Monitor your campaign: Monitor your campaign's performance regularly to see what is working and what is not. Use this information to tweak your campaign for better results.

By customizing your seller education drip campaign to your specific market and audience, you can establish yourself as a trusted resource for home sellers and increase your chances of closing more deals. Keep in mind that the key to success is providing valuable, relevant content that resonates with your audience and addresses their specific pain points and concerns. Use the tips and best practices outlined in this section to create a seller education drip campaign that sets you apart from your competitors and helps you build long-lasting relationships with your clients.

Conclusion

The Seller Education Drip Campaign is an effective way for real estate agents to educate their subscribers and guide them through the home selling process. By providing valuable information, helpful tips, and personalized assistance, agents can establish themselves as trusted advisors and help their clients achieve their goal of selling their home.

Throughout this chapter, we've covered the key components of a successful Seller Education Drip Campaign, including use cases, step-by-step templates, and tips for customizing the campaign to your specific market and audience. We've also discussed the importance of tracking the success of your campaign to ensure it's reaching and engaging your subscribers.

By implementing the strategies outlined in this chapter, agents can build stronger relationships with their clients, increase their brand awareness, and ultimately close more deals. We hope that the information provided here has been helpful and wish you success in your future real estate endeavors.

17

MORTGAGE EDUCATION/ UPDATES DRIP CAMPAIGN

As a real estate agent, keeping your clients informed about mortgage rates and lending requirements is critical to their decision-making process when buying or selling a property. But beyond just keeping your clients informed, this chapter will show you how to create a drip campaign that can generate and convert leads into buyers and sellers. By providing valuable and up-to-date information on mortgage rates and lending requirements through email and SMS templates, you can build trust and establish yourself as an authority in the industry. This chapter will provide a step-by-step guide on how to create and execute a successful drip campaign that will not only keep your clients informed, but also drive new business to your real estate practice.

User Scenario: Mortgage Education/Updates Drip Campaign

Lisa, a proactive real estate agent, understands the importance of keeping her clients informed about mortgage rates and lending requirements. To help her clients make informed decisions and stay updated on the latest mortgage trends, Lisa decides to implement a Mortgage Education/ Updates Drip Campaign. This campaign involves sending a series of personalized emails and SMS messages that provide valuable information on mortgage rates, types of mortgages, and tips for securing the best rates.

By offering consistent and relevant updates, Lisa can build trust with her clients and establish herself as a knowledgeable authority in the real estate industry. This approach not only helps her clients navigate the complexities of mortgages but also enhances their overall experience, making them more likely to refer her services to others.

Implementing this drip campaign can help you achieve similar success by educating your clients and keeping them engaged with timely and valuable mortgage information.

Mortgage Education/Updates Drip Campaign Use Cases

A mortgage is one of the biggest financial commitments a person can make in their lifetime. As a real estate agent or broker, it's important to keep your clients informed about mortgage rates and lending requirements to help them make informed decisions. One of the most effective ways to do this is through a Mortgage Updates Drip Campaign. In this section, we'll explore some use cases for Mortgage Updates Drip Campaigns and how they can help you generate and convert leads.

- Educate First-Time Homebuyers: First-time homebuyers are often new to the mortgage process and may not understand the intricacies of interest rates and lending requirements. A Mortgage Updates Drip Campaign can educate these buyers on the latest updates and trends in the mortgage industry, as well as provide tips on how to prepare for the application process.
- Nurture Prospective Buyers: Prospective buyers who have not yet committed to purchasing a home may need some encouragement to take the next step. A Mortgage Updates Drip Campaign can help to nurture these leads by providing them with valuable information on mortgage rates and lending requirements, while also demonstrating your expertise as a real estate professional.
- Follow-Up with Past Clients: Maintaining a relationship with past clients is essential for building a strong referral network. A Mortgage Updates Drip Campaign can be a great way to keep in touch with past clients, while also providing them with valuable information on the latest mortgage updates and trends.
- Engage with Referral Partners: Building relationships with referral partners, such as mortgage lenders and other real estate professionals, can be an effective way to generate new leads. A Mortgage Updates Drip Campaign can help to keep these partners informed on the latest mortgage updates and trends, while also demonstrating your expertise and value as a partner.

- Stay Top of Mind with Current Buyers: For clients who are in the process of purchasing a home, a Mortgage Updates Drip Campaign can provide regular updates on mortgage rates and lending requirements, as well as other relevant information that can help them to make informed decisions throughout the home buying process.

A Mortgage Updates Drip Campaign can be a valuable tool for generating and converting leads in the real estate industry. By providing valuable information on the latest mortgage updates and trends, you can demonstrate your expertise and value to clients and referral partners alike, while also staying top of mind with your current and past clients.

Step-By-Step Guide and Templates

As to provide the most relevant information and not overwhelm the lead, we will send an email once a week with periodic SMS messages sent 3 days after specific emails. Be sure to update the email with the most current mortgage rates. It is advised to monitor the rates frequently and update as frequently as possible. Freddie Mac is a government-sponsored enterprise that provides liquidity and stability to the US housing market by buying mortgages from lenders and packaging them into securities that are sold to investors. Their website provides up-to-date information on mortgage rates, including the average rate for a 30-year fixed mortgage, 15-year fixed mortgage, and 5/1 adjustable-rate mortgage. These rates are updated weekly and are based on data from mortgage lenders across the country. Checking Freddie Mac's website for current mortgage rates is a reliable and convenient way to stay informed about the latest rates and trends in the mortgage market. Their web address is https://www.freddiemac.com/pmms.

Step 1:

Send an email on day 1 with a subject line "Understanding Mortgage Basics: What You Need to Know." In this email, provide an overview of mortgage basics, including types of mortgages, current interest rates, factors affecting them, and loan terms. Encourage subscribers to contact your agency for personalized advice and assistance. Be sure to research

DRIP, DRIP, SOLD

and update the email with the most current interest rates at the time of your email. You can also include your agency's contact information for any questions or concerns.

Step 1 Email Template:

Subject: Understanding Mortgage Basics: What You Need to Know
Dear [Subscriber],

If you're planning to buy a home, understanding the basics of mortgages is crucial. In this email, we'll provide you with an overview of mortgage basics to help you make informed decisions.

Here are some key points to keep in mind:

Types of mortgages: Learn about the different mortgage options available, such as fixed-rate, adjustable-rate, and government-backed loans.

Current interest rates: Here's a snapshot of the current rates for popular mortgage types:

30-year fixed: 3.5%
15-year fixed: 2.9%
5/1 ARM: 3.1%

- Factors affecting mortgage rates: Understand how factors such as Federal Reserve policies, economic indicators, and global market trends affect interest rates.
- Loan terms: Get familiar with loan terms and how they impact your monthly payments and the overall cost of your loan.

We understand that navigating the mortgage process can be overwhelming, and that's why we're here to help. If you have any questions or need personalized advice, don't hesitate to reach out to us.

Best regards,
[Agent Signature Block with Contact Information]

Personalization:

Update the Subscriber Name and body with your links and phone numbers where appropriate.

Recommended Agent Action:

Follow up with a phone call to subscribers who reply to the email or express interest in discussing mortgage rates, buying or selling a property, or have questions about the home loan process. Offer your assistance and expertise to help them make the best decision for their needs.

Step 2:

Send an email on day 7 with a subject line "Current Mortgage Rates and Factors Affecting Them." Provide information on the current mortgage rates, including a sample rate, and discuss the factors affecting mortgage rates. You can also include your agency's contact information for any questions or concerns.

Step 2 Email Template:

Subject: Current Mortgage Rates and Factors Affecting Them
Dear [Subscriber],

Staying informed about current mortgage rates and the factors influencing them is crucial when buying a home. In this email, we'll provide you with information on the current mortgage rates and the key factors affecting them.

Here are some key points to keep in mind:

Sample mortgage rate: As of today, the average 30-year fixed mortgage rate is 3.25%. Keep in mind that this rate may vary depending on your credit score, loan amount, and other factors.

Factors affecting mortgage rates:

- Economic indicators: Key economic indicators, such as inflation, unemployment rates, and gross domestic product (GDP) growth, can influence mortgage rates.
- Federal Reserve policies: Changes in the Federal Reserve's monetary policy, like adjustments to the federal funds rate, can impact mortgage rates.
- Market conditions: Supply and demand dynamics in the mortgage market, along with investor sentiment, can affect the interest rates on home loans.

- Credit score: Your credit score plays a significant role in determining the mortgage rate you qualify for. Borrowers with higher credit scores tend to receive more favorable rates.
- Loan-to-Value ratio (LTV): A higher LTV ratio, which represents the percentage of the loan amount relative to the property's value, may result in a higher interest rate.

We understand that keeping track of mortgage rates and the factors influencing them can be challenging, and that's why we're here to help. If you have any questions or concerns, don't hesitate to reach out to us.

Best regards,

[Agent Signature Block with Contact Information]

Personalization:

Update the Subscriber Name and body with your links and phone numbers where appropriate. Be sure to update the sample mortgage rate with the most recent and accurate information at the time of sending the email.

Recommended Agent Action:

Follow up with a phone call to subscribers who reply to the email or express interest in buying or selling a property.

Step 3:

Send an email on day 15 with a subject line "Higher Interest Rates: Why Waiting May Not Be the Best Strategy." In this email, discuss the potential benefits of buying a home even when interest rates are higher, including the possibility of refinancing for lower payments in the future, and provide strategies for managing the situation. Encourage subscribers to contact your agency for personalized advice and assistance. You can also include your agency's contact information for any questions or concerns.

Step 3 Email Template:

Subject: Higher Interest Rates: Why Waiting May Not Be the Best Strategy

Dear [Subscriber],

While it's true that higher interest rates can affect the cost of your mortgage, waiting for rates to decrease may not always be the best strategy. In this email, we'll discuss the potential benefits of buying a home even when interest rates are higher, including the possibility of refinancing for lower payments in the future, and provide some strategies to help you navigate the situation.

Here are some key points to keep in mind:

- Future rates are uncertain: Predicting interest rates can be challenging, and waiting for them to decrease might mean missing out on a great home or facing even higher rates down the road.
- Building equity: When you buy a home, you start building equity, which can be a valuable long-term investment.
- Refinancing potential: Buying a home that you can afford when rates are high may allow you to refinance later when rates go down, leading to substantially lower payments.

Strategies for higher rates: Consider the following options if you're concerned about higher rates:

- Look for homes priced below your maximum budget to give you some flexibility with mortgage payments.
- Work on improving your credit score to potentially qualify for better rates.

We understand that navigating the mortgage process in times of higher interest rates can be challenging, and that's why we're here to help. If you have any questions or need personalized advice, don't hesitate to reach out to us.

Best regards,

[Agent Signature Block with Contact Information]

Personalization:

Update the Subscriber Name and body with your links and phone numbers where appropriate.

Recommended Agent Action:

Follow up with a phone call to subscribers who reply to the email or express interest in discussing mortgage rates, buying or selling a property, or have questions about the home loan process. Offer your assistance and expertise to help them make the best decision for their needs.

Step 4:

Send an SMS message on day 18, reminding subscribers about the importance of understanding mortgage options and that your agency is available for assistance. Encourage them to contact your agency for personalized advice or if they have any questions or concerns.

Step 4 SMS Template:

Hi [Subscriber], remember that understanding mortgage options is key when buying a home. Our team is here to help you navigate this process, answer any questions, and provide personalized advice. Don't hesitate to reach out to us!

Personalization:

Update the Subscriber Name and body with your links and phone numbers where appropriate.

Recommended Agent Action:

Follow up with a phone call to subscribers who reply to the SMS or express interest in discussing mortgage options, buying or selling a property, or have questions about the home loan process. Offer your assistance and expertise to help them make the best decision for their needs.

Step 5:

Send an email on day 25 with a subject line "How Credit Scores Affect Your Mortgage Rate." In this email, explain the impact of credit scores on mortgage rates, the importance of maintaining a good credit score, and tips for improving credit scores. Encourage subscribers to contact your agency for personalized advice or if they have any questions or concerns.

Step 5 Email Template:

Subject: How Credit Scores Affect Your Mortgage Rate

Dear [Subscriber],

Your credit score plays a significant role in determining the mortgage rate you'll receive when buying a home. In this email, we'll discuss how credit scores affect mortgage rates, the importance of maintaining a good credit score, and share some tips to help you improve your credit score.

Here are some key points to keep in mind:

- Higher credit scores lead to better rates: Lenders view borrowers with higher credit scores as less risky, so they often offer more favorable mortgage rates.
- Importance of a good credit score: Maintaining a good credit score can save you thousands of dollars over the life of your loan, making it easier to afford your dream home.

Tips for improving your credit score:

- Make all your payments on time.
- Keep your credit utilization low.
- Regularly check your credit report for errors and dispute any inaccuracies.
- Avoid opening new credit accounts or closing old ones right before applying for a mortgage.

We understand that navigating the mortgage process and maintaining a good credit score can be challenging, and that's why we're here to help. If you have any questions or need personalized advice, don't hesitate to reach out to us.

Best regards,

[Agent Signature Block with Contact Information]

Personalization:

Update the Subscriber Name and body with your links and phone numbers where appropriate.

Recommended Agent Action:

Follow up with a phone call to subscribers who reply to the email or express interest in discussing credit scores, mortgage rates, buying or selling a property, or have questions about the home loan process.

Offer your assistance and expertise to help them make the best decision for their needs.

Step 6:

Send an SMS message on day 28, reminding subscribers about the importance of maintaining a good credit score and how it can lead to better mortgage rates. Encourage them to contact your agency for personalized advice or if they have any questions or concerns.

Step 6 SMS Template:

Hi [Subscriber], a good credit score is crucial for securing better mortgage rates when buying a home. If you need guidance on improving your credit or have any questions about the process, don't hesitate to reach out to us. We're here to help!

Personalization:

Update the Subscriber Name and body with your links and phone numbers where appropriate.

Recommended Agent Action:

Follow up with a phone call to subscribers who reply to the SMS or express interest in discussing credit scores, mortgage rates, buying or selling a property, or have questions about the home loan process.

Offer your assistance and expertise to help them make the best decision for their needs.

Step 7:

Send an email on day 35 with a subject line "Mortgage Pre-Approval: Why It Matters and How to Get Started." In this email, explain the benefits of getting pre-approved for a mortgage, such as increased negotiating power and a faster home buying process. Provide guidance on how to start the pre-approval process and encourage subscribers to contact your agency for personalized advice or if they have any questions or concerns.

Step 7 Email Template:

Subject: Mortgage Pre-Approval: Why It Matters and How to Get Started
Dear [Subscriber],

Obtaining a mortgage pre-approval is an essential step in the home buying process. In this email, we'll discuss the benefits of getting pre-approved and provide guidance on how to start the pre-approval process.

Here are some key points to keep in mind:

- Benefits of mortgage pre-approval:
  - Increased negotiating power: Sellers are more likely to take your offer seriously if you're preapproved.
  - Faster home buying process: You'll have a better understanding of your budget and can focus on homes within your price range.
  - Improved chances of offer acceptance: Pre-approval signals to sellers that you're a serious buyer with financing in place.

How to start the pre-approval process:

- Gather necessary documentation: Collect pay stubs, tax returns, bank statements, and other financial documents.
- Contact a mortgage lender: Reach out to a reputable mortgage lender to discuss your financial situation and start the pre-approval process.
- Stay within your budget: Avoid making large purchases or taking on new debt, as this could affect your pre-approval status.

We understand that the mortgage pre-approval process can be overwhelming, and that's why we're here to help. If you have any questions or need personalized advice, don't hesitate to reach out to us.

Best regards,

[Agent Signature Block with Contact Information]

Personalization:

Update the Subscriber Name and body with your links and phone numbers where appropriate.

Recommended Agent Action:

Follow up with a phone call to subscribers who reply to the email or express interest in discussing mortgage pre-approval, buying or selling a property, or have questions about the home loan process.

Offer your assistance and expertise to help them make the best decision for their needs.

Step 8:

Send an SMS message on day 38, reminding subscribers about the benefits of working with a knowledgeable real estate agent, and how your agency can help guide them through the home buying process. Encourage them to reach out to your agency for personalized assistance or if they have any questions or concerns.

Step 8 SMS Template:

Hi [Subscriber], working with an experienced real estate agent can make a world of difference in your home buying journey. Our agency is here to provide guidance and support every step of the way. If you need any assistance or have questions, don't hesitate to reach out!

Personalization:

Update the Subscriber Name and body with your links and phone numbers where appropriate.

Recommended Agent Action:

Follow up with a phone call to subscribers who reply to the SMS or express interest in discussing their home buying needs, buying or selling a property, or have questions about the process. Offer your assistance and expertise to help them make the best decision for their needs.

Step 9:

Send an email on day 45 with a subject line "Mortgage Updates: Stay Informed and Make Informed Decisions." In this email, summarize the key points from the previous mortgage-related emails and stress the importance of staying informed about mortgage rates and lending requirements.

Encourage subscribers to contact your agency for personalized assistance, ongoing mortgage updates, or if they have any questions or concerns.

Step 9 Email Template:

Subject: Mortgage Updates: Stay Informed and Make Informed Decisions
Dear [Subscriber],

Over the past several weeks, we've shared valuable information about mortgage rates, lending requirements, and strategies to help you make the best decisions when buying or selling a property. Staying informed about mortgage updates is crucial for making smart financial decisions in the everchanging real estate market.

Here's a quick recap of the key points from our previous emails:

- Understand mortgage basics, including types of mortgages, interest rates, and loan terms.
- Stay up-to-date on current mortgage rates and factors that influence them.
- Consider strategies for buying a home when interest rates are higher, such as locking in a rate or refinancing when rates drop.
- Maintain a good credit score to secure better mortgage rates.
- Get pre-approved for a mortgage to increase negotiating power and streamline the home buying process.

Remember, our agency is here to provide ongoing guidance and support throughout your home buying or selling journey. If you have any questions or need personalized advice, don't hesitate to reach out to us.

Best regards,

[Agent Signature Block with Contact Information]

Personalization:

Update the Subscriber Name and body with your links and phone numbers where appropriate.

Recommended Agent Action:

Follow up with a phone call to subscribers who reply to the email or express interest in discussing mortgage updates, buying or selling a property, or have questions about the home loan process. Offer your assistance and expertise to help them make the best decision for their needs.

Tracking the Success of the Mortgage Updates Drip Campaign

To ensure that your Mortgage Updates Drip Campaign is effective, it's essential to track and analyze its performance. Here are some metrics and methods to track the success of your campaign:

- Open and click-through rates: Measure the open and click-through rates of your emails and SMS messages to determine how engaged your subscribers are with your campaign. If the rates are low, it may be an indication that you need to improve the content or timing of your communications.
- Response rate: Keep track of the number of subscribers who respond to your emails or SMS messages. This will help you gauge how interested they are in the mortgage updates you are providing.
- Conversion rate: Track how many of the leads generated from your campaign turned into actual clients. This will give you an idea of how effective your campaign is at generating quality leads.
- Referral rate: Keep track of the number of referrals generated from your campaign. This will help you gauge how effective your campaign is at generating referrals from your current clients.
- Feedback from clients: Ask your clients for feedback on the mortgage updates you are providing to get an idea of how effective your campaign is at providing valuable information.

To track these metrics, you can use email marketing tools or CRM software. You can also manually keep track of the number of leads, referrals, and conversions in a spreadsheet or document.

By tracking the success of your Mortgage Updates Drip Campaign, you can make data-driven decisions to improve its effectiveness and generate more quality leads for your agency.

Tips for Customizing Mortgage Updates Drip Campaign

In order to make the most out of a Mortgage Updates Drip Campaign, it is important to customize the campaign to fit your specific agency and audience. By making small tweaks and adjustments to the campaign, you can increase the effectiveness and success of the campaign. Here are some tips for customizing the Mortgage Updates Drip Campaign:

- Personalize your emails and SMS messages: Use the subscriber's name and any other relevant information you have about them to make your communications feel more personalized and engaging.
- Use a clear call to action: Encourage subscribers to contact your agency for more information or to schedule a consultation with a mortgage specialist.
- Offer incentives for referrals: While you cannot offer monetary rewards for referrals, you can offer incentives such as exclusive access to new listings or personalized mortgage consultations.
- Timing is key: Make sure to space out your messages appropriately and avoid bombarding subscribers with too many communications. Find a balance that works for your audience and your agency.
- Test and adjust: Continuously test and adjust your messaging to find what works best for your audience. Analyze metrics such as open rates and click-through rates to see what resonates with your subscribers and adjust accordingly.
- Make it easy to take action: Provide subscribers with easy-to-use tools and resources to contact your agency or learn more about the mortgage updates you are providing, such as a contact form on your website or social media.

By customizing your Mortgage Updates Drip Campaign, you can increase the likelihood of generating leads and expanding your client base.

Conclusion

The Mortgage Updates Drip Campaign can be an effective way for real estate agents to keep their clients informed and generate new leads. By providing valuable and up-to-date information on mortgage rates and lending requirements through email and SMS messages, agents can build trust and establish themselves as an authority in the industry. The key to success is to provide content that is personalized and relevant to your audience, and to make it easy for them to take action. By Tracking the Success of the campaign and making adjustments along the way, agents can ensure that they are maximizing their efforts and generating the best possible results.

18

CLIENT TESTIMONIAL DRIP CAMPAIGN

Client Testimonials Drip Campaign is a powerful tool for real estate agents to showcase their successes and build trust with potential clients. However, before beginning this drip campaign, it is essential to collect client testimonials.

To do so, it is recommended that agents request testimonials or reviews from all their clients after every closing. This will allow them to build a library of positive experiences from satisfied clients, which can be used in the Client Testimonials Drip Campaign.

Once an agent has a collection of testimonials, they can create a drip campaign that highlights the success stories of past clients. By sharing these testimonials via email and SMS messages, agents can demonstrate their credibility and build trust with leads who may be on the fence about working with them.

In this chapter, we will walk you through the steps for creating an effective Client Testimonials Drip Campaign, including how to collect client testimonials and how to use them in your marketing efforts. With this strategy, you can increase your chances of converting leads into clients and grow your real estate business.

Overall, the Client Testimonials Drip Campaign is a powerful marketing tool that can help agents build trust and credibility with potential clients. By showcasing the positive experiences of past clients, agents can demonstrate their expertise and build a strong reputation in their market.

User Scenario: Client Testimonials Drip Campaign

Michael, an experienced real estate agent, understands the power of social proof in building trust and credibility with potential clients. To leverage this, Michael decides to implement a Client Testimonials Drip Campaign. This campaign sends a series of emails and SMS messages featuring success stories and positive experiences from Michael's past clients.

By sharing these testimonials, Michael can demonstrate his expertise and the positive outcomes he has achieved for others. This approach not only builds trust with new leads but also reinforces Michael's reputation as a reliable and effective real estate professional.

Implementing this drip campaign can help you achieve similar success by showcasing your proven track record and building strong relationships with potential clients.

Client Testimonials Drip Campaign Use Cases

Client testimonials are a powerful way to build trust and generate new business in the real estate industry. By showcasing the positive experiences and outcomes of past clients, agents can effectively communicate their value and expertise to potential clients. Here are some key use cases for a Client Testimonials Drip Campaign:

- Generating Referrals: A Client Testimonials Drip Campaign can be an effective way to generate referrals from happy clients. By including a call to action in each testimonial email or message, agents can encourage past clients to refer their friends and family who may be in need of real estate services.

- Building Credibility: Testimonials from past clients can help agents establish credibility and build trust with potential clients. By sharing real stories and experiences, agents can demonstrate their expertise and track record of success.

- Showcasing Expertise: A Client Testimonials Drip Campaign can also help agents showcase their specific areas of expertise and the types of clients they serve. By featuring testimonials from clients in different neighborhoods, price ranges, or property types, agents can demonstrate their versatility and ability to meet a wide range of needs.

A Client Testimonials Drip Campaign can be a valuable addition to any real estate marketing strategy, helping agents generate new business, build credibility, and showcase their expertise. By carefully selecting testimonials and customizing messaging to meet the needs of different audiences, agents can create a campaign that generates results and helps them stand out in a crowded market.

Step-By-Step Guide and Templates Step 1

On Day 1, send an introductory email to your leads that highlights your expertise and success stories. The email should be friendly, informative, and focused on providing value to the recipient.

Step 1 Email Template:

Subject: Introducing [Agent Name] - Real Estate Expert
Dear [Subscriber],

I hope this email finds you well. My name is [Agent Name], and I am a real estate agent with [Agency Name]. I wanted to take a moment to introduce myself and share some of my recent success stories with you.

As a real estate expert, I have helped countless clients achieve their real estate goals, from finding their dream home to selling their property at the best possible price. I believe that every client is unique, and I work tirelessly to provide personalized solutions that meet their specific needs and requirements.

But don't just take my word for it - here are some testimonials from past clients that I have had the pleasure of working with:

[Testimonial 1]

[Testimonial 2]

[Testimonial 3]

If you're in the market to buy or sell a property, or simply have questions about the real estate market, I would be happy to chat with you. You can reach me at [Agent Contact Information].

Thank you for your time, and I look forward to hearing from you soon.

Best regards,

[Agent Signature Block with Contact Information]

DRIP, DRIP, SOLD

Personalization:

Update the Subscriber Name and body with your links and phone numbers where appropriate.

Recommended Agent Action:

Follow up with a phone call to subscribers who reply to the email or express interest in buying or selling a property.

Step 2

Send an SMS on Day 3 to reinforce the introduction and highlight the value of the upcoming testimonials.

SMS Template:

"Hello [Subscriber], it's [Agent Name] from [Agency Name]. Just wanted to say thank you for considering us. Stay tuned for some inspiring home buying/selling stories from our happy clients!"

Personalization:

Customize the email with the specific details of the client's story and update the contact information.

Recommended Agent Action:

Monitor responses and engage in follow-up conversations with subscribers who show interest. Offer to provide similar personalized service to them.

Step 3:

On Day 7 focus on sending out individual client testimonials in a dedicated email. This allows each story to shine and provides specific examples of how you've helped clients in various situations. These stories can range from first-time homebuyers to successful sales above the asking price.

Step 3 Email Template:

Subject: How We Helped [Client's Name] Find Their Dream Home
Dear [Subscriber],

I wanted to share a story that's close to my heart. Meet [Client's Name], who recently bought their dream home with our help. Their journey wasn't easy, but together, we navigated the challenges and celebrated a wonderful success.

[Insert Client's Testimonial Here]

Every client's story is unique, and I'm here to help write yours. Whether you're buying your first home, looking to sell, or just curious about the market, I'm here to help you every step of the way.

Feel free to reach out to me at [Agent Contact Information] for any real estate advice or assistance.

Warm regards,

[Agent Signature Block with Contact Information]

Personalization:

Customize the email with the specific details of the client's story and update the contact information.

Recommended Agent Action:

Monitor responses and engage in follow-up conversations with subscribers who show interest. Offer to provide similar personalized service to them.

Step 4

Send an SMS on Day 9 highlighting a key takeaway from the recent client stories.

SMS Template:

"Hi [Subscriber], hope you found [Client's Name]'s story(ies) inspiring! If you're looking for similar success in real estate, let's talk. - [Agent Name]"

Personalization:

Customize the email with the specific details of the client's story and update the contact information.

DRIP, DRIP, SOLD

Recommended Agent Action:

Monitor responses and engage in follow-up conversations with subscribers who show interest. Offer to provide similar personalized service to them.

Step 5:

Send an email on Day 15 that showcases a diverse range of testimonials. This helps to demonstrate your ability to cater to different client needs and preferences.

Step 5 Email Template:

Subject: See What Our Clients Say About Us
Dear [Subscriber],

Real estate is about people, and every person's story is different. Here's what a few of our clients had to say about their experiences working with us:

[Testimonial from a First-time Homebuyer]
[Testimonial from a Seller who Sold Above Asking Price]
[Testimonial from a Client who Bought an Investment Property]

These stories are just a few examples of how we tailor our approach to meet each client's unique needs.

If you're considering a move or just want to discuss your options, I'm here to help. Reach out anytime at [Agent Contact Information].

Best,
[Agent Signature Block with Contact Information]

Personalization:

Include a variety of testimonials that cover different aspects of your real estate services. Update with relevant contact details.

Recommended Agent Action:

Engage with subscribers who respond, offering insights and assistance based on their specific real estate interests.

200

Step 6:

On the 23rd day of this campaign send email with video testimonials to create a more dynamic and engaging experience. Videos can be more personal and relatable.

Step 6 Email Template:

Subject: Hear Our Clients' Success Stories

Dear [Subscriber],

Sometimes, seeing is believing. We're thrilled to share some video testimonials from clients who have found success with our help. Check out these stories:

[Link to Video Testimonial 1]

[Link to Video Testimonial 2]

[Link to Video Testimonial 3]

These videos highlight the real people and real stories behind each property transaction.

Interested in becoming our next success story? Contact me at [Agent Contact Information] to start your journey.

Warmly,

[Agent Signature Block with Contact Information]

Personalization:

Include links to video testimonials. Ensure each story reflects a different aspect of your service.

Recommended Agent Action:

Follow up with subscribers who engage with the videos, offering to discuss how you can support their real estate goals.

Step 7:

On the 28th day of this campaign, send an email to conclude the series of client testimonial narratives. This email should serve as a culmination of the shared experiences, emphasizing the value and expertise you bring to the real estate process. It's an opportunity to directly address potential clients, inviting them to begin their own journey with you. The template provided below is designed to encapsulate this message, offering a blend of reflection, invitation, and forward-looking optimism. Remember, this email is not just a closure but an open door to new beginnings and potential client relationships.

Step 7 Email Template

Subject: Your Journey to Real Estate Success
Dear [Subscriber],

As we reflect on the inspiring stories shared recently, I'm reminded of the unique journeys each of my clients embark upon in the realm of real estate. You've heard from individuals like [Client Name 1] and [Client Name 2], who have navigated the market's ebbs and flows, ultimately finding success with our help at [Agency Name].

Their experiences are more than just success stories; they represent the heart of what we do. Our commitment is rooted in providing personalized care, unwavering dedication, and professional expertise. Whether it's helping find the ideal family home or negotiating the best sale price, our aim is always to facilitate a seamless and rewarding experience in real estate.

Now, I invite you to think about your own real estate aspirations. Are you considering purchasing your first home, selling your current property, or maybe just pondering over your future options? Whatever your goals may be, I am here to offer guidance and support every step of the way.

I encourage you to reach out for a no-obligation consultation. Let's discuss your aspirations, answer any questions you may have, and explore how we can achieve your real estate objectives together. You can contact me at [Agent Contact Information] - I'm here to assist you in crafting your own success story in the world of real estate.

Thank you for engaging with the stories of those who have trusted us on their journey. I look forward to the possibility of working alongside you and adding your story to our ever-growing list of satisfied clients.

Warm regards,

[Agent Signature Block with Contact Information]

Personalization:

Ensure to tailor the email with specific names and stories featured in your campaign. Update with your contact details and any specific call-to-action you wish to include.

Tracking the Success of the Client Testimonials Drip Campaign

Tracking the success of a Client Testimonials Drip Campaign is important to determine the effectiveness of the campaign and make necessary adjustments for future campaigns. Here are some key metrics to track:

- Open Rates: Tracking the open rates of the testimonial emails can provide insights into the effectiveness of the subject line and timing of the emails. High open rates indicate that the subject line and timing resonate with the audience.
- Click-Through Rates: Tracking the click-through rates of the emails can provide insights into the effectiveness of the messaging and call to action. High click-through rates indicate that the messaging and call to action are engaging the audience.
- Referral Tracking: Tracking the number of referrals generated from the testimonial campaign can provide insights into the effectiveness of the campaign in generating new business.
- Conversion Rates: Tracking the conversion rates of leads generated from the testimonial campaign can provide insights into the effectiveness of the campaign in converting leads into clients.
- Client Feedback: Collecting feedback from clients who engage with the testimonial campaign can provide insights into what resonates with clients and what could be improved in future campaigns.

By tracking these metrics and making necessary adjustments, agents can create a Client Testimonials Drip Campaign that effectively generates new business, builds credibility, and showcases expertise.

Tips for Customizing the Client Testimonials Drip Campaign

Customizing a Client Testimonials Drip Campaign can help agents make the campaign more effective in generating new business and building credibility. Here are some tips for customizing the campaign:

- Segment Your Audience: Segmenting your audience based on their needs and interests can help you deliver more relevant testimonials and increase engagement.
- Personalize Your Messaging: Personalizing your messaging to the recipient can help you build rapport and increase the likelihood of conversion.
- Use Different Types of Testimonials: Using different types of testimonials such as video, written, or audio can help you cater to different types of learners and provide more variety.
- Showcase Specific Expertise: Showcasing specific expertise can help you target specific niches and attract more business in those areas.
- Highlight Success Stories: Highlighting success stories can help you showcase the benefits of working with you and provide social proof of your capabilities.

By customizing the Client Testimonials Drip Campaign, agents can create a more effective campaign that resonates with their audience and generates new business.

Conclusion

The Client Testimonials Drip Campaign can be a powerful tool for real estate agents to build credibility, generate new business, and convert leads into clients. By strategically using client testimonials in a drip campaign, agents can showcase their expertise, highlight their success stories, and provide social proof of their capabilities.

To make the most of this campaign, it's important to segment your audience, personalize your messaging, use different types of testimonials, showcase specific expertise, and highlight success stories. By customizing your Client Testimonials Drip Campaign to your audience's needs and interests, you can increase engagement and conversions, and ultimately grow your business.

Remember, the key to a successful Client Testimonials Drip Campaign is to create content that is relevant, informative, and valuable to your audience. By doing so, you can build trust with potential clients, establish yourself as an industry expert, and ultimately grow your real estate business.

19

BIRTHDAY WISHES DRIP CAMPAIGN

The Birthday Wishes Drip Campaign is a unique and personal way to engage with clients and leads. By acknowledging and celebrating their special day, real estate agents can foster a deeper, more personal connection with their audience. This chapter will guide you through the process of creating a memorable Birthday Wishes Drip Campaign.

User Scenario: Birthday Wishes Drip Campaign

Hassan, a dedicated real estate agent, wants to maintain a personal connection with his clients throughout the year. To achieve this, Hassan implements a Birthday Wishes Drip Campaign. This campaign sends personalized birthday greetings to his clients, showing them that he values and remembers their special day.

For example, a client named Sarah receives an email that reads:

"Happy Birthday, Sarah! Wishing you a day filled with joy and celebration. Thank you for trusting me with your real estate journey. If you'd like to catch up or have any questions about your property, I'm just a call away. Enjoy your special day!"

By acknowledging their birthdays with warm and sincere messages, Hassan strengthens his relationships with his clients, making them feel appreciated and remembered. This approach not only enhances client satisfaction but also fosters loyalty, increasing the likelihood of referrals and repeat business. Implementing this drip campaign can help you achieve similar success in maintaining personal connections with your clients and fostering long-term loyalty.

Birthday Wishes Drip Campaign Use Cases

In this section, we'll explore the simple applications of the Birthday Wishes Drip Campaign in real estate. These use cases illustrate how something as simple as a birthday greeting can be a powerful tool in strengthening client relationships and enhancing business outreach.

- Client Appreciation: Demonstrate appreciation for past and current clients, enhancing loyalty and encouraging repeat business.
- Lead Engagement: Re-engage cold leads or maintain contact with potential clients by showing attentiveness and personal care.
- Brand Personality Showcase: Use birthdays as an opportunity to showcase your brand's personal touch and attention to detail.

The Birthday Wishes Drip Campaign is a simple yet effective strategy to deepen client connections and maintain ongoing engagement. These use cases demonstrate the campaign's potential to add a personal touch to your real estate business, fostering loyalty and opening doors to new opportunities.

Step-By-Step Guide and Templates

Step 1

On the birthday of you client, send a personalized email acknowledging their special day with warmth and sincerity.

Step 1 Email Template:

Subject: Happy Birthday, [Client's Name]!

Dear [Client's Name],

I hope this message finds you well and ready to celebrate! Today is about you, and I wanted to take a moment to wish you a very Happy Birthday.

May your day be filled with joy, laughter, and wonderful moments. Birthdays are a fresh start, a time for new beginnings, and an opportunity to pursue new endeavors with new goals. I hope this year brings you everything you wish for.

If you're ever in need of real estate advice or just want to chat about your future plans, remember that I'm just a phone call or an email away. Enjoy your special day!

Best wishes,
[Agent Name]
[Agency Name]
[Agent Contact Information]

Personalization:

Update the Client's Name and body with your links and phone numbers where appropriate.

Recommended Agent Action:

Monitor responses to the birthday message and be prepared to engage in a friendly follow-up conversation.

Step 2

3 days after the birthday, send a follow-up email to inquire about their celebration and gently reintroduce your real estate services.

Step 2 Email Template:

Subject: Hope You Had a Memorable Birthday, [Client's Name]!
Dear [Client's Name],

I trust you had a wonderful birthday celebration filled with happiness and good company. Birthdays are a time of reflection and looking forward, and as you embark on another year, I wanted to remind you that I'm here to assist with any real estate needs you may have.

Whether you're considering buying a new property, selling your current home, or just curious about the latest market trends, I'm just an email or a call away. Let's make this year even more successful and fulfilling.

Best regards,
[Agent Name]
[Agency Name]
[Agent Contact Information]

Personalization:

Update the Client's Name and body with your links and phone numbers where appropriate.

Recommended Agent Action:

Engage with clients who respond, offering personalized real estate assistance or scheduling meetings as needed.

Tracking the Success of the Birthday Wishes Drip Campaign

Understanding the impact of your Birthday Wishes Drip Campaign is crucial in gauging its effectiveness. In this section, we will delve into key metrics and methods that help in accurately tracking the success of your birthday greetings. This process is vital for optimizing your approach and ensuring that your campaign resonates well with your clients.

- Open and Response Rates: Monitor the open rates of your emails and responses to assess engagement levels.
- Client Feedback: Collect feedback through informal conversations or follow-up surveys to gauge the personal impact of the campaign.
- Referral Tracking: Keep track of any referrals that stem from clients who received birthday wishes, as a measure of deepened client relationships.

To wrap up, effectively tracking the success of your Birthday Wishes Drip Campaign is an essential step in refining your marketing strategy. By closely monitoring response rates, client feedback, and overall engagement, you gain valuable insights that can be used to enhance future campaigns. This evaluation not only helps in improving your approach but also ensures that your efforts in building client relationships are as impactful and genuine as possible.

Tips for Customizing the Birthday Wishes Drip Campaign

Customizing your Birthday Wishes Drip Campaign is pivotal in maximizing its impact. This section offers practical tips to tailor your birthday messages, ensuring they resonate with each client's unique preferences and enhance the overall effectiveness of the campaign. These strategies are designed to add a personal touch, making each greeting feel special and thoughtfully crafted.

- Personalize Messages: Use client data to personalize messages, possibly including a reference to their preferred neighborhoods or property types.
- Integrate with CRM: Automate the campaign using CRM software to schedule messages efficiently.
- Offer Exclusive Deals: Include special birthday offers or incentives, like a consultation discount or a complimentary home valuation.

The art of customizing your Birthday Wishes Drip Campaign holds the key to its success. By implementing these tips, you can transform a simple birthday message into a powerful tool for client engagement and relationship building. Personalization, thoughtful timing, and relevant content are the cornerstones of a successful campaign that not only acknowledges a special day but also reinforces your commitment to providing personalized and attentive service in your real estate business.

Conclusion

The Birthday Wishes Drip Campaign is more than just a marketing tactic; it's a bridge to heartfelt client relationships. By acknowledging such a personal occasion, real estate agents can transcend the traditional client-agent dynamic, embedding themselves as a thoughtful and caring presence in their clients' lives. This campaign not only nurtures existing relationships but also opens doors to new opportunities through referrals and repeat business.

DRIP, DRIP, SOLD

20

HOME IMPROVEMENT TIPS DRIP CAMPAIGN

The Home Improvement Tips Drip Campaign is designed to provide valuable information and resources to homeowners looking to improve their homes. This campaign can be used by real estate agents or home improvement professionals to generate leads and establish themselves as experts in the industry. The campaign consists of a series of emails and SMS messages that provide tips and advice on various home improvement projects, as well as resources for finding professionals and products. By providing valuable content to subscribers, agents can build trust and credibility with potential clients, leading to increased business and referrals.

User Scenario: Home Improvement Tips Drip Campaign

Amina, a dedicated real estate agent, wants to stay connected with her clients and provide ongoing value even after they have purchased their homes. To achieve this, Amina implements a Home Improvement Tips Drip Campaign. This campaign involves sending a series of emails and SMS messages that offer practical and creative home improvement tips, ranging from simple DIY projects to more extensive renovations.

By consistently providing useful and engaging content, Amina helps her clients maintain and enhance their homes, demonstrating her commitment to their long-term satisfaction. This approach not only strengthens client relationships but also positions Amina as a knowledgeable and trusted advisor in the real estate market.

Implementing this drip campaign can help you achieve similar success by keeping your clients engaged and providing them with valuable information that enhances their homeownership experience.

Home Improvement Drip Campaign Use Cases

The Home Improvement Drip Campaign can be used by real estate agents and home improvement professionals to provide value to their clients and prospects. Here are some use cases for this type of campaign:

- Real estate agents can use this campaign to provide helpful tips and advice to clients who are preparing to sell their homes. By providing valuable content on how to improve their homes, agents can help their clients increase the value of their properties and attract more potential buyers.
- Home improvement professionals such as contractors or interior designers can use this campaign to establish themselves as experts in their field and showcase their services. By providing helpful tips and advice on home improvement projects, they can demonstrate their knowledge and expertise to potential clients.
- Homeowners can use this campaign to receive regular home improvement tips and advice that can help them maintain and improve their homes. This can include tips on DIY projects, home maintenance, and energy efficiency.

Overall, the Home Improvement Drip Campaign can be a valuable tool for anyone in the real estate or home improvement industry to provide value to their clients and prospects and establish themselves as experts in their field.

Step-By-Step Guide and Templates

Step 1:

Send an email on day 1 with a subject line "Transform Your Home: Easy DIY Home Improvement Projects." In this email, provide an overview of simple DIY home improvement projects that homeowners can do themselves to improve their homes. You can also include your agency's contact information for any questions or concerns.

Step 1 Email Template:

Subject: Transform Your Home: Easy DIY Home Improvement Projects
Dear [Subscriber],

If you're looking to improve your home but don't want to break the bank, there are many simple DIY home improvement projects you can do yourself. In this email, we'll provide you with an overview of some of these projects to help you transform your home.

Here are some key ideas to consider:

- Fresh coat of paint: Painting is an easy way to give your home a fresh, updated look.
- Kitchen backsplash: Adding a new backsplash to your kitchen can be a cost-effective way to update the space.
- Lighting fixtures: Updating your lighting fixtures can make a big difference in the look and feel of a room.

We understand that improving your home can be overwhelming, and that's why we're here to help. If you have any questions or concerns about the home improvement process, don't hesitate to reach out to us.

Best regards,

[Agent Signature Block with Contact Information]

Personalization:

Update the Subscriber Name and body with your links and phone numbers where appropriate.

Recommended Agent Action:

Follow up with a phone call to subscribers who reply to the email or express interest in buying or selling a property.

Step 2:

Send an email on day 7 with a subject line "Top Home Improvement Projects for Resale Value." In this email, provide tips and ideas for home improvement projects that can increase the resale value of a home, such as kitchen and bathroom renovations, landscaping, and energy-efficient upgrades. You can also include your agency's contact information for any questions or concerns.

Step 2 Email Template:

Subject: Top Home Improvement Projects for Resale Value
Dear [Subscriber],

If you're planning to sell your home in the future, you may want to consider making some home improvements to increase its resale value. In this email, we'll provide you with tips and ideas for home improvement projects that can boost your home's value.

Here are some top home improvement projects for resale value:

- Kitchen and bathroom renovations: Upgrading your kitchen and bathrooms can add significant value to your home, as these are areas that potential buyers pay close attention to.
- Landscaping: Improving your home's curb appeal with landscaping upgrades can increase its overall value and make a great first impression on potential buyers.
- Energy-efficient upgrades: Adding energy-efficient features to your home, such as new windows, insulation, or appliances, can not only increase its resale value but also save you money on energy bills in the meantime.

We understand that home improvement projects can be overwhelming, and that's why we're here to help. If you have any questions or concerns about the home improvement process, don't hesitate to reach out to us.

Best regards,
[Agent Signature Block with Contact Information]

Personalization:

Update the Subscriber Name and body with your links and phone numbers where appropriate.

Recommended Agent Action:

Follow up with a phone call to subscribers who reply to the email or express interest in selling their property.

Step 3:

Send an email on day 14 with a subject line "Small Bathroom, Big Impact: Tips for a Quick Refresh." In this email, provide tips and ideas for refreshing a small bathroom, such as replacing fixtures, updating the lighting, and adding a fresh coat of paint. You can also include your agency's contact information for any questions or concerns.

Step 3 Email Template:

Subject: Small Bathroom, Big Impact: Tips for a Quick Refresh
Dear [Subscriber],

If you're looking to update your home, a small bathroom is a great place to start. With a few simple changes, you can create a big impact. In this email, we'll provide you with tips and ideas for refreshing a small bathroom.

Here are some key points to keep in mind:

- Replace fixtures: Swapping out old fixtures for new ones, such as faucets, showerheads, and towel racks, can make a big difference in the look and feel of your bathroom.
- Update lighting: Improving the lighting in your bathroom can make it feel brighter and more welcoming. Consider adding new fixtures or updating bulbs to create a warm, inviting atmosphere.
- Add a fresh coat of paint: A new paint color can completely transform a small bathroom. Choose a light, neutral color to make the space feel larger and more open.

We understand that updating your home can be overwhelming, and that's why we're here to help. If you have any questions or concerns, don't hesitate to reach out to us.

Best regards,

[Agent Signature Block with Contact Information]

Personalization:

Update the Subscriber Name and body with your links and phone numbers where appropriate.

Recommended Agent Action:

Follow up with a phone call to subscribers who reply to the email or SMS and express interest in home improvement or renovation projects.

Step 4:

Send an email on day 21 with a subject line "Adding Value to Your Home: Home Improvement Projects That Increase Resale Value." In this email, provide information on home improvement projects that can increase the resale value of a home, including kitchen and bathroom renovations, landscaping, and energy-efficient upgrades. You can also include your agency's contact information for any questions or concerns.

Step 4 Email Template:

Subject: Adding Value to Your Home: Home Improvement Projects That Increase Resale Value

Dear [Subscriber],

If you're a homeowner, you likely want to make sure that your home retains its value and potentially increases in value over time. In this email, we'll provide you with information on home improvement projects that can increase the resale value of your home.

Here are some key projects to consider:

- Kitchen and bathroom renovations: Updating these rooms can make a big impact on the overall value of your home.
- Landscaping: Curb appeal is important when it comes to selling your home. Invest in your landscaping to make your home more attractive to potential buyers.
- Energy-efficient upgrades: Making your home more energy-efficient can not only increase its value but also save you money on utility bills.

We understand that taking on home improvement projects can be overwhelming, and that's why we're here to help. If you have any questions or concerns, don't hesitate to reach out to us.

Best regards,

[Agent Signature Block with Contact Information]

Personalization:

Update the Subscriber Name and body with your links and phone numbers where appropriate.

Recommended Agent Action:

Follow up with a phone call to subscribers who reply to the email or express interest in buying or selling a property.

Step 5:

Send an email on day 21 with a subject line "Maximizing Curb Appeal: Tips for Improving Your Home's Exterior." In this email, provide tips for improving the exterior of a home to increase its curb appeal, including landscaping, painting, and making necessary repairs. You can also include your agency's contact information for any questions or concerns.

Step 5 Email Template:

Subject: Maximizing Curb Appeal: Tips for Improving Your Home's Exterior

Dear [Subscriber],

The exterior of your home is the first thing potential buyers see, so it's important to make a good impression. In this email, we'll provide you with tips and strategies for improving your home's exterior to increase its curb appeal.

Here are some key points to keep in mind:

- Landscaping: A well-manicured lawn and neatly trimmed hedges and trees can make a big impact on the appearance of your home.
- Painting: A fresh coat of paint on the front door or shutters can add a pop of color and make your home look more inviting.
- Necessary repairs: Fixing any visible issues, such as cracks in the driveway or broken windows, can make your home more appealing and help increase its value.

DRIP, DRIP, SOLD

We understand that improving your home's exterior can be overwhelming, and that's why we're here to help. If you have any questions or concerns about the home improvement process, don't hesitate to reach out to us.

Best regards,
[Agent Signature Block with Contact Information]

Personalization:

Update the Subscriber Name and body with your links and phone numbers where appropriate.

Recommended Agent Action:

Follow up with a phone call to subscribers who reply to the email or express interest in selling their home.

Step 6:

Send an email on day 28 with a subject line "Planning Your Next Home Improvement Project." In this email, provide tips and strategies for planning your next home improvement project, including setting a budget, researching materials and contractors, and creating a timeline. You can also include your agency's contact information for any questions or concerns.

Step 6 Email Template:

Subject: Planning Your Next Home Improvement Project
Dear [Subscriber],

Are you thinking about starting a home improvement project? Whether you want to update your kitchen, remodel your bathroom, or add a new room to your house, planning ahead is key to ensure a successful outcome. In this email, we'll provide you with some tips and strategies for planning your next home improvement project.

First and foremost, it's important to set a budget for your project. Determine how much you can afford to spend and stick to it. Be sure to include any unforeseen expenses or unexpected costs in your budget to avoid any surprises down the line.

Next, research materials and contractors to find the best options for your project. Take the time to compare prices and quality to ensure you're getting the best value for your money. Consider asking for recommendations from friends and family or reading online reviews to find reputable contractors in your area.

Finally, create a timeline for your project. Establishing a timeline will help ensure that your project stays on track and is completed on time. Be sure to factor in any potential delays or setbacks that may arise along the way.

We understand that planning a home improvement project can be overwhelming, and that's why we're here to help. If you have any questions or concerns, don't hesitate to reach out to us. Our team of experts can provide you with guidance and support every step of the way.

Thank you for your time, and we look forward to helping you with your home improvement project.

Best regards,

[Agent Signature Block with Contact Information]

Personalization:

Update the Subscriber Name and body with your links and phone numbers where appropriate.

Recommended Agent Action:

Follow up with a phone call to subscribers who reply to the email or express interest in starting a home improvement project.

Step 7:

Send an email on day 42 with a subject line "Top Home Improvement Projects to Increase Your Home's Value." In this email, provide insights on home improvement projects that can increase the value of a home, such as kitchen and bathroom renovations, adding a deck or patio, or landscaping improvements. You can also include your agency's contact information for any questions or concerns.

Step 7 Email Template:

Subject: Top Home Improvement Projects to Increase Your Home's Value

Dear [Subscriber],

Are you considering home improvement projects that can increase the value of your home? In this email, we'll provide you with insights on some of the top home improvement projects that can add value to your home.

Here are some key projects to consider:

- Kitchen and bathroom renovations: Updating these areas can greatly increase the value of your home and make it more appealing to potential buyers.
- Adding a deck or patio: Outdoor living spaces are in high demand, and adding a deck or patio can significantly boost your home's value.
- Landscaping improvements: Improving your curb appeal can make a big impact on the value of your home.

We understand that deciding which projects to tackle can be overwhelming, and that's why we're here to help. If you have any questions or concerns, don't hesitate to reach out to us.

Best regards,

[Agent Signature Block with Contact Information]

Personalization:

Update the Subscriber Name and body with your links and phone numbers where appropriate.

Recommended Agent Action:

Follow up with a phone call to subscribers who reply to the email or express interest in starting a home improvement project that can increase their home's value.

Tracking the Success of the Home Improvement Drip Campaign

Tracking the success of your home improvement drip campaign is crucial to understanding its effectiveness and making necessary adjustments to improve its performance. Here are some metrics and methods to track the success of your campaign:

- Open and click-through rates: Measure the open and click-through rates of your emails to determine how engaged your subscribers are with your campaign. If the rates are low, it may be an indication that you need to improve the content or timing of your emails.

- Conversion rate: Track how many subscribers take action on the information provided in your emails. For instance, you could track how many subscribers purchase products or services recommended in your emails or how many of them carry out the home improvement tasks you suggest.
- Feedback from subscribers: Request feedback from your subscribers on how useful they find the tips and advice you provide in your emails. You can use surveys or forms to collect this feedback.
- Social media engagement: Monitor engagement with your social media posts related to the home improvement tips campaign, such as likes, shares, and comments.
- Sales growth: Monitor your sales growth during the campaign period to assess the campaign's impact on your bottom line.

To track these metrics, you can use email marketing tools or CRM software. You can also manually keep track of the metrics in a spreadsheet or document.

By tracking the success of your home improvement drip campaign, you can make data-driven decisions to improve its effectiveness and generate more leads for your business.

Tips for Customizing the Home Improvement Drip Campaign

To customize the home improvement drip campaign for your audience and business, consider the following tips:

- Personalize your emails: Use your subscribers' names and any other relevant information to make your communications feel more personalized and engaging.
- Offer relevant tips: Tailor your tips and advice to the specific needs and interests of your audience. For example, if you have a segment of subscribers who are interested in landscaping, provide tips related to gardening and outdoor spaces.
- Use a clear call to action: Encourage subscribers to take action on the information provided in your emails, whether it's by purchasing

a product or service, carrying out a DIY task, or contacting you for professional help.

- Timing is key: Space out your messages appropriately and avoid bombarding subscribers with too many communications. Find a balance that works for your audience and your business.
- Test and adjust: Continuously test and adjust your messaging to find what works best for your audience. Analyze metrics such as open rates and click-through rates to see what resonates with your subscribers and adjust accordingly.

By customizing the home improvement drip campaign to meet the needs and interests of your audience, you can increase its effectiveness and generate more leads for your business.

Conclusion

A home improvement drip campaign can be an effective way to establish yourself as a trusted source of advice and generate leads for your business. By providing valuable tips and advice, you can build a loyal subscriber base and encourage them to take action on the information you provide. By tracking the success of your campaign and making adjustments along the way, you can ensure that you are maximizing its impact on your business.

21

TEST DRIVE THE NEIGH-BORHOOD

The Test Drive the Neighborhood campaign is designed to help potential homebuyers get a better sense of the neighborhoods they're considering. By providing them with useful information about the community, including local attractions, schools, and amenities, you can help them make a more informed decision about where to live. The campaign can also help establish your agency as a trusted resource for homebuyers, increasing the likelihood that they will choose to work with you.

A test drive of the neighborhood can consist of various activities that allow potential homebuyers to get a better feel for the community they are considering moving to. Some examples of activities could include:

- Driving around the neighborhood to get a feel for the layout and location of key amenities like schools, grocery stores, and parks.
- Walking or biking around the community to get a better sense of the neighborhood's vibe and to explore potential walking or biking routes.
- Visiting local cafes, restaurants, or shops to get a sense of the area's character and culture.
- Attending local events or festivals to experience the community's unique traditions and social gatherings.
- Meeting and chatting with current residents to gain insight into the community's strengths and weaknesses.

These activities can help potential homebuyers get a better sense of the community and whether it's a good fit for their lifestyle and needs.

User Scenario: Test Drive the Neighborhood Drip Campaign

Kenji, a knowledgeable real estate agent, wants to help his clients get a genuine feel for different neighborhoods before making a purchase decision. To achieve this, Kenji implements a Test Drive the Neighborhood Drip Campaign. This campaign involves sending a series of emails and SMS messages designed to encourage potential buyers to explore neighborhoods of interest, offering tips on what to look for and providing insights into local amenities, schools, and community events.

By guiding his clients through this exploratory phase, Kenji helps them make informed decisions about where they want to live. This approach not only builds trust and rapport with his clients but also positions Kenji as a valuable resource and expert in the local real estate market.

Implementing this drip campaign can help you achieve similar success in assisting your clients to find their ideal neighborhood, ultimately leading to higher client satisfaction and more successful transactions.

Test Drive the Neighborhood Drip Campaign Use Cases

The Test Drive the Neighborhood Drip Campaign can be useful for real estate agents who want to help potential homebuyers get a better understanding of the neighborhoods in which they may be interested. Some use cases include:

- Providing a personalized experience for potential homebuyers: By offering a personalized experience, agents can build trust and rapport with potential clients. By tailoring the Test Drive the Neighborhood Drip Campaign to their clients' interests and needs, agents can create a more engaging experience.
- Generating interest and engagement: A Test Drive the Neighborhood Drip Campaign can generate interest and engagement with potential homebuyers who may not have previously considered certain neighborhoods or areas. By showcasing the unique features and attractions of a neighborhood, agents can attract new clients and generate leads.
- Providing valuable information: By providing valuable information about a neighborhood, including things to do, local amenities, and

transportation options, agents can help potential homebuyers make informed decisions about where to live.

- Establishing expertise: By demonstrating their knowledge of the neighborhoods they serve, agents can establish themselves as experts in the industry. This can help to build credibility and trust with potential clients, leading to more business in the future.

Step-By-Step Guide and Templates

Step 1:

Send an email on day 1 with a subject line "Discover Your Dream Neighborhood: A Guide to Choosing the Perfect Community". In this email, provide an overview of factors to consider when choosing a neighborhood, such as safety, schools, commute time, and community amenities. You can also include your agency's contact information for any questions or concerns.

Step 1 Email Template:

Subject: Discover Your Dream Neighborhood: A Guide to Choosing the Perfect Community

Dear [Subscriber],

Choosing the right neighborhood is one of the most important decisions you'll make when looking for a new home. That's why we've put together this guide to help you choose the perfect community for you and your family.

Here are some key factors to consider:

- Safety: Make sure the neighborhood is safe and has low crime rates.
- Schools: Research the quality of schools in the area if you have children or plan to start a family.
- Commute time: Consider your commute time to work and other important destinations.
- Community amenities: Look for neighborhoods that offer amenities like parks, restaurants, and shopping centers.

DRIP, DRIP, SOLD

We understand that choosing a neighborhood can be overwhelming, and that's why we're here to help. If you have any questions or concerns, don't hesitate to reach out to us.

Best regards,

[Agent Signature Block with Contact Information]

Personalization:

Update the Subscriber Name and body with your links and phone numbers where appropriate.

Recommended Agent Action:

Follow up with a phone call to subscribers who reply to the email or express interest in test driving a neighborhood.

Step 2:

Send an email on day 7 with a subject line "Discover [Neighborhood Name]: A Guide to the Best Local Hotspots." In this email, provide information about the best local restaurants, parks, and other attractions in the neighborhood. You can also include your agency's contact information for any questions or concerns.

Step 2 Email Template:

Subject: Discover [Neighborhood Name]: A Guide to the Best Local Hotspots

Dear [Subscriber],

Welcome to [Neighborhood Name]! As you settle into your new home, we wanted to provide you with a guide to the best local hotspots in the area.

Here are some of our top recommendations:

- Restaurants: From farm-to-table dining to ethnic cuisine, [Neighborhood Name] has something for everyone. Check out [Restaurant 1], [Restaurant 2], and [Restaurant 3] for some of the best eats in town.
- Parks: Take a break from the hustle and bustle of city life and enjoy the great outdoors at [Park 1], [Park 2], or [Park 3].

- Attractions: Whether you're a history buff or an art lover, [Neighborhood Name] has plenty of attractions to explore, such as [Attraction 1], [Attraction 2], and [Attraction 3].

We hope you enjoy exploring all that [Neighborhood Name] has to offer. If you have any questions or concerns, don't hesitate to reach out to us.

Best regards,

[Agent Signature Block with Contact Information]

Personalization:

Update the Subscriber Name and body with your links and phone numbers where appropriate.

Recommended Agent Action:

Follow up with a phone call to subscribers who reply to the email or express interest in learning more about the neighborhood.

Step 3:

Send an SMS message on day 10 after the initial email with a reminder to take a test drive of the neighborhood. Provide tips and strategies for conducting a successful test drive, such as identifying the most important factors in a neighborhood, mapping out a route, and taking notes or photos. You can also include your agency's contact information for any questions or concerns.

Step 3 SMS Template:

Hi [Subscriber], just a friendly reminder to take a test drive of the neighborhood. We recommend identifying the most important factors in a neighborhood, mapping out a route, and taking notes or photos to help with your decision-making process. If you have any questions or concerns, don't hesitate to reach out to us.

Personalization:

Update the Subscriber Name and body with your links and phone numbers where appropriate.

DRIP, DRIP, SOLD

Recommended Agent Action:

Provide the lead with information on the neighborhood, such as local amenities, schools, and community events to help them conduct their own test drive. Follow up with a phone call to subscribers who reply to the SMS or express interest in learning more about the neighborhood.

Step 4:

Send an email on day 14 with a subject line "Discovering Your Perfect Neighborhood." In this email, provide tips for discovering the perfect neighborhood, including researching school districts, checking out local amenities and attractions, and taking a walk or drive through the neighborhood. You can also include your agency's contact information for any questions or concerns.

Step 4 Email Template:

Subject: Discovering Your Perfect Neighborhood
Dear [Subscriber],

Choosing the perfect neighborhood can be just as important as finding the perfect home. In this email, we'll provide you with tips for discovering your perfect neighborhood.

Here are some key points to keep in mind:

- Research school districts: If you have children or are planning to have children, researching the quality of the local school district is crucial.
- Check out local amenities and attractions: Consider what local amenities and attractions are important to you, such as parks, shopping centers, or restaurants.
- Take a walk or drive through the neighborhood: Get a feel for the neighborhood by taking a walk or drive through the area at different times of the day to see what it's like.

We understand that finding the perfect neighborhood can be overwhelming, and that's why we're here to help. If you have any questions or concerns, don't hesitate to reach out to us.

Best regards,

[Agent Signature Block with Contact Information]

230

Personalization:

Update the Subscriber Name and body with your links and phone numbers where appropriate.

Recommended Agent Action:

Follow up with a phone call to subscribers who reply to the email or express interest in discovering their perfect neighborhood. Provide additional tips and resources to help them with their search.

Step 5:

Send an email on day 30 with a subject line "Wrapping Up Your Neighborhood Test Drive." In this email, thank the subscriber for taking the time to explore the neighborhood and provide them with additional resources, such as a neighborhood guide or a list of local events. You can also include your agency's contact information for any questions or concerns.

Step 5 Email Template:

Subject: Wrapping Up Your Neighborhood Test Drive
Dear [Subscriber],

We wanted to thank you for taking the time to explore the neighborhood and test drive its features. We hope you enjoyed your experience and gained valuable insights into what the area has to offer.

As promised, we've put together some additional resources to help you get even more acquainted with the neighborhood. Here are some of the materials we think you'll find helpful:

- Neighborhood guide: Our comprehensive guide will provide you with information on the area's history, local businesses, and popular attractions.
- Local events: Check out our list of upcoming events in the neighborhood and surrounding areas.

We're here to help you make the most of your home search, so if you have any questions or concerns, don't hesitate to reach out to us.

Best regards,

[Agent Signature Block with Contact Information]

Personalization:

Update the Subscriber Name and body with your links and phone numbers where appropriate.

Recommended Agent Action:

Follow up with a phone call to subscribers who reply to the email or express interest in a particular neighborhood. Offer to answer any questions they may have and assist them with their home search.

Tracking the Success of the Test Drive the Neighborhood Drip Campaign

Tracking the success of your Test Drive the Neighborhood Drip Campaign is essential to understanding how well it is performing and making adjustments to improve its effectiveness. Here are some metrics and methods to track the success of your campaign:

- Number of Test Drive requests: This is the most obvious metric to track. Keep a record of the number of Test Drive requests you receive during the campaign period.
- Conversion rate: Track how many of the Test Drive requests turned into actual clients. This will give you an idea of how effective your campaign is at generating quality leads.
- Open and click-through rates: Measure the open and click-through rates of your emails and SMS messages to determine how engaged your subscribers are with your campaign. If the rates are low, it may be an indication that you need to improve the content or timing of your emails.
- Response rate: Keep track of the number of subscribers who respond to your emails or SMS messages. This will help you gauge how interested they are in test driving the neighborhood.
- Feedback from clients: Ask your clients about their test driving experience and the information you provided to improve your campaign's effectiveness.

TEST DRIVE THE NEIGHBORHOOD

To track these metrics, you can use email marketing tools or CRM software. You can also manually keep track of the number of test drives and conversions in a spreadsheet or document.

By tracking the success of your Test Drive the Neighborhood Drip Campaign, you can make data-driven decisions to improve its effectiveness and generate more quality leads for your agency.

Tips for Customizing the Test Drive the Neighborhood Drip Campaign

In order to make the most out of the Test Drive the Neighborhood Drip Campaign, it is important to customize the campaign to fit your specific agency and audience. By making small tweaks and adjustments to the campaign, you can increase the effectiveness and success of the campaign. Here are some tips for customizing the Test Drive the Neighborhood Drip Campaign:

- Personalize your emails and SMS messages: Use the subscriber's name and any other relevant information you have about them to make your communications feel more personalized and engaging.
- Use a clear call to action: Encourage subscribers to test drive the neighborhood with a clear call to action, such as "Get your free guide to the best routes to test drive our neighborhood today!"
- Offer incentives for Test Driving: Offer incentives such as a personalized guide to the neighborhood or a free consultation with one of our agents to encourage subscribers to test drive the neighborhood.
- Timing is key: Make sure to space out your messages appropriately and avoid bombarding subscribers with too many communications. Find a balance that works for your audience and your agency.
- Test and adjust: Continuously test and adjust your messaging to find what works best for your audience. Analyze metrics such as open rates and click-through rates to see what resonates with your subscribers and adjust accordingly.

By customizing your Test Drive the Neighborhood Drip Campaign, you can increase the likelihood of receiving Test Drive requests from your subscribers and grow your client base.

Conclusion

The Test Drive the Neighborhood Drip Campaign can be an effective way for real estate agents to generate new leads and expand their client base. By providing valuable information and encouraging subscribers to explore the neighborhood, agents can showcase their knowledge and expertise. The key to success is to provide valuable content and incentives that encourage subscribers to request a Test Drive. By Tracking the Success of the campaign and making adjustments along the way, agents can ensure that they are maximizing their efforts and generating the best possible results.

22

CONTINUED CLIENT CARE DRIP CAMPAIGN

The "Continued Client Care: Post-Transaction and Home Anniversary Drip Campaign" is a comprehensive approach designed to maintain and deepen relationships with clients after the completion of a real estate transaction. This campaign thoughtfully combines immediate post-transaction follow-ups with annual acknowledgments of home purchase anniversaries. It serves not only to express gratitude and offer support following a property sale but also to celebrate key milestones in homeownership each year. This dual-strategy campaign is focused on long-term client engagement, reinforcing the agent's commitment to their clients' ongoing satisfaction and success in their real estate journey. Through personalized communication and timely gestures, this campaign establishes a foundation for enduring professional relationships and a thriving real estate practice.

User Scenario: Continued Client Care: Post-Transaction Drip Campaign

Mariana, a dedicated real estate agent, understands the importance of maintaining relationships with her clients even after the transaction is complete. To ensure her clients feel appreciated and supported, Mariana implements a Continued Client Care: Post-Transaction Drip Campaign. This campaign involves sending a series of personalized emails and SMS messages to clients immediately after the sale and on key anniversaries, such as the one-year anniversary of their home purchase.

By consistently checking in and providing valuable information, Mariana helps her clients feel valued and remembered. This thoughtful approach not only enhances client satisfaction but also increases the likelihood of repeat business and referrals.

Implementing this drip campaign can help you achieve similar success in maintaining strong, long-term relationships with your clients and fostering ongoing engagement.

Post-Transaction Follow-Up Drip Campaign Use Cases

The "Continued Client Care: Post-Transaction and Home Anniversary Drip Campaign" can be effectively utilized in various scenarios within the real estate sector. Each use case demonstrates the campaign's versatility and its ability to foster enduring relationships with clients. Here are some key use cases:

- Strengthening Client Loyalty: By consistently reaching out to clients after the transaction and on each anniversary of their home purchase, you reinforce their decision to choose your services, enhancing loyalty and the likelihood of repeat business.
- Generating Referrals: Satisfied clients who feel valued and remembered are more likely to refer your services to friends and family. Personalized anniversary wishes and follow-ups can turn past clients into active referrers.
- Building a Reputation for Thoughtfulness: Regularly acknowledging significant milestones in your clients' lives positions you as a thoughtful and caring professional, which can enhance your reputation in the community and industry.
- Re-engaging Past Clients: The annual anniversary wishes offer an opportunity to re-engage clients who may be considering another real estate transaction, ensuring you remain their go-to real estate professional.
- Market Presence Reinforcement: Each touchpoint in the campaign keeps your name and brand in front of clients, reinforcing your presence in the market and keeping you top of mind for any future real estate needs.

- Client Satisfaction and Feedback: The post-transaction follow-up is an excellent opportunity to gather feedback, helping you refine your services and client experience.
- Opportunities for Upselling Services: These regular communications can be used to inform clients about additional services you offer, such as property management, market analysis, or investment opportunities.

By strategically implementing these use cases, the "Continued Client Care" campaign becomes a powerful tool in cultivating lasting client relationships, driving business growth, and establishing a network of satisfied, loyal clients.

Step-By-Step Guide and Templates

Step 1: Immediate Post-Transaction Follow-Up

Send an email on Day 1 with the subject line "Congratulations on Your New Home!" to express gratitude and offer continued support.

Step 1 Email Template:

Subject: Congratulations on Your New Home!
Dear [Client's Name],

Congratulations on your new home! It's been a pleasure assisting you in this journey. As you embark on this exciting new chapter, know that my support continues. Should you have any questions or need assistance, I'm just a call away.

Warm regards,
[Agent Name]
[Agency Name]
[Agent Contact Information]

Personalization:

Adjust the Client's Name and include specific details about the transaction.

DRIP, DRIP, SOLD

Recommended Agent Action:

Monitor the email for responses and be ready to engage in further conversations or provide additional support as needed.

Step 2: Three-Month Check-In

On Day 90 post-transaction, send a follow-up email to inquire about the client's settling-in experience and offer any assistance they might need.

Step 2 Email Template:

Subject: How's Life in Your New Home, [Client's Name]?
Dear [Client's Name],

It's been three months since you began this exciting chapter in your home. I hope you are finding comfort and joy in your new surroundings.

If you have any questions about homeownership, need local recommendations, or if there's anything else I can assist you with, please don't hesitate to reach out.

Best wishes,
[Agent Name]
[Agency Name]
[Agent Contact Information]

Personalization:

Adapt the email to include the Client's Name and make references to specific aspects of their home or the transaction.

Recommended Agent Action:

Be proactive in responding to any queries that come from this check-in, providing personalized support, and maintaining a strong client-agent relationship.

Step 3: Six-Month Local Market Update

Send an informative email six months after the transaction, providing a local real estate market update to keep your client informed and engaged.

Step 3 Email Template:

Subject: Staying Informed: Your 6-Month Market Update

Dear [Client's Name],

I hope you're settling in well in your new home! As we reach the six-month mark since your home purchase, I thought it would be a great time to update you on the current real estate market trends in [Client's Area/Neighborhood].

[Insert Brief Market Update]

This information can be valuable whether you're considering future investments or just staying informed about your community. If you have any questions about this update or need further insights, please feel free to reach out.

Warm regards,

[Agent Name]

[Agency Name]

[Agent Contact Information]

Personalization:

Tailor the email to include specific information about the Client's neighborhood or area, making the update relevant and useful.

Recommended Agent Action:

Engage with clients who show interest in the market update, offering detailed insights or consultations to discuss their potential real estate plans or queries.

Step 4: First Anniversary of Home Purchase

On the first anniversary of the client's home purchase, send a celebratory email to acknowledge this important milestone and reaffirm your availability for any real estate assistance.

Step 4 Email Template:

Subject: Celebrating One Year in Your Home, [Client's Name]!

Dear [Client's Name],

Time flies! Today marks the first anniversary of your home purchase – a milestone worth celebrating. I hope this past year in your home has been filled with happiness and cherished memories.

As you look forward to more years in your wonderful home, remember that I am always here to assist with any real estate needs or provide insights into the current market.

Best wishes for continued joy in your home,

[Agent Name]

[Agency Name]

[Agent Contact Information]

Personalization:

Adjust the email to include the Client's Name and reference any specific memories or highlights from their home-buying experience.

Recommended Agent Action:

Be attentive to any responses from this email, ready to engage in conversations and offer customized real estate advice or services as needed.

Additional Steps for Annual Follow-Ups:

As part of the "Continued Client Care: Post-Transaction and Home Anniversary Drip Campaign," it's important to maintain a connection with clients beyond the first year. Each subsequent anniversary offers an opportunity to touch base, reaffirm your relationship, and provide ongoing value. Here's how you can structure these annual follow-ups:

Annual Home Anniversary Email:

On the anniversary of the home purchase each year include a personalized message celebrating the anniversary, reflecting on any significant changes in their lives or the community, and offering insights or updates relevant to their homeownership.

Home Anniversary Email Template:

Subject: [X] Years in Your Beloved Home, [Client's Name]!

Dear [Client's Name],

Congratulations on another wonderful year in your home! As time passes, homes evolve into spaces rich with memories and stories. I hope this year has added many more to your collection.

In case you're curious about the current market or pondering future real estate decisions, here's a brief update on [Market/News/Trends].

Here's to many more years of happiness and comfort in your home. As always, if you need any assistance or have questions, I'm just a call or email away.

Best regards,

[Agent Name]

[Agency Name]

[Agent Contact Information]

Annual Home Anniversary SMS:

A few days after the anniversary email send a brief, friendly SMS to reinforce the anniversary message and remind them of your availability.

Annual Home Anniversary SMS Template:

Hi [Client's Name], hope you enjoyed reflecting on your [X] years in your home! If you have any real estate queries or need assistance, feel free to reach out. Best, [Agent Name]

By implementing these additional steps, you ensure that the relationship with your clients remains strong and dynamic. Regular, thoughtful communication not only keeps you top-of-mind but also demonstrates your commitment to their long-term satisfaction and success as homeowners.

Tracking the Success of the Post-Transaction Follow-Up Drip Campaign

A well-executed post-transaction follow-up drip campaign can enhance customer relationships, drive repeat purchases, and increase overall brand loyalty. However, tracking its success is essential to ensure its effectiveness and identify areas for improvement. Here are key strategies and metrics to measure the success of your campaign:

1. **Define Clear Goals**

Objective: Establish measurable goals such as increasing repeat purchases, improving customer satisfaction, or reducing churn rates.

Key Result Areas (KRAs): Outline specific outcomes like a 20% increase in repeat sales or a 10% boost in customer lifetime value.

2. Measure Email Engagement Metrics

Open Rates: Indicates how effectively the subject line and timing of your email captured attention.

Click-Through Rates (CTR): Shows the percentage of recipients who clicked on links within the email, reflecting content relevance.

Conversion Rates: Tracks how many recipients completed a desired action, such as purchasing or signing up for a loyalty program.

3. Monitor Customer Retention

Repeat Purchase Rate: Measure the percentage of customers who make additional purchases after the initial transaction.

Customer Lifetime Value (CLV): Evaluate how the campaign influences the long-term value of your customers.

4. Analyze Feedback and Sentiment

Use post-transaction surveys to gauge customer satisfaction and pinpoint areas for improvement.

Monitor responses to personalized messages, noting whether customers express positive sentiment or concerns.

5. Track Behavioral Data

Website Traffic: Monitor if campaign recipients revisit your website and explore additional products or services.

Cart Abandonment Rates: Determine if follow-up emails encourage customers to return and complete their purchases.

6. Segment-Specific Performance

Break down results by customer segments (e.g., first-time buyers vs. loyal customers) to understand which groups respond best to the campaign.

7. Return on Investment (ROI)

Calculate the ROI by comparing the campaign's cost to the revenue generated from its outcomes.

Include factors like the time spent crafting emails, automation software fees, and the resulting sales.

8. Test and Optimize

Conduct A/B tests for subject lines, email content, and timing to identify what works best.

Regularly update your campaign based on data insights to continually improve performance.

By systematically tracking these metrics and analyzing data, you can refine your post-transaction drip campaign to maximize its impact and ensure sustainable customer engagement and loyalty.

Tips for Customizing the Post-Transaction Follow-Up Drip Campaign

Customization is key to making your Post-Transaction Follow-Up Drip Campaign resonate with each client. Here are some tips to personalize and enhance your campaign:

- Know Your Client: Keep notes on personal details shared by your clients during the transaction process. Use this information to personalize your messages, whether it's mentioning their favorite room in the house or acknowledging significant life events.
- Vary Your Content: Not every client will have the same interests or needs. Mix up your content to include market updates, home maintenance tips, community events, or even local real estate trends. This variety keeps your messages fresh and relevant.
- Celebrate Milestones: Beyond the home purchase anniversary, acknowledge other important dates in your clients' lives, like birthdays or significant holidays. This shows attentiveness to their personal lives, strengthening the relationship.
- Use Feedback: Encourage and utilize feedback from clients. Their responses can guide you in tailoring future communications to better meet their preferences and interests.
- Offer Value in Every Interaction: Whether it's a market update, a home maintenance tip, or just a friendly check-in, ensure that each interaction provides value to your client. This could be in the form of useful information, services, or even just a moment of delight in their day.
- Leverage Technology for Personalization: Use CRM tools to automate aspects of your campaign, but ensure that Personalization doesn't get lost in automation. Tools like dynamic content insertion can help make each message feel tailor-made.
- Stay Informed About the Local Market: Keep yourself updated with the latest real estate trends and news in your client's area. This ensures that the information you provide is timely and pertinent.

- Be Responsive: Always be ready to respond to any replies or queries generated by your campaign. Prompt and thoughtful responses are key to maintaining trust and engagement.

By incorporating these tips, your Post-Transaction Follow-Up Drip Campaign becomes more than just a series of emails or messages; it transforms into a personalized, engaging, and ongoing conversation with your clients. This personalized approach not only deepens client relationships but also enhances your reputation as a caring, attentive professional.

Conclusion

The "Continued Client Care: Post-Transaction and Home Anniversary Drip Campaign" represents a holistic approach to real estate client relations, emphasizing the importance of sustained engagement beyond the closing of a transaction. This campaign is more than a series of communications; it's a commitment to nurturing lifelong relationships with clients.

Key Insights:
- Long-Term Relationship Building: The essence of this campaign lies in its ability to foster enduring connections. By staying in touch after the transaction and commemorating home anniversaries, you demonstrate ongoing care and commitment, reinforcing the trust your clients have placed in you.
- Enhanced Client Experience: Regular check-ins, market updates, and anniversary wishes contribute to a superior client experience. They reflect a level of service that goes beyond the expected, elevating your position in the clients' eyes from a mere agent to a trusted advisor in all things real estate.
- Creating Opportunities for Future Business: By maintaining regular contact, you stay top-of-mind, which can lead to repeat business and referrals. Clients are more likely to return to agents who have shown consistent interest in their well-being and satisfaction.
- Building a Strong Personal Brand: This campaign is an extension of your brand, showcasing your dedication, professionalism, and

client-first approach. It reinforces your reputation as an agent who values relationships and goes the extra mile.

- Feedback and Adaptation: The campaign provides opportunities to gather feedback and adapt your services to meet evolving client needs. This iterative process ensures that your approach remains relevant and effective.

The Continued Client Care: Post-Transaction and Home Anniversary Drip Campaign is an indispensable strategy in today's competitive real estate landscape. It embodies a comprehensive, client-centric approach that transcends the traditional boundaries of agent-client interactions. By implementing this campaign, you not only enhance client satisfaction and loyalty but also lay a robust foundation for a thriving, referral-rich real estate business. This strategy underscores the fact that in real estate, the true measure of success is not just in transactions completed, but in relationships nurtured and sustained over time.

23

NEW CONSTRUCTION DRIP CAMPAIGN

The New Construction Drip Campaign is a technologically advanced yet accessible strategy, designed specifically for real estate professionals aiming to capitalize on the lucrative new construction market segment. While this campaign incorporates more technical aspects, such as real-time data integration and automated content delivery, it is a valuable asset that can significantly enhance your marketing efforts.

This campaign isn't just about sending emails; it's about leveraging the latest digital marketing tools to provide personalized, up-to-the-minute information on new construction projects. It's a game-changer for agents who want to stay ahead in a competitive market, offering a unique way to engage with clients who are particularly interested in new homes.

By adopting this approach, you can tap into a profitable segment of the market with efficiency and precision. The campaign is designed to be user-friendly, ensuring that even those new to digital marketing can successfully implement and benefit from it. It's a perfect blend of cutting-edge technology and practical real estate marketing, aimed at keeping your clients informed and engaged with the latest developments in the new home market.

The New Construction Drip Campaign is an indispensable tool for real estate agents looking to offer exceptional value to their clients. It demonstrates a commitment to providing the latest market information, showcasing your role not just as a real estate agent, but as a knowledgeable advisor in the realm of new construction.

For agents, this campaign represents an opportunity to stand out by offering something beyond the traditional property listings – a focused, data-driven, and client-centric approach to new home sales. It's an innovative way to connect with clients, offering them a tailored experience that aligns with their specific interests in the new construction market.

In summary, this campaign is more than a marketing strategy; it's a reflection of your dedication to meeting client needs with the most current and relevant information available. It's an approach that resonates with a growing segment of the market, making it a key component of a modern real estate professional's toolkit.

User Scenario: New Construction Drip Campaign

Sofia, a passionate real estate agent, specializes in helping clients find their dream homes in new construction developments. To keep her clients informed about the latest projects, Sofia decides to implement a New Construction Drip Campaign. This campaign sends a series of well-timed emails and SMS messages, providing clients with up-to-date information on new construction projects, including timelines, customization options, and neighborhood amenities.

By leveraging this campaign, Sofia can offer her clients valuable insights and personalized updates, making the home-buying process smoother and more exciting. This approach not only establishes Sofia as an expert in new construction but also enhances her relationships with clients, increasing their trust and satisfaction.

Implementing this drip campaign can help you achieve similar success by keeping your clients informed and engaged with the latest developments in the new construction market.

New Construction Drip Campaign Use Cases

In the realm of real estate marketing, the New Construction Drip Campaign stands as a pivotal tool, especially for those looking to tap into the unique and profitable segment of new home construction. This campaign is not just about sharing listings; it's about crafting a narrative that resonates with specific client needs and market dynamics. The following use cases illustrate how this campaign can be effectively utilized to capture various aspects of the new construction market.

- Market Entry for First-Time Buyers: Tailor content to educate and guide first-time homebuyers through the process of purchasing new construction homes. This can include timelines, what to expect during each phase of construction, and how to customize their new home.
- Investment Opportunities for Seasoned Investors: Highlight the potential benefits of investing in new construction projects. Provide insights on market trends, expected ROI, and long-term benefits of investing in newly developed areas.
- Upselling to Existing Homeowners: Reach out to homeowners who might be considering an upgrade. Showcase the advantages of moving to a newly constructed home, like modern amenities, energy efficiency, and customization options.
- Relocation Opportunities for Corporate Clients: For clients moving due to work, focus on the convenience, modern facilities, and lifestyle benefits of living in newly constructed communities, especially those close to major business centers.
- Local Area Development Updates: Keep the local community informed about new construction projects and their impact on the local economy and lifestyle. This can build a sense of anticipation and interest among residents.

The versatility of the New Construction Drip Campaign makes it an indispensable component of a real estate agent's marketing arsenal. Whether it's introducing first-time buyers to the nuances of new homes, guiding investors towards profitable ventures, or assisting homeowners in upgrading their living experience, this campaign serves as a bridge connecting various client needs with the right new construction opportunities. By leveraging these use cases, agents can not only boost their clientele but also establish themselves as authoritative voices in the new construction real estate market.

Step-By-Step Guide and Templates

Step 1: Selecting a Suitable Platform and Setting Up Integration

- Choose a Platform: Select an email marketing platform like Mailchimp, HubSpot, or ActiveCampaign for their robust integration capabilities.
- API Integration: Integrate the platform with a real estate data source API, such as Zillow's. This connection will allow your campaign to automatically pull the latest information on new constructions.
- Integration Setup: In the platform's settings, find the section for API integrations. Enter your API key from the data source (e.g., Zillow). This step might vary slightly depending on the platform but generally involves navigating to an 'Integrations' or 'API' section and following the prompts to add a new data source.

Step 2: Creating a Dynamic Email Template

- Designing the Template: Create an email template that includes placeholders for dynamic content. These placeholders will be automatically filled with data from your integrated source.
- Inserting Dynamic Blocks: Most email platforms offer a drag-and-drop interface to insert dynamic content blocks. In these blocks, specify the data fields to be filled with API data, such as property name, location, features, and price.

Email Template Example:

Subject: "Explore Newly Built Homes in [Area Name] - Curated Just for You!"

Hi [Recipient's Name],

Exciting news in [Area Name]! We have handpicked the latest new construction homes for you. Discover modern living spaces designed with your lifestyle in mind:

1. [API: Project Name]
    - Location: [API: Location]
    - Features: [API: Key Features]

- Price: [API: Price Range]
- Details: [API: Direct Link to Listing]

[Repeat For Additional Properties]

Interested in a property or need more options? I'm here to help.

Best,

[Agent Signature Block with Contact Information]

Step 3: Setting Up Automated Data Updates

Automate Data Refresh: Configure the system to periodically check and update the data from the API source. This ensures your emails always include the latest property listings.

Step 4: Audience Segmentation and Campaign Launch

- Segment Your Contacts: Use your platform's segmentation tools to target clients interested in new constructions.
- Launch and Monitor: Start your campaign and use the platform's analytics to track its performance, looking for engagement metrics like open and click-through rates.

Simplifying the Technical Aspects

This enhanced guide aims to make the technical aspects of setting up a New Construction Drip Campaign more approachable, even for those new to digital marketing. By following these detailed steps and utilizing the dynamic email template provided, you'll be able to deliver timely and relevant new construction listings to your clients, positioning yourself as a knowledgeable and resourceful real estate professional. Remember, most platforms offer support and tutorials, making it easier to navigate and implement these advanced features.

Tracking the Success of the New Construction Drip Campaign

To ensure your New Construction Drip Campaign is hitting its mark and effectively engaging your audience, it's crucial to track and analyze its performance. Here's how you can measure the success of your campaign:

Key Metrics to Monitor

- Open Rates: This metric indicates how many recipients are opening your emails. A high open rate suggests your subject lines are compelling and relevant to your audience.
- Click-Through Rates (CTR): CTR measures how many recipients clicked on links within your emails. A high CTR is a strong indicator that your content, especially the dynamically updated listings, is engaging and of interest to your audience.
- Conversion Rates: Track how many recipients take action, such as inquiring about a property, scheduling a viewing, or subscribing to more listings. This metric is crucial for understanding the direct impact of your emails on generating leads or sales.
- Bounce Rates: Monitor the number of emails that weren't delivered successfully. A high bounce rate may indicate issues with your email list or content being flagged as spam.
- Feedback and Responses: Pay attention to direct replies and feedback from your clients. This qualitative data can provide insights into what they find most useful or areas that need improvement.

Tools and Techniques for Tracking

- Most email marketing platforms offer built-in analytics to track these metrics. Utilize these tools to gather data on each email blast.
- Consider integrating your email platform with your CRM to have a more consolidated view of how email interactions translate into client engagement or sales.
- Use A/B testing to experiment with different email formats, content, and subject lines to see what resonates best with your audience.

Analyzing and Interpreting Data

- Regularly review these metrics to understand the trends and patterns in your campaign's performance.
- If open rates are low, experiment with different subject lines. Personalized or localized subject lines can often yield better open rates.

- A low CTR could indicate that the content is not as relevant or engaging as it could be. In this case, consider refining your dynamic content or the overall design of your email.

Adjusting the Campaign Based on Data

- Use the insights gained from these metrics to make informed decisions about adjusting your campaign. This might include changing the frequency of emails, the type of content shared, or the segmentation of your audience.
- Continuously evolving your strategy based on this data ensures that your New Construction Drip Campaign remains effective and relevant, and aligns with the evolving interests and needs of your audience.

By effectively tracking the performance of your New Construction Drip Campaign, you can fine-tune your approach to better meet the needs of your clients and maximize your campaign's impact. This ongoing process of monitoring, analyzing, and adjusting is key to maintaining a successful and dynamic drip campaign in the fast-paced real estate market.

Tips for Customizing the New Construction Drip Campaign

Customizing your New Construction Drip Campaign is crucial for ensuring that it resonates with your specific audience and meets their unique needs. Here are some strategies to tailor your campaign effectively:

1. **Understand Your Audience**
- Segmentation: Classify your audience into different segments based on their preferences, such as location, budget, or type of property. This allows for more targeted and relevant communication.
- Buyer Personas: Create detailed buyer personas to understand the needs, challenges, and motivations of your potential clients. This insight can guide the tone and content of your emails.
2. **Personalize Your Messages**
- Dynamic Content: Utilize dynamic content that not only updates with the latest listings but also personalizes based on the recipient's interests or past interactions.

- Personal Touch: Include personalized greetings and references to previous interactions or inquiries, making each email feel more individualized and less like a mass mailing.

3. Leverage Local Insights

- Area-Specific Information: Share insights specific to the areas where the new constructions are located, such as neighborhood features, upcoming developments, or local market trends.
- Community Highlights: Include information about local schools, amenities, and community events to give a well-rounded view of what living in that area would be like.

4. Optimize Email Content and Design

- Visual Appeal: Use high-quality images and a clean layout to showcase new construction properties attractively.
- Clear and Concise: Keep your content clear, concise, and focused on providing value. Avoid overwhelming your audience with too much information in a single email.

5. Regular Updates and Fresh Content

- Market Changes: Regularly update your content to reflect changes in the market, new listings, and other relevant news.
- Variety of Content: Mix up your content to include not just listings, but also tips for new homeowners, financing options for new constructions, and success stories of recent buyers.

6. Call to Action (CTA)

- Effective CTAs: Include clear and compelling calls to action in every email, whether it's to view more details about a listing, schedule a viewing, or contact you for more information.
- Test and Refine CTAs: Experiment with different types of CTAs to see which ones generate the most response and refine them based on performance.

7. Feedback Loop

- Request Feedback: Encourage recipients to provide feedback on the listings and information you are sharing. This can provide valuable insights for future customization.
- Surveys and Polls: Use surveys or polls to gather information about your clients' preferences and use this data to refine your campaign.

Customizing your New Construction Drip Campaign requires a blend of Personalization, market knowledge, and attention to detail. By understanding and adapting to your audience's preferences, and continually refining your approach based on feedback and performance, you can create a campaign that not only informs but also engages and resonates with potential clients. Remember, the goal is to establish yourself not just as a source of listings, but as a knowledgeable and trustworthy guide in the new construction real estate market.

Conclusion

The New Construction Drip Campaign represents a significant leap in real estate marketing, merging the latest in digital technology with traditional customer engagement strategies. This campaign is not just about sending out emails; it's a comprehensive approach to keeping clients informed and engaged in the ever-evolving world of new construction properties.

By harnessing real-time data and integrating it into personalized emails and SMS messages, this campaign ensures that potential buyers receive the most current and relevant information about new construction opportunities. It demonstrates a commitment to providing value-added services, positioning you as a forward-thinking real estate professional who understands the importance of timely and relevant information in the decision-making process.

Customization and regular updates in the New Construction Drip Campaign help build trust with clients. By providing them with the latest information tailored to their interests and needs, you establish yourself as an authority in the new construction market. This trust is crucial in nurturing long-term relationships with clients who will turn to you for guidance and support in their real estate endeavors.

The technical aspects of this campaign, while initially daunting, offer a competitive edge. Modern CRM and email marketing platforms have made these advanced features more accessible, enabling you to efficiently target and engage with your audience. Embracing these tools can significantly enhance your marketing capabilities, allowing you to reach a wider audience with less effort and cost.

The New Construction Drip Campaign is more than a marketing tactic; it's a growth strategy. It aligns with the evolving expectations of clients in a digital age, where access to up-to-date information is paramount. By adopting this approach, you are not only catering to current market demands but also positioning yourself for future success in an increasingly digital and data-driven real estate landscape.

The New Construction Drip Campaign is an indispensable tool in today's real estate market. It embodies a perfect blend of technology, Personalization, and market insight, enabling you to deliver exceptional service to clients interested in new constructions. As you continue to navigate the dynamic world of real estate, this campaign serves as a beacon, guiding your efforts to connect with clients, build lasting relationships, and establish a strong presence in the new construction market.

24

AGENT INTRODUCTION DRIP CAMPAIGN

Introducing yourself to potential clients can be a daunting task, but with the help of an Agent Introduction Drip Campaign, it can be an effective way to generate and convert leads. In this chapter, we'll show you how to create a drip campaign that will introduce you to potential clients and help establish you as a trusted authority in the real estate industry. By providing valuable information and personalized communication, you can build a relationship with potential clients that can lead to long term business growth.

User Scenario: Agent Introduction Drip Campaign

Leroy, a proactive real estate agent, aims to introduce himself to potential clients and build a robust pipeline of leads. To achieve this, Leroy implements an Agent Introduction Drip Campaign. This campaign involves sending a series of emails and SMS messages designed to introduce Leroy, highlight his expertise, and establish a connection with prospects.

By providing valuable information and demonstrating his professional background, Leroy can nurture these leads and encourage them to consider his services when they are ready to buy or sell property. This approach not only builds trust but also positions Leroy as a knowledgeable and approachable real estate professional.

Implementing this drip campaign can help you achieve similar success in establishing strong initial connections with potential clients and growing your client base effectively.

Agent Introduction Drip Campaign Use Cases

An Agent Introduction Drip Campaign can be used in several ways to generate and convert leads, including:

- Nurturing prospects: Potential clients who have not yet committed to working with a specific agent may need some encouragement to take the next step. An Agent Introduction Drip Campaign can help to nurture these leads by providing them with valuable information and demonstrating your expertise as a real estate professional.
- Follow-up with past clients: Maintaining a relationship with past clients is essential for building a strong referral network. An Agent Introduction Drip Campaign can be a fantastic way to keep in touch with past clients and remind them of your services.
- Engage with referral partners: Building relationships with referral partners, such as mortgage lenders and other real estate professionals, can be an effective way to generate new leads. An Agent Introduction Drip Campaign can help to keep these partners informed on your services, while also demonstrating your expertise and value as a partner.

Step-By-Step Guide and Templates

Step 1:

Send an email on day 1 with a subject line "Introducing [Agent Name]." In this email, introduce yourself to the lead and provide a brief overview of your background and experience in the real estate industry.

Step 1 Email Template:

Subject: Introducing [Agent Name]

Dear [Subscriber],

My name is [Agent Name], and I am a licensed real estate agent with [Agency Name]. I wanted to take a moment to introduce myself and share a little bit about my background and experience in the real estate industry.

[Include a brief overview of your experience, such as any certifications, years in the industry, or areas of specialization.]

I am passionate about helping my clients achieve their real estate goals and would love the opportunity to work with you. If you have any questions or concerns about the home buying or selling process, don't hesitate to reach out to me.

Best regards,

[Agent Signature Block with Contact Information]

Personalization:

Update the Subscriber Name and body with your links and phone numbers where appropriate.

Step 2:

Send an SMS message on day 5 after the initial email with a personalized introduction to the agent. In this SMS, introduce yourself and your real estate agency, and provide a brief overview of your experience and expertise. Encourage subscribers to reach out to you with any questions or concerns they may have.

Step 2 SMS Template:

Hi [Subscriber], this is [Agent Name] from [Agency Name]. I wanted to personally introduce myself and let you know that I'm here to help with any of your real estate needs. With [Number] years of experience in the industry, I've helped countless clients find their dream homes. If you have any questions or concerns, don't hesitate to reach out to me.

Personalization:

Update the Subscriber Name, Agent Name, Agency Name, and experience details where appropriate.

Recommended Agent Action:

Follow up with a phone call to subscribers who reply to the SMS or express interest in buying or selling a property.

Step 3:

Send an email on day 7 with a subject line "Our Agency's Services and Expertise." In this email, provide information about your agency's services and expertise, including your experience, areas of specialization, and unique selling points. You can also include your agency's contact information for any questions or concerns.

Step 3 Email Template:

Subject: Our Agency's Services and Expertise

Dear [Subscriber],

Thank you for subscribing to our Agent Introduction Drip Campaign. In this email, we want to introduce you to our agency's services and expertise.

At [Agency Name], we are dedicated to providing our clients with exceptional service and expertise. Here are some of the areas in which we specialize:

- [Area of Specialization 1]: Briefly describe your area of specialization and why you excel in this area.
- [Area of Specialization 2]: Briefly describe your area of specialization and why you excel in this area.
- [Area of Specialization 3]: Briefly describe your area of specialization and why you excel in this area.

In addition, here are some of our unique selling points:

- [Unique Selling Point 1]: Briefly describe your unique selling point and how it benefits your clients.
- [Unique Selling Point 2]: Briefly describe your unique selling point and how it benefits your clients.

We understand that choosing the right real estate agent is a crucial decision, and that's why we're here to help. If you have any questions or concerns about our agency's services, don't hesitate to reach out to us.

Best regards,

[Agent Signature Block with Contact Information]

Personalization:

Update the Subscriber Name and body with your links and phone numbers where appropriate.

Recommended Agent Action:

Follow up with a phone call to subscribers who reply to the email or express interest in buying or selling a property.

AGENT INTRODUCTION DRIP CAMPAIGN

Step 4:

Send an email on day 14 with a subject line "How I Can Help You Achieve Your Real Estate Goals." In this email, provide an overview of your expertise and services as a real estate agent, and how you can help the lead achieve their real estate goals. You can also include a call to action for the lead to contact you for more information or to schedule a consultation.

Step 4 Email Template:

Subject: How I Can Help You Achieve Your Real Estate Goals
Dear [Subscriber],

As a licensed real estate agent, I have the knowledge and expertise to help you achieve your real estate goals. Whether you're looking to buy or sell a home, or simply need advice on the real estate market, I'm here to help.

Here's how I can assist you:

- Landscaping: A well-manicured lawn and neatly trimmed hedges and trees can make a big impact on the appearance of your home
- Expertise: I have years of experience in the industry and am up-to-date on the latest trends and best practices.
- Services: I offer a wide range of services to help you with your real estate needs, including home buying and selling, property management, and more.
- Personalized approach: I work closely with my clients to understand their unique needs and develop a personalized plan to help them achieve their goals.

If you're interested in learning more about how I can help you, don't hesitate to contact me for a consultation.

Best regards,
[Agent Signature Block with Contact Information]

Personalization:

Update the Subscriber Name and body with your links and phone numbers where appropriate.

DRIP, DRIP, SOLD

Recommended Agent Action:

Follow up with a phone call to subscribers who reply to the email or express interest in buying or selling a property.

Step 5:

Send an email on day 21 with a subject line "How We Can Help You Achieve Your Real Estate Goals." In this email, provide an overview of how your agency can help clients achieve their real estate goals, including services offered and areas of expertise. You can also include client testimonials to showcase your agency's success in helping others.

Step 5 Email Template:

Subject: How We Can Help You Achieve Your Real Estate Goals
Dear [Subscriber],

At [Agency Name], we are dedicated to helping our clients achieve their real estate goals. In this email, we want to provide you with an overview of how we can help you with your real estate needs.

Here are some of the services we offer:

- Home buying and selling: We can assist you with every step of the home buying or selling process, from finding the right property to negotiating the best deal.
- Property management: If you're a landlord, we can manage your properties and help you maximize your rental income.
- Real estate investment: Our team can help you identify and acquire investment properties that meet your financial goals.

We also have expertise in various areas, including [Insert Areas of Expertise]. Our team is committed to providing you with the highest level of service and expertise to help you achieve your real estate goals.

Don't just take our word for it - here's what some of our clients have to say:

[Insert Client Testimonials]

We understand that every client is unique, and that's why we offer personalized solutions to meet your specific needs. If you have any questions or would like to discuss your real estate goals further, don't hesitate to reach out to us.

Best regards,
[Agent Signature Block with Contact Information]

Personalization:

Update the Subscriber Name and body with your links and phone numbers where appropriate.

Recommended Agent Action:

Follow up with a phone call to subscribers who reply to the email or express interest in buying or selling a property.

Step 6:

Send an SMS message on day 28 with a reminder to subscribers about the services and benefits of working with your agency and encouraging them to contact your agent for more information.

Step 6 SMS Template:

Hi [Subscriber], just a quick reminder of the many services and benefits our agency offers when it comes to buying or selling a home. Our experienced agents are here to provide you with expert guidance every step of the way. Don't hesitate to contact us for more information or to schedule a consultation. We look forward to hearing from you soon.

Personalization:

Update the Subscriber Name and body with your links and phone numbers where appropriate.

Recommended Agent Action:

Follow up with a phone call to subscribers who reply to the SMS or express interest in buying or selling a property.

Tracking the Success of the Agent Introduction Drip Campaign

Tracking the success of your Agent Introduction Drip Campaign is essential to understanding how well it is performing and making adjustments to improve its effectiveness. Here are some metrics and methods to track the success of your campaign:

- Open and click-through rates: Measure the open and click-through rates of your emails and SMS messages to determine how engaged your subscribers are with your campaign. If the rates are low, it may be an indication that you need to improve the content or timing of your communications.
- Response rate: Keep track of the number of subscribers who respond to your emails or SMS messages. This will help you gauge how interested they are in your services and give you an opportunity to follow up with them.
- Conversion rate: Track how many of the subscribers who responded to your communications turned into actual clients. This will give you an idea of how effective your campaign is at generating quality leads.
- Feedback from clients: Ask your clients how they heard about your agency to get an idea of how effective your Agent Introduction Drip Campaign is at generating leads.

To track these metrics, you can use email marketing tools or CRM software. You can also manually keep track of the number of responses and conversions in a spreadsheet or document.

By tracking the success of your Agent Introduction Drip Campaign, you can make data-driven decisions to improve its effectiveness and generate more quality leads for your agency.

Tips for Customizing the Agent Introduction Drip Campaign

In order to make the most out of an Agent Introduction Drip Campaign, it is important to customize the campaign to fit your specific agency and audience. By making small tweaks and adjustments to the campaign, you can increase the effectiveness and success of the campaign. Here are some tips for customizing the Agent Introduction Drip Campaign:

- Personalize your communications: Use the subscriber's name and any other relevant information you have about them to make your communications feel more personalized and engaging.
- Use a clear call to action: Encourage subscribers to contact your agency for more information or to schedule a consultation with a

clear call to action, such as "Call us today to schedule your consultation."

- Offer incentives: Offer incentives such as exclusive access to new listings or personalized home buying or selling consultations.
- Timing is key: Make sure to space out your messages appropriately and avoid bombarding subscribers with too many communications. Find a balance that works for your audience and your agency.
- Test and adjust: Continuously test and adjust your messaging to find what works best for your audience. Analyze metrics such as open rates and click-through rates to see what resonates with your subscribers and adjust accordingly.

By customizing your Agent Introduction Drip Campaign, you can increase the likelihood of generating quality leads and growing your client base.

Conclusion

The Agent Introduction Drip Campaign can be an effective way for real estate agents to introduce themselves to potential clients and generate new leads. By providing valuable information and incentives, agents can engage with their audience and build trust and credibility. The key to success is to customize the campaign to fit your specific audience and track the success of the campaign to make data-driven decisions to improve its effectiveness. By following these tips and best practices, agents can maximize the success of their Agent Introduction Drip Campaign and generate the best possible results.

25

AREA GUIDES DRIP CAMPAIGN

The Area Guides Drip Campaign is designed to engage and nurture leads by showcasing the unique aspects and highlights of various neighborhoods or communities in your target market. This campaign aims to help leads develop a deeper connection to the local area, increasing the likelihood that they will choose you as their real estate agent when they're ready to buy or sell a property.

By providing valuable information about local attractions, amenities, schools, and other essential features, you'll establish yourself as an expert in the area and a trusted resource for your leads. This drip campaign typically consists of multiple emails and SMS messages, each focusing on a specific neighborhood or community in your target area.

User Scenario: Area Guides Drip Campaign

Brian, a real estate agent specializing in relocating families, wants to provide potential clients with valuable information about different neighborhoods in his area. To achieve this, Brian implements an Area Guides Drip Campaign. This campaign sends a series of emails and SMS messages that highlight the unique aspects, amenities, and lifestyle of various neighborhoods.

By offering in-depth insights and useful information, Brian helps his clients make informed decisions about where to move. This approach not only builds trust but also positions Brian as an expert in his market, increasing his chances of converting leads into clients.

Implementing this drip campaign can help you achieve similar success in educating your clients and showcasing your knowledge of the local real estate market.

Area Guides Drip Campaign Use Cases

The Area Guides Drip Campaign can be employed in various scenarios to engage and nurture leads by providing them with valuable information about different neighborhoods or communities. Here are some common use cases for implementing this campaign:

- New leads: When you acquire new leads, especially those who are new to the area or unfamiliar with the local market, the Area Guides Drip Campaign can help them get acquainted with the neighborhoods and communities that might be of interest to them. By providing valuable insights into each area, you'll be able to guide them towards the right location for their needs and preferences.

- Relocation clients: Clients who are relocating to a new city or region will benefit greatly from the information provided in this drip campaign. By showcasing the unique features of each neighborhood or community, you'll help them make informed decisions about where they'd like to settle down in their new home.

- Nurturing cold leads: Re-engage cold leads by offering them useful information about the local area. The Area Guides Drip Campaign can help you regain their interest by demonstrating your expertise and providing them with valuable content that can help them better understand the local market.

- Increasing brand awareness: By creating well-researched, informative, and visually appealing area guides, you can effectively boost your brand awareness and establish yourself as a go-to resource for local real estate knowledge. Sharing these guides on social media, your website, or through email marketing can help you reach a wider audience and attract new leads.

- Targeting specific buyer personas: Tailor your Area Guides Drip Campaign to focus on specific buyer personas, such as families with children, retirees, or young professionals. By providing relevant and targeted information about the neighborhoods or communities that cater to their unique needs, you'll increase the likelihood of converting these leads into clients.

Overall, the Area Guides Drip Campaign serves as a versatile tool for engaging and nurturing leads by showcasing the distinct aspects of various neighborhoods and communities. By providing valuable, targeted content, you'll establish yourself as an expert in the local market and increase the chances of converting these leads into active clients.

Step-By-Step Guide and Templates

Step 1:

Send an email on day 1 with a subject line "Discover the Best of [Area] - Your Exclusive Area Guides!" This email introduces the Area Guides Drip Campaign and sets the expectation for the valuable content your leads will receive.

Step 1 Email Template:

Subject: Discover the Best of [Area] - Your Exclusive Area Guides!
Dear [Subscriber],

Welcome to our exclusive Area Guides series, where we'll be showcasing the best neighborhoods and communities in [Area] over the next few weeks. As a local real estate expert, I'm excited to share with you the unique aspects, attractions, and amenities that make each area special.

Keep an eye on your inbox for our in-depth guides, which will cover:
- Local attractions and points of interest
- Top-rated schools and educational facilities
- Recreation options and outdoor activities • Dining, shopping, and entertainment venues
- And much more!

I hope you find these guides helpful as you explore and get to know [Area]. If you have any questions or need assistance with your real estate needs, please don't hesitate to reach out.

Best regards,

[Agent Signature Block with Contact Information]

Personalization:

Update the Subscriber Name, Area, and body with your contact information where appropriate.

Recommended Agent Action:

Follow up with subscribers who express interest.

Step 2:

Send the first Area Guide email on day 5, focusing on a specific neighborhood or community. Provide valuable information and highlight the unique aspects of the area.

Step 2 Email Template:

Subject: [Area] Area Guide: Discover [Neighborhood/Community]!
Dear [Subscriber],

Today, we're excited to introduce you to [Neighborhood/Community], a vibrant and sought-after area in [Area]. In this guide, you'll learn about the unique features, attractions, and amenities that make [Neighborhood/Community] a great place to call home.

[Provide a brief overview of the neighborhood/community and include links or attachments to your in-depth area guide.]

If you have any questions about [Neighborhood/Community] or need assistance with your real estate needs, please don't hesitate to reach out. I'm here to help!

Best regards,
[Agent Signature Block with Contact Information]

Personalization:

Update the Subscriber Name, Area, Neighborhood/Community, and body with your links and contact information where appropriate.

Recommended Agent Action:

Follow up with subscribers who express interest.

Step 3:

Send an SMS message on day 7, reminding your leads about the first Area Guide email and offering additional assistance.

Step 3 SMS Template:

Hi [Subscriber], it's [Agent Name] from [Agency Name]. I hope you enjoyed learning about [Neighborhood/Community] in our recent Area Guide email. If you have any questions or need more information, feel free to reach out. Have a wonderful day!

Personalization:

Update the Subscriber Name and body with the Neighborhood/Community and your contact information where appropriate.

[Repeat Steps 2 and 3 for each additional neighborhood or community you want to cover in your campaign.]

Recommended Agent Action:

Follow up with subscribers who express interest.

Step 4:

Send a concluding email on day 14, recapping the Area Guides series and offering further assistance with your leads' real estate needs.

Step 4 Email Template:

Subject: Wrapping Up Our Exclusive [Area] Area Guides - How Can I Help You?

Dear [Subscriber],

Over the past few weeks, we've explored some of the best neighborhoods and communities in [Area] through our exclusive Area Guides series. I hope you found these guides informative and helpful in getting to know the unique aspects of each area.

As your local real estate expert, I'm here to help you with all your real estate needs. Whether you're looking to buy, sell, or simply have questions about the market or a specific neighborhood, please don't

DRIP, DRIP, SOLD

hesitate to reach out. My goal is to provide you with the best possible support and guidance throughout your real estate journey.

If you'd like to revisit any of our Area Guides, you can find them here:
[Link to Neighborhood/Community Guide 1]
[Link to Neighborhood/Community Guide 2]
[Link to Neighborhood/Community Guide 3]
[And so on...]

Thank you for allowing me to share my knowledge of [Area] with you. I look forward to the opportunity to work with you and help you achieve your real estate goals.

Best regards,
[Agent Signature Block with Contact Information]

Personalization:

Update the Subscriber Name, Area, and body with your links and contact information where appropriate.

Recommended Agent Action:

Continue to monitor your leads' engagement with the Area Guides Drip Campaign and follow up with those who express interest in specific neighborhoods or communities. Use this opportunity to learn more about their needs and preferences, and offer personalized solutions that meet their requirements. Additionally, be sure to keep your CRM system updated with their contact information and preferences, ensuring that you are reaching out to them in the most effective way possible.

Tracking the Success of the Area Guides Drip Campaign

Tracking the Success of the Area Guides Drip Campaign is essential to determine its effectiveness and make any necessary adjustments to improve its performance. Here are some key metrics and strategies you can use to track the success of your campaign:

- Open rates and click-through rates: Monitor the open rates and click-through rates of your email campaign to gauge the level of engagement and interest from your leads. High open rates indicate that your subject lines are compelling, while high click-through rates show that your content is valuable and relevant to your audience.

- Lead engagement: Track the number of leads who respond to your emails or SMS messages, request more information, or engage with your content (e.g., downloading an area guide or watching a video). This will help you identify which neighborhoods or communities are generating the most interest and adjust your campaign accordingly.
- Conversion rates: Measure the number of leads who progress through the sales funnel as a result of the Area Guides Drip Campaign. This includes leads who schedule property viewings, request home evaluations, or ultimately buy or sell a property. High conversion rates indicate that your campaign is effectively engaging your audience and driving them to take action.
- Website traffic: Monitor the traffic to your website, specifically the pages related to the area guides, to determine the level of interest in your content. Analyze metrics such as page views, time spent on the page, and bounce rates to evaluate the performance of your area guide content.
- Social media engagement: If you're sharing your area guides on social media platforms, track the number of likes, shares, and comments your posts receive. High engagement rates indicate that your content resonates with your audience and can help you reach new leads.
- Customer feedback: Gather feedback from leads and clients who have engaged with your Area Guides Drip Campaign. This will provide valuable insights into the strengths and weaknesses of your campaign, allowing you to make improvements based on their experiences and preferences.

By regularly tracking and analyzing these metrics, you can continuously refine and optimize your Area Guides Drip Campaign to ensure its effectiveness in engaging leads and driving them towards conversion.

As you gain a deeper understanding of your audience's needs and preferences, you'll be better equipped to provide valuable content that showcases your expertise and strengthens your position as a trusted real estate professional in your target market.

Tips for Customizing the Area Guides Drip Campaign

Customizing your Area Guides Drip Campaign can significantly increase its effectiveness. Consider these strategies:

- Personalize Your Communications: Use personal information such as subscribers' preferred neighborhoods, property types, or previously viewed listings to make emails more relevant.
- Offer Area-Specific Information: Tailor your guides to address the unique attributes of different areas. Include local market trends, upcoming developments, or community features relevant to each segment.
- Clear Call to Action: Encourage your audience to act on the information provided, whether it's exploring more listings in the area, scheduling a neighborhood tour, or attending local open houses.
- Optimal Timing: Distribute your content at strategic times. Consider the local real estate cycle, seasonal trends, or community events that may impact interest in specific areas.
- Experiment and Adapt: Regularly test different aspects of your emails, such as layouts, content types, and subject lines, to determine what resonates most with your audience.

Conclusion

An Area Guides Drip Campaign is a strategic tool for real estate professionals to establish expertise in local markets and engage potential clients. By providing insightful, localized content, you can foster a connection with your audience, encouraging them to explore real estate opportunities in their areas of interest. Continuously tracking and refining your campaign ensures it remains a valuable resource in your marketing toolkit, driving interest and conversions in your real estate business.

26

HOLIDAY GIFT DRIP CAMPAIGN

The Holiday Gift Guide Drip Campaign is a strategic approach to engaging with clients during the festive season. This campaign aims to provide value-added content that goes beyond real estate, focusing on the spirit of giving and celebration. It's an opportunity for real estate agents to connect with their clients on a more personal level, strengthening relationships and fostering a sense of community and goodwill. This campaign should be updated yearly to include the most recent trending gifts in the identified sectors.

This campaign typically involves sending a series of emails and SMS messages that feature curated gift ideas, holiday home decorating tips, and local holiday event information. The content is designed to be informative, festive, and engaging, helping clients navigate the holiday season with ease and enjoyment.

Key Elements:
- Personalization: Tailoring content to reflect local traditions, client interests, and unique holiday themes.
- Timing: Strategically scheduling communications to coincide with key holiday shopping dates and events.
- Diverse Content: Including a mix of gift suggestions, holiday home decor ideas, and local event information.

User Scenario: Holiday Gift Guide Drip Campaign

Lena, a dedicated real estate agent, wants to stay connected with her clients during the holiday season and show her appreciation for their business. To do this, Lena decides to implement a Holiday Gift Guide Drip Campaign. This campaign sends a series of well-timed communications that provide clients with thoughtful and creative gift ideas for the holiday season, tailored to their preferences and needs.

By providing valuable and festive content, Lena can strengthen her relationships with her clients, demonstrate her appreciation, and keep her brand top-of-mind. This approach not only enhances client satisfaction but also increases the likelihood of receiving referrals and repeat business.

Implementing this drip campaign can help you achieve similar success in engaging with your clients and spreading holiday cheer.

Holiday Gift Guide Drip Campaign Use Cases

The Holiday Gift Guide Drip Campaign serves as a versatile tool for real estate professionals, allowing them to engage with their client base in a unique and festive manner. This campaign caters to a wide range of client needs and interests, making it a valuable asset for real estate agents during the holiday season. Below, we explore various use cases that demonstrate how this campaign can be effectively implemented to maintain client relationships, offer practical value, and spread holiday cheer.

- For Home Buyers: Provide gift ideas that are perfect for new homeowners, such as home improvement tools, decor items, or smart home gadgets.
- For Sellers: Share suggestions on how to stage homes festively for the holidays, enhancing appeal for potential buyers.
- Local Community Focus: Include a guide to local holiday markets, craft fairs, or unique local gift shops, encouraging support for small businesses in the community.
- DIY Enthusiasts: Offer a guide on DIY holiday crafts or home decoration projects, appealing to clients who enjoy hands-on activities.
- Family-Oriented Ideas: Suggest family-friendly gifts and activities, catering to clients with children or large families.
- Luxury Market: Curate a list of high-end gift ideas for clients in the luxury market segment, including exclusive experiences or premium home accessories.

- Eco-Conscious Gifts: For environmentally conscious clients, offer a guide to sustainable and ecofriendly gift options.
- Post-Holiday Guide: Provide ideas for organizing and decluttering post-holidays, which can be particularly valuable for those looking to sell their homes in the new year.
- Referral Encouragement: Use the holiday spirit to gently encourage satisfied clients to refer your services to friends and family as a gift idea.
- Investment Clients: For clients interested in real estate investment, offer insights into the market trends for the upcoming year as a holiday 'gift' of knowledge.

The Holiday Gift Guide Drip Campaign presents a multitude of opportunities for real estate agents to connect with their clients during a season that resonates with warmth and generosity. Whether it's aiding new homeowners, supporting local businesses, or providing thoughtful ideas for family activities, this campaign is adaptable to various client segments. It not only reinforces your role as a knowledgeable real estate professional but also highlights your commitment to fostering community spirit and personalized service. Engaging your clients through this campaign can strengthen relationships, encourage referrals, and set the stage for a productive new year in real estate.

Step-By-Step Guide and Templates

Step 1:

Send an email on November 15th with a subject line "Get Ready for the Holidays: Exclusive Gift Ideas Inside!"

In this email, introduce your Holiday Gift Guide, highlighting the variety of gift ideas that will be featured in the upcoming weeks.

Step 1 Email Template:

Subject: Get Ready for the Holidays: Exclusive Gift Ideas Inside!
Dear [Subscriber],

DRIP, DRIP, SOLD

As the holiday season approaches, we're excited to present our exclusive Holiday Gift Guide! Stay tuned for unique gift ideas that will delight your loved ones.

Best regards,

[Your Agency Name] [Contact Information]

Personalization:

Customize the SMS with your client's name and your agency contact information.

Recommended Agent Action:

Monitor responses and engagement with the gift guide and be prepared to offer additional home decor suggestions or assist in finding specific items.

Step 2:

Send an SMS on November 18th to remind subscribers about the upcoming gift guide.

Keep the message short and engaging to spark curiosity.

Step 2 SMS Template:

Hi [Subscriber]! Our Holiday Gift Guide is coming soon with fantastic gift ideas. Keep an eye on your inbox! - [Your Agency Name]

Personalization:

Customize the SMS with your client's name and your agency contact information.

Recommended Agent Action:

Monitor responses and engagement with the gift guide and be prepared to offer additional home decor suggestions or assist in finding specific items.

Step 3:

Send an email on November 22nd with the subject line "Holiday Gift Guide: Week 1 - Home Decor Delights."

Focus this edition on home decor items that could make great gifts.

Step 3 Email Template:

Subject: Holiday Gift Guide: Week 1 - Home Decor Delights
Dear [Subscriber],

Happy holidays! This week, we're excited to share with you our curated selection of home decor gifts that will bring joy and warmth to any space. Whether you're shopping for family, friends, or even a treat for your own home, these delightful finds are sure to impress.

- Artisanal Scented Candles: Elevate any room with the soothing ambiance and exquisite fragrances of handcrafted candles.
- Elegant Throw Pillows: Add a touch of comfort and style with these beautifully designed throw pillows, perfect for cozy evenings.
- Decorative Vases: From sleek modern designs to classic elegance, these vases make a charming addition to any home decor collection.
- Wall Art Prints: Bring walls to life with stunning art prints that cater to all tastes, from abstract to landscapes.
- Stylish Table Lamps: Illuminate spaces with chic and functional table lamps that blend seamlessly with any interior design.

Find more inspiring home decor gift ideas in our full guide: [Link to Full Gift Guide].

Warm regards,
[Your Agency Name] [Contact Information]

Personalization:

Customize the email with images of the featured products and links to where they can be purchased. Include a personal message or recommendation based on the subscriber's known preferences.

Recommended Agent Action:

Monitor responses and engagement with the gift guide, and be prepared to offer additional home decor suggestions or assist in finding specific items.

Step 4:

Send an SMS on November 24th as a follow-up to the first edition. Encourage subscribers to check their emails if they haven't already.

DRIP, DRIP, SOLD

Step 4 SMS Template:

Hello [Subscriber]! Have you checked our first Holiday Gift Guide edition? Find the perfect home decor gifts! - [Your Agency Name]

Personalization:

Customize the SMS with your clients name and your agency contact information.

Recommended Agent Action:

Monitor responses and engagement with the gift guide and be prepared to offer additional home decor suggestions or assist in finding specific items.

Step 5:

Send an email on November 29th with the subject line "Week 2 of Our Holiday Gift Guide: Tech Gadgets for Everyone!"

This edition should focus on popular technology gadgets.

Step 5 Email Template:

Subject: Week 2 of Our Holiday Gift Guide: Tech Gadgets for Everyone!
Dear [Subscriber],

Welcome to Week 2 of our Holiday Gift Guide! This week, we're delving into the world of technology to bring you an exciting selection of gadgets that are perfect for gift-giving this season. Whether you're shopping for the tech enthusiast in your life or looking to upgrade your own tech collection, these gadgets are sure to be a hit.

- Smart Home Assistants: Enhance everyday life with voice-activated smart home devices that can play music, control smart home features, and provide information.
- Wireless Earbuds: Offer the gift of high-quality sound and convenience with the latest in wireless earbud technology.
- Fitness Trackers: For the health-conscious, a fitness tracker is a thoughtful gift that encourages a healthy lifestyle.
- E-Readers: Perfect for book lovers, modern e-readers provide a portable and convenient way to enjoy their favorite books.
- Portable Chargers: A practical and highly useful gift, portable chargers ensure your loved ones' devices never run out of power.

Discover more fantastic tech gadgets in our full guide: [Link to Full Gift Guide].

Happy holidays and happy gifting!

Best,

[Your Agency Name] [Contact Information]

Personalization:

Add images and links to each tech gadget for easy browsing and purchasing. Personalize the message with a brief note on why these tech gifts are a must-have this holiday season.

Recommended Agent Action:

Keep track of which gadgets garner the most interest and be ready to provide further information or tech gift suggestions based on subscriber inquiries and responses.

Step 6:

Send an SMS on December 1st, reminding subscribers about the tech gadget edition.

Step 6 SMS Template:

Hi [Subscriber], don't miss out on our tech gadget gift ideas in this week's Holiday Gift Guide! - [Your Agency Name]

Personalization:

Customize the SMS with your client's name and your agency contact information.

Recommended Agent Action:

Monitor responses and engagement with the gift guide and be prepared to offer additional home decor suggestions or assist in finding specific items.

Step 7:

Send an email on December 17th with the subject line "Final Edition: Last-Minute Gift Ideas."

This email should focus on last-minute gift ideas for those who are still looking.

Step 7 Email Template:

Subject: Final Edition: Last-Minute Gift Ideas
Dear [Subscriber],

As the holiday season reaches its peak, we understand that finding the perfect gift at the last minute can be a challenge. That's why we've curated a selection of thoughtful and easy-to-acquire last-minute gift ideas in our final edition of the Holiday Gift Guide. These gifts are not only delightful but also easily accessible for those last-minute shopping needs.

- Subscription Services: Gift subscriptions like streaming services, book clubs, or gourmet food deliveries offer a present that keeps on giving.
- Gift Cards: An ever-popular choice, gift cards to favorite stores or experiences allow your loved ones to choose their own perfect gift.
- DIY Gift Baskets: Create a personalized gift basket filled with a variety of treats and items tailored to the recipient's interests.
- E-books or Online Courses: For the lifelong learner, an e-book or an online course in an area of their interest can be a unique and enriching gift.
- Local Artisan Products: Support local businesses while giving a unique gift, such as handcrafted jewelry, art, or home decor.

Check out our full list of last-minute gift ideas here: [Link to Full Gift Guide].
Happy Holidays and happy last-minute gifting!
Regards,
[Your Agency Name] [Contact Information]

Personalization:

Customize the email with images and direct links to the products or services for easy access. Include a personal note on the joy and excitement of finding the perfect last-minute gifts.

Recommended Agent Action:

Monitor the responses and inquiries to gauge interest in different types of last-minute gifts. Be prepared to offer additional suggestions or guidance on where to find these items locally.

Step 8:

Send a Post-Holiday Email on December 26th with subject line: "Unwind After the Holidays: Home Relaxation Ideas"

Step 8 Email Template:

Subject: Unwind After the Holidays: Home Relaxation Ideas
Dear [Subscriber],

The holiday season is a whirlwind of activity, but now it's time to slow down and enjoy some well deserved relaxation at home. To help you create a sanctuary where you can unwind and recharge, here are some home relaxation ideas:

- Create a Cozy Reading Nook: Set up a comfortable corner with soft lighting, a plush chair, and a stack of your favorite books. It's the perfect spot to lose yourself in a good story.
- Indulge in Aromatherapy: Use essential oils or scented candles to fill your home with calming fragrances like lavender, chamomile, or sandalwood.
- Designate a Meditation Space: Dedicate a quiet area in your home for meditation or yoga. Add some cushions, a yoga mat, and perhaps some calming nature sounds for an enhanced experience.
- Install Soft, Warm Lighting: Swap bright lights for softer, warmer bulbs to create a tranquil atmosphere in your living spaces.
- Invest in Comfortable Bedding: Upgrade your bedding with high-quality sheets and plush pillows for a luxurious sleep experience.
- Set Up a DIY Spa: Treat yourself to an at-home spa day with homemade face masks, a warm bath, and some soothing music.

For more tips on turning your home into a relaxation haven, explore our full guide here: [Link to Relaxation Tips].
Relax and enjoy,
[Agent Signature Block with Contact Information]

Personalization:

Customize the email with photos of serene home setups and links to recommended products for creating a relaxing atmosphere.

Recommended Agent Action:

Keep track of the responses and feedback to understand the relaxation preferences of your subscribers. Offer personalized tips or resources based on their interests and feedback.

Step 8 SMS Template:

Hey [Subscriber]! It's not too late for holiday gifts. Check our final Holiday Gift Guide for great lastminute ideas! - [Your Agency Name]

Personalization:

Customize the SMS with your client's name and your agency contact information.

Recommended Agent Action:

Monitor responses and engagement with the gift guide and be prepared to offer additional home decor suggestions or assist in finding specific items.

Step 9:

Send a Post-Holiday Email on December 26th with subject line: "Unwind After the Holidays: Home Relaxation Ideas"

Step 9 Email Template:

Subject: Unwind After the Holidays: Home Relaxation Ideas
Dear [Subscriber],

The holiday season is a whirlwind of activity, but now it's time to slow down and enjoy some well deserved relaxation at home. To help you create a sanctuary where you can unwind and recharge, here are some home relaxation ideas:

- Create a Cozy Reading Nook: Set up a comfortable corner with soft lighting, a plush chair, and a stack of your favorite books. It's the perfect spot to lose yourself in a good story.
- Indulge in Aromatherapy: Use essential oils or scented candles to fill your home with calming fragrances like lavender, chamomile, or sandalwood.

- Designate a Meditation Space: Dedicate a quiet area in your home for meditation or yoga. Add some cushions, a yoga mat, and perhaps some calming nature sounds for an enhanced experience.
- Install Soft, Warm Lighting: Swap bright lights for softer, warmer bulbs to create a tranquil atmosphere in your living spaces.
- Invest in Comfortable Bedding: Upgrade your bedding with high-quality sheets and plush pillows for a luxurious sleep experience.
- Set Up a DIY Spa: Treat yourself to an at-home spa day with homemade face masks, a warm bath, and some soothing music.

For more tips on turning your home into a relaxation haven, explore our full guide here: [Link to Relaxation Tips].
Relax and enjoy,
[Agent Signature Block with Contact Information]

Personalization:

Customize the email with photos of serene home setups and links to recommended products for creating a relaxing atmosphere.

Recommended Agent Action:

Keep track of the responses and feedback to understand the relaxation preferences of your subscribers. Offer personalized tips or resources based on their interests and feedback.

Tracking the Success of the Holiday Gift Guide Drip Campaign

Monitoring the effectiveness of your Holiday Gift Guide Drip Campaign is essential for understanding its impact on your audience and refining future marketing efforts. By analyzing specific metrics, you can gain insights into subscriber engagement and behavior.

Key Metrics to Track:

- Open Rates: Keep an eye on how many subscribers are opening your emails. A high open rate indicates that your subject lines are capturing attention and your timing is resonating with the audience.

DRIP, DRIP, SOLD

- Click-Through Rates (CTR): Measure the rate at which subscribers click on the links within your emails. A high CTR suggests that your content is engaging and your gift suggestions are appealing.
- Conversion Rate: Track the number of subscribers who take a specific action, such as visiting your website or contacting you for real estate services, after receiving the email.
- Subscriber Feedback: Gather direct feedback from your subscribers. This can be done through surveys within the email, encouraging subscribers to share their thoughts on the gift suggestions and overall content.
- Engagement on Social Media: Monitor likes, shares, and comments on your social media posts related to the Holiday Gift Guide. This engagement can provide additional insights into the campaign's reach and impact.

By regularly assessing these metrics, you can fine-tune your campaign for maximum effectiveness. Understanding your audience's preferences and behaviors allows you to create more targeted and compelling content for future campaigns.

Tips for Customizing the Holiday Gift Drip Campaign

Customizing your Holiday Gift Guide Drip Campaign is key to connecting with your audience on a more personal level. Tailoring the content to reflect the interests and needs of your subscribers can significantly boost engagement and response rates. Here are some strategic tips:

- Segment Your Audience: Divide your email list based on demographics, past interactions, or property interests. This allows you to send more relevant gift suggestions to different groups.
- Personalize the Content: Use the recipient's name and reference their specific interests or past interactions with your agency in the emails.
- Localize Your Suggestions: Include gift ideas from local businesses or artisans to promote community engagement and add a personal touch.

- Incorporate Interactive Elements: Add polls or quizzes in your emails to gather preferences, which can be used to personalize future communications.
- Include a Personal Note: Share a brief message or story in your emails to create a more personal connection with your subscribers.

A well-customized Holiday Gift Guide Drip Campaign not only enhances the holiday experience for your subscribers but also strengthens your relationship with them. By showing that you understand and cater to their interests, you can foster loyalty and trust.

Conclusion

The Holiday Gift Guide Drip Campaign is a unique way to engage with your audience during the festive season. This campaign adds a personal touch to your marketing efforts, setting you apart from competitors and enhancing your brand image. These are some benefits of the campaign:

- Enhances Client Relationships: The campaign shows clients that you value them beyond just business interactions, fostering long-term relationships.
- Boosts Brand Visibility: By offering valuable and enjoyable content, your brand stays top of mind even during the off-peak real estate season.
- Encourages Engagement: The gift guide can stimulate interaction and feedback from clients, providing valuable insights for future marketing strategies.

The Holiday Gift Guide Drip Campaign is a creative and effective way to maintain client engagement and showcase your brand's unique approach. By blending real estate professionalism with a personal touch, this campaign can significantly contribute to client satisfaction and loyalty.

27

MOVING DAY CHECKLIST DRIP CAMPAIGN

Moving can be one of the most stressful events in a person's life, but with proper planning and organization, it can be a smooth and seamless process. The Moving Day Checklist Drip Campaign is designed to guide your clients through every step of their moving journey, ensuring they are well-prepared and informed. This campaign includes a series of emails and SMS messages that provide timely reminders, valuable tips, and comprehensive checklists to help clients stay on track and reduce moving-related stress. Implementing this drip campaign will not only enhance your client's moving experience but also demonstrate your commitment to their well-being, fostering long-term relationships and increasing client satisfaction.

User Scenario: Moving Day Checklist Drip Campaign

Michael, a real estate agent, has several clients who are about to move into their new homes. To help them through this stressful period, Michael implements a Moving Day Checklist Drip Campaign. This campaign includes a series of emails and SMS messages that provide clients with timely reminders, valuable tips, and comprehensive checklists to ensure they are well-prepared for moving day.

By guiding his clients through each stage of the moving process, Michael helps them stay organized and reduces their stress. This thoughtful approach not only improves the moving experience for his clients but also reinforces their trust and satisfaction with his services.

Implementing this drip campaign can help you achieve similar success in assisting your clients with a smooth and efficient move.

Moving Day Checklist Drip Campaign Use Cases

A Moving Day Checklist Drip Campaign is an invaluable tool for real estate agents to help clients navigate the complex process of moving. By providing timely and organized information, you can ensure that your clients have a smooth and stress-free moving experience. Here are the key use cases for this campaign:

- First-Time Homebuyers: First-time homebuyers often feel overwhelmed by the moving process. This campaign provides them with step-by-step guidance, helping them feel more confident and in control.
- Clients with Busy Schedules: For clients with demanding jobs or busy personal lives, this campaign serves as a helpful reminder of important tasks, ensuring nothing is overlooked.
- Out-of-Town Buyers: Clients moving from a different city or state may be unfamiliar with the local resources and logistics. The campaign can include information about local movers, utility companies, and other essential services.
- Families: Families moving with children or elderly members need extra preparation and coordination. This campaign can include tips for making the move easier for all family members, ensuring a smooth transition.
- Clients Downsizing: Clients who are downsizing may need additional help with decluttering and organizing. The campaign can provide tips and resources for managing this process effectively.
- Investment Property Buyers: Investors who purchase properties to rent out can use this campaign to prepare the property for new tenants. This ensures that the property is move-in ready and that the transition is smooth for future renters.

By customizing the Moving Day Checklist Drip Campaign to fit these various scenarios, you can provide personalized support that meets the unique needs of each client. This level of service not only enhances the client experience but also strengthens your reputation as a reliable and caring real estate professional.

Step-By-Step Guide and Templates

Step 1: Initial Moving Preparation Email

Send an email with the subject "30-Day Countdown to Your Move: Your Detailed Moving Checklist" 30 days before the move.

Step 1 Email Template:

Subject: 30-Day Countdown to Your Move: Your Detailed Moving Checklist
Dear [Subscriber],

As your moving day approaches, we want to ensure you're fully prepared. Here's a detailed 30-day moving checklist to guide you through this busy period:

Week 4: Planning and Organization
- Begin sorting and decluttering your belongings.
- Create an inventory of items to move.
- Research and book a reliable moving company.

Week 3: Early Packing and Address Updates
- Start packing non-essential items like books, out-of-season clothes, and decor.
- Use this time to also gather packing supplies – boxes, tape, labels, etc.
- Begin updating your address with banks, subscriptions, and notify friends and family.

Week 2: Address Changes and Utility Arrangements
- Confirm transfer or setup of utilities at your new home (electricity, water, internet).
- Continue packing, focusing on less frequently used items.

Week 1: Final Preparations
- Pack a 'first night' box with essentials like toiletries, change of clothes, and important documents.
- Confirm all moving day logistics with movers.
- Do a final walkthrough of your home to ensure nothing is left behind.

Remember, moving can be a complex process, but with this checklist, you're on track for a smoother transition.

Best wishes,
[Agent's Name]
[Agency Name]
[Contact Information]

Personalization:

Customize with the subscriber's name and include any specific moving services or local resources offered by your agency.

Recommended Agent Action:

Follow up with a phone call or email to clients who engage with the checklist, offering assistance or answering any queries they might have regarding their move.

Step 2: Final Packing and Moving Tips

14 days before the move send an email with the subject "Your Moving Day is Approaching: Final Packing Tips and Checklist.

Step 2 Email Template

Subject: Your Moving Day is Approaching: Final Packing Tips & Detailed Checklist

Dear [Subscriber],

As your moving day rapidly approaches, here's a comprehensive checklist to guide you through these final two weeks:

- Deep Packing:
  - Finish packing all items except daily necessities.
  - Clearly label each box with its contents and the room it belongs to in your new home.

- Movers Confirmation:
  - Re-confirm the moving date, time, and any special instructions with your moving company.

MOVING DAY CHECKLIST DRIP CAMPAIGN

- o Ensure the movers have your new address and a contact number for moving day.

- Pack an essentials bag for moving day, including:
  - o Snacks and bottled water
  - o Chargers for your electronic devices
  - o Basic toiletries and a change of clothes
  - o Any necessary medication
  - o Important documents related to the move

- Utilities Check:
  - o Confirm the setup of utilities at your new home and the disconnection date at your current residence.

- Address Updates:
  - o Notify banks, employers, and subscription services of your new address.
  - o Arrange for mail forwarding through the postal service.

- • Final Home Check:
  - o Do a final walkthrough of each room to ensure nothing is left behind.
  - o Plan for the disposal of any remaining items you're not taking with you.

Remember, while moving can be stressful, staying organized will make the process smoother.

Best regards,

[Agent's Name]

Personalization:

Tailor the email with the subscriber's name and add any local moving resources or services provided by your agency.

DRIP, DRIP, SOLD

Recommended Agent Action:

Follow up with a phone call or email to clients who may need last-minute assistance or have concerns about the move. Offer reassurance and practical help where needed.

Step 3: Moving Day SMS Reminder

One day before the move send an SMS reminding the client to double check their lists and ensure everything is ready for their move tomorrow. Let them know you are there to help if they need you.

Step 3 SMS Template:

"Hi [Subscriber], it's [Agent's Name]. Just a quick reminder: your moving day is tomorrow! Remember your essentials bag and double-check your inventory. Good luck, and if you need any assistance, just give us a call!"

Personalization:

Include the clients name and the agents contact information.

Recommended Agent Action:

Be available for any last-minute assistance or queries from clients.

Step 4: Moving Day SMS Send on the day of the move.

Step 4 SMS Template:

"Hi [Subscriber], it's [Agent's Name] from [Agency Name]. Wishing you a smooth moving day! Remember, your 'first night' box is your best friend today. Call us if you need anything!"

Personalization:

Include the clients name and the agents contact information.

Recommended Agent Action:

Be ready to provide assistance or advice if clients reach out on their moving day.

MOVING DAY CHECKLIST DRIP CAMPAIGN

Step 5: Post-Move Follow-Up Email

Send an email 7 days after the move with the subject "Welcome to Your New Home! Post-Move Tips".

Step 5 Email Template:

Subject: Welcome to Your New Home! Post-Move Tips
Dear [Subscriber],

Congratulations on your move! As you settle in, here are some tips to help:

- Unpacking Strategy: Start with essentials and then move room by room.
- Home Personalization: Add personal touches to make your new space feel like home.
- Community Exploration: Familiarize yourself with your new neighborhood and local amenities.

All the best,
[Agent's Name]
[Agency Name]
[Contact Information]

Personalization:

Include the subscriber's name and any local recommendations or resources that may help them in their new neighborhood.

Recommended Agent Action:

Check-in with clients to ensure they are settling in well and offer any further assistance they might need.

Tracking the Success of the Moving Day Checklist Drip Campaign

Effectively monitoring the performance of your Moving Day Checklist Drip Campaign is essential for understanding its impact and optimizing future iterations. This tracking is not just about numbers; it's about ensuring a seamless and stress-free moving experience for your clients, which in turn, enhances your reputation and client satisfaction.

Key Metrics to Monitor:

- Open and Click-Through Rates: These metrics are vital to evaluate the engagement level of your emails. High open rates indicate that your subject lines are resonating with your audience, while high click-through rates suggest that your content is compelling and useful.
- Feedback and Queries: Pay attention to the responses and questions you receive from clients. This feedback is a goldmine for insights into how well your checklist is addressing client needs and areas where it could be improved.
- Conversion Rates: Monitor how many clients engage in further actions, like scheduling additional services, consultations, or sending referrals. This indicates the campaign's effectiveness in driving client action beyond just reading the email.
- SMS Engagement: If SMS messages are part of your campaign, track their open and response rates. SMS engagement can offer a more immediate measure of client interaction and interest.
- Client Satisfaction Surveys Post-Move: After the move, sending out a survey to gauge client satisfaction can provide invaluable feedback on the usefulness of the checklist and areas for improvement.

Regularly tracking and analyzing these metrics allows you to refine and enhance your Moving Day Checklist Drip Campaign, ensuring it continually meets the evolving needs of your clients. This proactive approach not only bolsters the efficiency of your campaign but also plays a crucial role in building lasting client relationships and establishing your reputation as a supportive and resourceful real estate agent.

Tips for Customizing the Moving Day Checklist Drip Campaign

Customization is key to making your Moving Day Checklist Drip Campaign resonate with your clients. A one-size-fits-all approach rarely works, especially when dealing with something as personal and varied as moving homes. By tailoring your campaign, you can address the specific concerns and needs of your clients, making the moving process less stressful and more efficient for them.

Customization Tips:

- Segment Your Audience: Different clients have different needs. Segment your audience based on factors like the size of the move (e.g., moving from an apartment vs. a large family home), distance (local vs. long-distance), or whether they're first-time homebuyers or seasoned movers. Tailor your checklists and advice to each segment.
- Localize Your Content: Include information relevant to the area your clients are moving to or from. Local moving tips, utility company information, or local service providers can be incredibly useful.
- Personalization: Use your clients' names and reference any specific conversations or preferences you might know about. This personal touch can make your communications feel more relevant and engaging.
- Include Interactive Elements: Consider adding interactive elements like checkable boxes or links to online resources. This can make your checklist more engaging and useful.
- Timing Adjustments: Adjust the timing of your emails and SMS messages based on client feedback and engagement data. Some clients may appreciate more frequent reminders as the moving day approaches, while others may prefer less frequent, more comprehensive communications.
- Feedback Loop: Encourage feedback on your checklists and communications. This can not only provide valuable insights for future customization but also keep the lines of communication open with your clients.
- Use of Visuals: Enhance your emails with visuals like infographics or short videos. Visual aids can make complex information more digestible and engaging.

A well-customized Moving Day Checklist Drip Campaign can significantly reduce the stress associated with moving for your clients. By taking the time to understand and address their unique needs, you not only provide valuable assistance but also reinforce your commitment to offering personalized, client focused service. This approach can lead to higher client satisfaction, better engagement with your campaign, and increased referrals and repeat business.

Conclusion

The Moving Day Checklist Drip Campaign plays a pivotal role in enhancing the moving experience for clients. By providing structured and timely guidance, this campaign transforms a typically chaotic and stressful period into an organized and manageable process.

Key Takeaways:

- Client-Centric Approach: Tailoring the campaign to address individual client needs ensures that each client feels valued and supported. This approach not only assists them during the move but also cements a lasting positive impression of your agency.
- Efficient Communication: The campaign's systematic structure ensures that clients receive the right information at the right time. This eliminates information overload and enhances the effectiveness of each communication.
- Building Long-Term Relationships: By supporting clients through one of life's major milestones, you foster trust and loyalty. This relationship-building strategy can lead to future business opportunities and referrals.
- Adaptability and Improvement: The campaign's structure allows for adaptability and improvement based on client feedback and success tracking. Continuous refinement ensures the campaign remains relevant and effective.

In essence, the Moving Day Checklist Drip Campaign is more than just a set of reminders and tips. It represents your agency's commitment to exceptional client service, going beyond the transaction to provide meaningful support. Such initiatives not only elevate your client's moving experience but also position your agency as a caring and indispensable resource in the real estate industry. As the campaign concludes, it leaves a lasting impact, paving the way for ongoing client relationships and sustained business growth.

28

REKINDLING COLD LEADS DRIP CAMPAIGN

R e-engaging cold leads is an important part of any real estate agent's business. These are leads that may have shown interest in the past, but for one reason or another, did not convert into clients. By reengaging these leads through a targeted drip campaign, agents can potentially turn these leads into active clients and generate more business.

This drip campaign focuses on warming up cold leads through a series of email and SMS messages. The messages will be designed to re-introduce the agent to the lead, provide value-added content, and gently nudge the lead towards re-engaging with the agent.

Re-engaging cold leads can be an extremely valuable tactic for converting leads into active clients, and this drip campaign will provide agents with the tools and strategies they need to make the most out of their cold lead database.

User Scenario: Rekindling Cold Leads Drip Campaign

Aisha, a seasoned real estate agent, has accumulated a substantial database of leads over the years. However, many of these leads have gone cold, meaning they showed initial interest but did not follow through with any real estate transactions. Recognizing the potential value in these dormant leads, Aisha decides to implement a Rekindling Cold Leads Drip Campaign. This campaign aims to re-engage these leads through a series of emails and SMS messages that reintroduce Aisha, provide valuable content, and gently encourage the leads to reconnect and consider their real estate needs.

By systematically reaching out to these cold leads with personalized and relevant content, Aisha hopes to reignite their interest and convert them

299

DRIP, DRIP, SOLD

into active clients. Implementing this drip campaign can help you achieve similar success in reviving dormant leads and expanding your client base.

Rekindling Cold Leads Drip Campaign Use Cases

This drip campaign can be used by real estate agents who have a database of cold leads that they have not been able to convert into clients. The campaign can be used to re-engage these leads and potentially turn them into active clients.

This drip campaign can also be used by agents who have a large database of leads that have gone cold over time. By re-engaging these leads, agents can potentially generate more business and increase their overall client base.

Step-By-Step Guide and Templates

Step 1:

Send an email on day 1 with a subject line "Re-Introducing [Agent Name] - Let's Catch Up!" In this email, re-introduce yourself to the lead, explain why you are reaching out, and offer some value-added content such as an industry report or recent market updates. You can also include your agency's contact information for any questions or concerns.

Step 1 Email Template:

Subject: Re-Introducing [Agent Name] - Let's Catch Up!
Dear [Subscriber],

It's been some time since we've been in touch, and I wanted to reach out and say hello. As a reminder, my name is [Agent Name] and I am a real estate agent with [Agency Name]. I'm reaching out today because I wanted to provide you with some valuable content and see if there is anything I can do to assist you with your real estate needs.

Here are some recent market updates and industry reports that you may find helpful:

- [Market Update 1]
- [Industry Report 1]

We understand that life gets busy, and that's why we're here to help. If you have any questions or concerns about the real estate market or need

300

any assistance with buying or selling a property, please don't hesitate to reach out to us.

Best regards,
[Agent Signature Block with Contact Information]

Personalization:

Update the Subscriber Name and body with your links and phone numbers where appropriate.

Recommended Agent Action:

Follow up with a phone call to subscribers who reply to the email or express interest in buying or selling a property.

Step 2:

Send an SMS message on day 5 with a friendly reminder that you are available to help with any real estate needs or questions. You can also offer some value-added content such as a guide to local attractions or restaurants to help the lead feel more connected to the area.

Step 2 SMS Template:

Hi [Subscriber], this is [Agent Name] with [Agency Name]. Just wanted to touch base and see if you have any questions or needs regarding the real estate market. Let me know if there's anything I can assist you with. Also, check out this guide to local attractions and restaurants [Link]. Have a great day!

Personalization:

Update the Subscriber Name and body with your links and phone numbers where appropriate.

Recommended Agent Action:

Follow up with a phone call to subscribers who respond to the SMS or express interest in re-engaging. Use the opportunity to listen to their needs and offer personalized solutions that meet their requirements. Also, make sure to update their contact information and preferences in your CRM system to ensure you are reaching out to them in the most effective way possible.

DRIP, DRIP, SOLD

Step 3:

Send an email on day 14 with a subject line "What's New in the Real Estate Market?" In this email, provide updates on the current state of the real estate market, including trends in pricing, inventory, and interest rates. Also, include any recent success stories or testimonials from satisfied clients. This will demonstrate your expertise and remind the subscriber of the value you can provide.

Step 3 Email Template:

Subject: What's New in the Real Estate Market?
Dear [Subscriber],

I hope this email finds you well. As a real estate agent, it's my job to keep you updated on the latest trends and changes in the market. Here are some recent updates you may find helpful:

- Pricing trends: The median home price in our area has increased by [Percentage] since [Date].
- Inventory levels: Currently, there are [Number] homes available for sale in our area, which is [Percentage] higher than this time last year.
- Interest rates: The current interest rate for a [Type of Loan] is [Percentage], which is [Higher/Lower] than last month.

In addition to these updates, I wanted to share a recent success story from one of my clients who found their dream home using my services. [Insert Client Testimonial or Success Story].

If you have any questions or concerns about the current state of the real estate market, don't hesitate to reach out to me. I'm always here to help.

Best regards,
[Agent Signature Block with Contact Information]

Personalization:

Update the Subscriber Name and body with your links and phone numbers where appropriate.

302

Recommended Agent Action:

Follow up with a phone call to subscribers who reply to the email or express interest in re-engaging. Use this opportunity to offer your services and schedule a meeting or consultation to discuss their specific needs.

Step 4:

Send an email on day 28 with a subject line "Are You Still Interested in Real Estate?" In this email, address any potential concerns or objections the subscriber may have, and offer additional resources or information to help them make an informed decision. Also, provide examples of successful deals you have closed and any awards or recognition you have received.

Step 4 Email Template:

Subject: Are You Still Interested in Real Estate?
Dear [Subscriber],

It's been a few weeks since we last spoke, and I wanted to check in and see if you are still interested in the real estate market. I understand that you may have concerns or objections, and I'm here to address any of them. Here are some common concerns and how I can help:

- "I don't have enough money for a down payment." There are many financing options available that require little or no down payment, and I can help you explore them.
- "I'm not sure I'm ready to commit to a mortgage." I can provide you with resources and information to help you make an informed decision.
- "I'm worried about finding the right property." As an experienced agent, I have helped many clients find their dream home, and I'm confident I can help you too.

In addition, I wanted to share some recent success stories with you. [Insert examples of successful deals you have closed, awards or recognition you have received, or positive reviews from satisfied clients.]

If you have any questions or concerns about the real estate market, don't hesitate to reach out to me. I'm always here to help.

Best regards,

[Agent Signature Block with Contact Information]

Personalization:

Update the Subscriber Name and body with your links and phone numbers where appropriate.

Recommended Agent Action:

Follow up with a phone call to subscribers who reply to the email or express interest in exploring their options in the real estate market. Offer to set up a consultation to discuss their needs and concerns. Use the success stories you included in the email to showcase your expertise and build trust with the lead.

Step 5:

Send an SMS message on day 32 with a friendly reminder about an upcoming local event or community activity. This message shows that you're not only knowledgeable about the real estate market but also engaged with the local community, making you a valuable resource for your leads.

Step 5 SMS Template:

Hi [Subscriber], it's [Agent Name] from [Agency Name]. I wanted to let you know about an upcoming event in our community: [Event Name] at [Location] on [Date/Time]. It's a great opportunity to enjoy [A brief description of the event and its benefits]. If you have any questions or need more information, feel free to reach out. Have a great day!

Personalization:

Update the Subscriber Name and body with your event details and any relevant links where appropriate.

Recommended Agent Action:

Monitor responses from subscribers and be prepared to answer any questions they may have about the event or local community. If they express interest in attending, consider joining them at the event to further build rapport and strengthen your relationship. Continue to engage with your leads by sharing valuable resources, offering personalized advice, and keeping them updated on real estate market trends. This consistent and helpful approach will increase your chances of converting these cold leads into active clients.

Step 6:

Send an email on day 35 with a subject line "What's Your Home Worth? Get a Free Home Evaluation!" This email will pique the interest of leads who are considering selling their property by offering a valuable service that helps them determine their home's current market value.

Step 6 Email Template:

Subject: What's Your Home Worth? Get a Free Home Evaluation!
Dear [Subscriber],

Whether you're thinking about selling your property or just curious about its current market value, knowing the worth of your home can be incredibly helpful. That's why I'm offering you a free, no obligation home evaluation to give you an accurate estimate of your property's worth in today's market.

To get started, simply click the link below and fill out the brief form with your property details. I'll then prepare a detailed report for you, including comparisons to other recently sold homes in your area, to help you better understand your home's value.

[Link to Home Evaluation Form]

If you have any questions or need assistance, please don't hesitate to reach out to me. I'm here to help with all your real estate needs!

Best regards,

[Agent Signature Block with Contact Information]

Personalization:

Update the Subscriber Name and body with your links and contact information where appropriate.

Recommended Agent Action:

Follow up with a phone call to subscribers who request a home evaluation or express interest in selling their property. Provide personalized guidance on the best strategies for selling their home, including staging tips, pricing, and marketing tactics. Continue to support them throughout the process,

DRIP, DRIP, SOLD

from preparing their property for sale to negotiating offers and closing the deal. This level of service will help you establish a strong relationship with your leads, ultimately converting them into satisfied clients.

Step 7:

Send a final email on day 30 with a subject line "Your Personal Real Estate Concierge - Here to Help!" This email serves as a reminder of your commitment to assisting your leads with their real estate needs and encourages them to reach out if they have any questions or concerns.

Step 7 Email Template:

Subject: Your Personal Real Estate Concierge - Here to Help!
Dear [Subscriber],

I hope you've found the information I've shared over the past month to be helpful and informative. As your personal real estate concierge, my goal is to provide you with the best possible support and guidance throughout your real estate journey.

Whether you're looking to buy, sell, or simply have questions about the market, I'm always here to help. Please don't hesitate to reach out if you need assistance or if you have any concerns.

To make it easier for you, here's a quick recap of the resources and services I can provide:

- Free home evaluations
- Personalized property searches
- Local market updates
- Expert advice on buying and selling strategies • Assistance with financing and mortgage options
- And much more!

Thank you for considering me as your real estate partner. I look forward to the opportunity to work with you and help you achieve your real estate goals.

Best regards,
[Agent Signature Block with Contact Information]

Personalization:

Update the Subscriber Name and body with your contact information where appropriate.

Recommended Agent Action:

Even after the drip campaign ends, continue to monitor your leads' engagement and follow up with them periodically. It's essential to maintain an open line of communication and be available to assist them whenever they're ready to take action. By providing value and demonstrating your expertise, you'll be their top choice when it comes time to buy or sell a property. Keep nurturing these relationships, and you'll see higher conversion rates and long-term success in your real estate business. If there is no response to this email, it may be best to focus on other leads. However, you can keep the lead on your mailing list and continue to provide valuable content to stay top-of-mind for any future real estate needs.

Tracking the Success of the Rekindling Cold Leads Drip Campaign

To measure the effectiveness of your Rekindling Cold Leads Drip Campaign, it's essential to track specific metrics and analyze the results. This will help you determine whether the campaign is meeting your goals and identify areas for improvement. Here are some key metrics to track:

- Open Rates: Monitor the open rates of your email messages to assess the level of engagement from your cold leads. An increase in open rates indicates that your subject lines and content are capturing the interest of your audience.
- Click-Through Rates (CTR): Track the click-through rates on the links provided within your email and SMS messages. High CTRs indicate that your content is relevant and valuable to the recipients, encouraging them to take action.
- Response Rates: Measure the response rates of your leads, including those who provide their correct phone numbers, reply to your emails or SMS messages, or express interest in re-engaging with your services. High response rates signify that your campaign is effectively re-engaging cold leads.

- Conversion Rates: Track the number of cold leads that ultimately convert into clients by either buying or selling a property with your assistance. This is the most important metric, as it directly reflects the success of your campaign in generating new business.
- Return on Investment (ROI): Calculate the ROI of your campaign by comparing the cost of implementing the drip campaign (including email and SMS service fees, content creation, and time spent) against the revenue generated from converted leads.

To optimize the success of your Rekindling Cold Leads Drip Campaign, regularly review these metrics and make data-driven adjustments to your content, messaging, and follow-up strategies. This will help you fine-tune your campaign, maximize engagement, and ultimately convert more cold leads into clients.

Tips for Customizing the Rekindling Cold Leads Drip Campaign

Customizing the Rekindling Cold Leads Drip Campaign is essential for maximizing its effectiveness and making it resonate with your target audience. Here are some tips to help you personalize the campaign to better engage your cold leads:

- Segment your leads: Group your cold leads based on their preferences, behaviors, or demographics. This will allow you to tailor your messaging and content to address the unique needs and interests of each segment, making the campaign more relevant and engaging.
- Use personalized subject lines and greetings: Include the lead's name in the subject line and greeting of your emails to create a more personal connection. Personalized subject lines have been shown to improve open rates and overall engagement.
- Offer valuable, relevant content: Ensure that the content you share, such as market reports, industry updates, and local guides, is relevant to your leads' interests and needs. Providing valuable information will demonstrate your expertise and commitment to their success.
- Leverage local knowledge: Customize your campaign by incorporating local market trends, property listings, and area-specific

resources. This will show that you have a deep understanding of the community and can provide insights that other agents may not have.
- Test and optimize: Monitor the performance of your campaign and conduct A/B tests to identify the most effective subject lines, content, and follow-up strategies. Continuously refine your campaign based on data-driven insights to maximize engagement and conversions.
- Automate where possible: Use email marketing and CRM platforms to automate the delivery of your campaign, while still maintaining a level of personalization. This will save you time and ensure that your messages are delivered consistently and on schedule.
- Keep track of lead preferences: Update your CRM system with any new information or preferences provided by your leads during the campaign. This will help you better tailor future communications and improve the overall effectiveness of your marketing efforts.

By customizing your Rekindling Cold Leads Drip Campaign and incorporating these tips, you can create a more personalized experience for your leads, increasing the likelihood of re-engaging them and converting them into clients.

Conclusion

The Rekindling Cold Leads Drip Campaign is a powerful tool for real estate agents to reconnect with leads who may have fallen off their radar. By implementing a well-crafted and personalized campaign that utilizes a mix of email and SMS messages, you can reignite interest, showcase your expertise, and provide value to your leads.

To maximize the effectiveness of your campaign, it's essential to segment your leads, offer relevant and valuable content, leverage local knowledge, and continuously optimize your messaging and follow-up strategies. Furthermore, automating the process and tracking key metrics will allow you to efficiently manage your campaign and gauge its success.

By re-engaging your cold leads through this targeted drip campaign, you can build stronger relationships, demonstrate your commitment to their real estate needs, and ultimately convert more leads into clients, boosting your business success in the competitive real estate industry.

29

BEST PRACTICES FOR REAL ESTATE DRIP CAMPAIGN

Drip campaigns play a significant role in engaging and nurturing leads in the real estate industry. They can help you maintain consistent communication with your audience, provide valuable content, and encourage leads to take action. To maximize the success of your drip campaigns, it's essential to follow best practices that align with your audience's needs, preferences, and behaviors. In this section, we will outline several best practices to ensure your real estate drip campaigns are effective and drive increased engagement and conversions.

Tips for Creating Effective Real Estate Drip Campaigns

These are a summary of tips for creating campaigns that work:

- Know Your Target Audience: Understanding your target audience is the foundation for creating successful drip campaigns. Gather information about your leads, such as their preferences, property requirements, and communication preferences. Use this data to segment your leads and create personalized campaigns that resonate with each group.
- Craft Compelling Content: The content of your drip campaigns should be relevant, informative, and engaging. Focus on providing value to your leads by sharing market updates, industry reports, and useful resources. Include strong calls-to-action that encourage leads to take the next step, whether that's scheduling a consultation, attending an open house, or requesting a property valuation.
- Personalize Your Messages: Personalization is key to increasing engagement and conversions. Address your leads by their names,

tailor your messages to their preferences, and use dynamic content to make each message feel unique. This will help your leads feel more connected to your brand and increase the likelihood of them taking action.

- Test and Optimize: Continually test and optimize your drip campaigns for maximum performance. Experiment with different subject lines, email designs, and content types to determine what resonates best with your audience. Use analytics to track the performance of your campaigns, and make data-driven adjustments as needed.
- Monitor and Adjust Frequency: The frequency of your drip campaign messages can significantly impact engagement and conversions. Avoid overwhelming your leads with too many messages, and find the optimal frequency that keeps your leads engaged without causing fatigue. Monitor your campaign metrics and adjust the frequency as needed based on your audience's response.
- Leverage Marketing Automation: Marketing automation platforms can streamline the creation, execution, and analysis of your drip campaigns. By automating time-consuming tasks and providing actionable insights, these platforms allow you to focus on crafting compelling content and nurturing your leads more effectively.
- Analyze Campaign Performance: Regularly reviewing your campaign performance is crucial for understanding what works and what doesn't. Track key metrics, such as open rates, click-through rates, and conversion rates, to identify areas for improvement. Use these insights to optimize your campaigns and drive better results.

By following these best practices, you can create highly effective real estate drip campaigns that engage and nurture your leads. Understanding your target audience, crafting compelling content, personalizing your messages, and leveraging marketing automation are all essential components of a successful drip campaign. Continuously analyze and optimize your campaigns to ensure they deliver the desired results and help you build lasting relationships with your leads.

Choosing the Right Type of Drip Campaign for Your Audience

Selecting the appropriate drip campaign for your audience in real estate is a nuanced process. It involves understanding your audience's unique needs and preferences and tailoring your campaign to address these effectively. Here's a comprehensive guide to help you choose the right type of drip campaign for your audience:

Analyze Your Audience

- Demographics and Preferences: Start by analyzing the demographics of your audience, including age, location, and economic status. Understanding their preferences, such as communication style (email vs. SMS), is also crucial.
- Buying Stage and Intent: Determine the stage your audience is in their buying journey. Are they early-stage researchers, actively looking to buy, or considering selling their property? Their stage dictates the type of information they need.

Define Your Objectives

- Awareness, Education, or Conversion: Define what you want to achieve with your campaign. Are you looking to build brand awareness, educate potential clients, or drive conversions? Your goal will guide your campaign type.

Choose the Campaign Type

- Educational Campaigns for Early-Stage Leads: If your audience is at the early stage of buying or selling, consider educational campaigns. Provide valuable information, guides, and tips relevant to the real estate process.
- Listing Updates for Active Buyers: For leads actively seeking properties, a campaign focusing on new listings, open houses, and price changes will keep them engaged and informed.
- Market Updates for Sellers and Investors: If your audience consists of sellers or investors, periodic market updates about pricing trends, market conditions, and investment opportunities are valuable.

DRIP, DRIP, SOLD

- Testimonial and Success Story Campaigns for Trust Building: Share success stories and testimonials to build trust among potential clients who are considering your services.
- Post-Transaction Campaigns for Ongoing Engagement: After a transaction, continue to engage clients with content that helps them in their new phase of homeownership. This can include home maintenance tips, local community events, and annual market analysis. These campaigns help maintain a strong relationship, encouraging repeat business and referrals.

Personalization is Key

- Tailor Content to Needs: Customize your content based on the client's specific needs and interests. Personalized content resonates more and can drive better engagement.
- Use Data Effectively: Utilize CRM data to segment your audience and tailor campaigns accordingly. This could involve different messages for first-time buyers versus repeat clients.

Engagement and Follow-Up

- Interactive Content: Use interactive content like quizzes, polls, or surveys in your campaigns to engage your audience and gather more insights about their preferences.
- Prompt Follow-Up: Set up a system for prompt follow-ups based on the responses or interactions with your campaign. Personal interaction can significantly boost conversion rates.

Measure and Optimize

- Track Performance Metrics: Monitor open rates, click-through rates, and conversion rates to understand how your campaigns are performing.
- Adjust Based on Feedback: Be prepared to adjust your campaigns based on the feedback and data. What works for one segment may not work for another.

Choosing the right type of drip campaign requires a deep understanding of your audience and a clear definition of your marketing objectives.

314

By aligning your campaign strategy with the needs and preferences of your audience, and continuously refining your approach based on performance data, you can effectively engage, nurture, and convert leads in the real estate market. Remember, the most successful drip campaigns are those that resonate personally with the recipient and add real value to their real estate journey.

How to Analyze and Adjust Your Drip Campaigns for Maximum Effectiveness

Effective analysis and adjustment of your drip campaigns are essential for achieving maximum impact in the real estate market. This process involves a continuous cycle of monitoring, evaluating, and refining your strategies. Here's a guide to help you optimize your drip campaigns for peak performance:

Step 1: Set Clear Goals and Key Performance Indicators (KPIs)

- Define Campaign Objectives: Establish what you aim to achieve with each campaign - be it lead generation, client engagement, or post-transaction relationships.
- Identify Relevant KPIs: Choose KPIs that align with your objectives, such as open rates, click-through rates, conversion rates, and lead quality.

Step 2: Collect and Analyze Data

- Utilize Analytics Tools: Implement tools to track and analyze the performance of your campaigns. This can include email marketing software analytics, CRM tracking, or specialized marketing analysis tools.
- Monitor Engagement Metrics: Pay close attention to open rates, click-through rates, and engagement time. Low engagement may indicate issues with content relevance or email subject lines.

Step 3: Assess Lead Quality and Conversion Rates

- Track Lead Progression: Monitor how leads move through the sales funnel post-campaign. Are they converting at the expected rate?

- Evaluate Lead Quality: Assess the quality of leads generated. High-quality leads are more likely to engage with your content and move further along the sales funnel.

Step 4: Seek Feedback and Conduct Surveys
- Direct Feedback from Clients: Reach out to clients for their feedback on your campaign content and its relevance to their needs.
- Surveys and Questionnaires: Conduct surveys or questionnaires to gather broader insights from your audience.

Step 5: Test and Experiment
A/B Testing: Experiment with different aspects of your emails, such as subject lines, content formats, and call-to-action buttons. This helps identify what resonates best with your audience.
- Segmentation Tests: Test different content with various audience segments to determine the most effective strategies for each group.

Step 6: Make Informed Adjustments
- Refine Content and Messaging: Based on your analysis, adjust the content, tone, and messaging of your campaigns to better suit your audience's preferences.
- Optimize Sending Times and Frequency: Adjust the timing and frequency of your campaigns based on when your audience is most responsive.

Step 7: Implement Changes and Monitor Results
- Apply Adjustments: Implement the changes based on your analysis and observations.
- Continuous Monitoring: Continuously monitor the performance post-adjustment to assess the impact of your changes.

Step 8: Stay Updated with Market Trends
- Market Awareness: Keep abreast of changing real estate market trends and adjust your campaigns accordingly to remain relevant and effective.
- Analyzing and adjusting your drip campaigns is a dynamic and ongoing process. It requires a keen understanding of your audience,

a willingness to experiment, and a commitment to continuous improvement. By regularly assessing and refining your approach, you can ensure that your drip campaigns remain effective tools for engaging clients, nurturing leads, and growing your real estate business.

Conclusion

Real estate drip campaigns are a cornerstone of effective marketing, allowing agents to engage leads, nurture relationships, and build long-term client loyalty. By implementing the best practices outlined in this chapter, you can transform your campaigns into powerful tools that drive meaningful results.

The foundation of a successful drip campaign lies in understanding your audience. Tailoring content to their needs, preferences, and stage in the real estate journey ensures relevance and increases engagement. Personalization, compelling content, and clear calls-to-action further enhance the effectiveness of your campaigns.

Consistency and strategic use of automation streamline your marketing efforts while maintaining a personal touch. Regular analysis and optimization of your campaigns ensure they stay aligned with your goals and audience expectations. Metrics like open rates, click-through rates, and conversion rates provide actionable insights to refine your approach.

Ultimately, the success of your real estate drip campaigns depends on their ability to resonate with your audience and add value to their journey. By committing to these best practices, you position yourself as a trusted, knowledgeable real estate professional who consistently delivers an exceptional client experience.

DRIP, DRIP, SOLD

30

LEAD CONVERSIONS IN DRIP CAMPAIGN

Integrating lead conversion strategies into your drip campaigns is pivotal for turning prospects into clients in real estate. A well-structured drip campaign not only nurtures leads but also gently guides them towards making a decision. Here's how you can enhance lead conversion through your drip campaigns.

Understanding Lead Conversion

- Lead Conversion Defined: Lead conversion in real estate is the process of transforming potential leads into active clients who are ready to buy, sell, or invest in property. It's a crucial measure of the effectiveness of your marketing efforts.
- Importance in Real Estate: In a competitive market, effective lead conversion strategies set successful real estate agents apart from the rest. It's not just about attracting leads, but about converting them into revenue-generating clients.

Strategies for Enhancing Lead Conversion

Targeted Content: Deliver content that addresses the specific concerns and interests of your leads. For instance, send detailed guides on the home buying process to first-time buyers, and investment analysis to real estate investors.

- Consistent Engagement: Keep your leads engaged with regular updates. Consistency in communication builds trust and keeps you top-of-mind, increasing the likelihood of conversion.

DRIP, DRIP, SOLD

- Personalization: Use the data you have about your leads to personalize your communications. Personalized messages have a higher engagement and conversion rate.
- Call-to-Actions (CTAs): Incorporate clear and compelling CTAs in your drip campaigns. Encourage your leads to take the next step, be it scheduling a viewing, attending an open house, or setting up a consultation.
- Follow-Up Strategies: Automate follow-ups based on lead interactions. For instance, if a lead clicks on a property link, follow up with more information on similar properties or an invitation for a showing.

Measuring and Optimizing Lead Conversion

Conversion Rate Tracking: Keep track of how many leads convert into clients. Use this data to measure the effectiveness of your drip campaigns.

- A/B Testing: Experiment with different email formats, subject lines, content types, and sending times to see what works best for your audience.
- Feedback Loops: Encourage feedback from leads and clients. This feedback can provide valuable insights into what's working and what's not.
- Continuous Improvement: Use analytics and feedback to continuously refine your drip campaigns for better lead conversion.

Conclusion

Incorporating lead conversion strategies into your drip campaigns is essential for success in the real estate industry. By understanding your audience, delivering targeted and personalized content, engaging consistently, and optimizing based on performance, you can effectively convert leads into loyal clients. The key lies in maintaining a balance between informative content and persuasive calls to action, ensuring that each interaction moves the lead closer to a decision. With a focus on lead conversion, your drip campaigns can become a powerful tool in your real estate marketing arsenal.

31

THE ROLE OF AI IN CRAFTING "DRIP DRIP SOLD"

D rip Drip Sold" is a comprehensive guidebook designed to help real estate professionals master the art of drip campaigns. A significant aspect of this guidebook's development involved leveraging advanced AI technology. This chapter not only reveals AI's role in the book's development, but also highlights its transformative impact in the broader realm of real estate marketing. In an era where Artificial Intelligence is reshaping industries, its application in creating "Drip Drip Sold" exemplifies the synergy of technology and human expertise.

AI's Contribution to the Book

AI technology was instrumental in various stages of creating "Drip Drip Sold." This included:

- Strategic Timing and Data Analysis for Effective Campaigns: AI algorithms play a pivotal role in the strategic timing of email and SMS messages, analyzing vast data sets to pinpoint the most effective times for sending communications, thereby ensuring higher open and response rates. Concurrently, these algorithms excel in data analysis and pattern recognition, processing extensive amounts of information to identify successful patterns and trends in real estate drip campaigns. This dual capability of AI allows for the integration of proven strategies and optimal timing, making each campaign not only more relevant but also more likely to engage the target audience at the most opportune moments.

- Content Generation and Assistance: AI tools have been instrumental in drafting the content of "Drip Drip Sold," ensuring that not only is the language tailored for impact but also the structure and format of the campaigns are optimized for maximum lead engagement and conversion. By evaluating successful campaign formats, AI suggests structures and layouts most likely to capture attention and prompt decisive action from leads. This approach harmonizes content creation with strategic design, ensuring that every aspect of the campaigns is finely tuned to meet the needs and preferences of the target audience effectively.
- Language Optimization for Engagement: Utilizing the sophisticated techniques of natural language processing, AI plays a pivotal role in refining the language used in our templates to deeply resonate with the intended audience. This optimization is key in boosting engagement and enhancing the potential for lead conversion. Furthermore, AI's capabilities extend to structuring the content in a manner that is not only efficient but also easily digestible, ensuring that readers can effortlessly grasp and apply the information presented. This seamless integration of language and structure is crucial in making "Drip Drip Sold" a user-friendly and effective guide for real estate professionals.

Expanding the Role of AI in Real Estate: Insights from "Drip Drip Sold"

The utilization of AI in "Drip Drip Sold" is indicative of its increasingly integral role in the real estate sector:

- AI Chatbots for Enhanced Client Engagement: AI chatbots, integrated into real estate websites, offer immediate and round-the-clock client interaction. These advanced chatbots are equipped to handle a wide array of inquiries, from scheduling appointments to providing specific property details. This not only improves customer service efficiency but also significantly boosts lead generation efforts.
- Data-Driven Insights for Refined Marketing Strategies: The core of AI's impact lies in its ability to meticulously analyze large datasets. In the context of "Drip Drip Sold," this capability was vital for pinpointing successful patterns and strategies in drip campaigns.

This ensures that the guidebook's strategies are not only based on solid data but also fine-tuned for effectiveness.

- Predictive Analytics for Market Foresight: AI's predictive analysis tools empower real estate professionals with the ability to anticipate market trends, property valuations, and even client behaviors.

This foresight is crucial for strategic planning and allows for more targeted and effective marketing campaigns.

- Personalization at Scale with AI: One of the standout features of AI in real estate marketing, as showcased in "Drip Drip Sold," is the ability to personalize communication on a large scale. AI tools can tailor marketing efforts to meet the specific needs and preferences of individual clients, thereby enhancing the relevance and impact of each communication.
- Automated Valuation Models (AVMs): AI-driven AVMs provide real estate professionals with quick property valuations, utilizing historical data and current market trends. This aids in accurate pricing strategies and market analysis.
- Virtual Property Tours and AI Imaging: AI has revolutionized property showcasing with virtual tours and enhanced imaging techniques. This not only makes properties more accessible to potential buyers but also offers a more engaging viewing experience.
- Efficiency in Property Management: For real estate agents dealing with property management, AI systems can automate and streamline tasks like rent collection, maintenance scheduling, and tenant communication, leading to enhanced operational efficiency.
- Integration with Smart Home Technologies: AI's synergy with smart home technology provides real estate professionals with additional selling points, emphasizing convenience, safety, and energy efficiency in modern homes.

The integration of AI in "Drip Drip Sold" is not just a testament to the technology's current capabilities but also a glimpse into its potential to transform the real estate industry in more profound ways. As AI continues to evolve, its applications in real estate are expected to expand, bringing more innovative solutions and strategies to the forefront.

Conclusion

- "Drip Drip Sold" represents a pioneering integration of AI technology with real estate expertise, illustrating a forward-thinking approach in creating a comprehensive guidebook for real estate professionals. This chapter provides insights into the significant role AI played in the development of the guide, emphasizing its critical contribution to enhancing the content's accuracy, relevance, and practicality.

- Rationale Behind AI's Use: The decision to incorporate AI into the creation of "Drip Drip Sold" was driven by the goal to offer the most effective and up-to-date strategies in real estate marketing. AI's involvement ranged from analyzing large datasets for optimal campaign timing to refining the language and structure of content. This strategic use of AI ensures that the guidebook is not only rich in quality but also resonates with current industry trends and practices.

- AI's Transformative Role in Real Estate: The application of AI in "Drip Drip Sold" reflects its broader, transformative impact on the real estate industry. The book mirrors the extensive use of AI in various real estate facets, such as chatbots for improved client interactions, predictive analytics for market foresight, and AI-driven tools for personalizing marketing efforts at scale. These examples highlight AI's capacity to revolutionize industry practices, offering more efficient, accurate, and client focused solutions.

- Looking Ahead: AI as a Catalyst in Real Estate: The integration of AI in this guidebook is indicative of its expanding role in the real estate sector. From optimizing property management tasks to enhancing property showcasing with virtual tours, AI is poised to introduce more innovative solutions and strategies. "Drip Drip Sold" serves as an example of how embracing AI can lead to a deeper understanding and more proficient application of real estate marketing strategies.

- Commitment to Excellence: The inclusion of AI in the development of "Drip Drip Sold" aligns with a commitment to excellence. It ensures that the guidebook is a cutting-edge resource, equipped with data-backed strategies and insights. This approach not only enhances the guide's utility but also positions it as a leading resource in an industry that is increasingly influenced by technological advancements.

In sum, "Drip Drip Sold" exemplifies the effective synergy of AI and expert knowledge in the realm of real estate marketing. It stands as a testament to the progressive application of technology in enhancing professional resources, ensuring that real estate agents are equipped with the most current and effective tools for success. As the real estate landscape continues to evolve, AI's role in shaping industry practices and resources will undoubtedly expand, ushering in a new era of innovation and efficiency.

32

NAVIGATING LEGAL AND ETHICAL GUIDELINES

This chapter delves into the vital legal and ethical aspects of real estate drip campaigns. While CRM and email marketing tools offer helpful compliance features, it's imperative to understand and actively manage these aspects.

1. Understanding Consent in Communication:

Obtaining consent for communication is critical. While CRM and email tools track consent, the responsibility for legal compliance rests with the user.

Actionable Tips:

- Use CRM features to document consent accurately.
- Regularly update your understanding and practice of consent acquisition.

2. Opt-Out Mechanisms:

Ensure your CRM and email tools provide clear, functional opt-out mechanisms in all communications.

Actionable Tips:

- Verify the visibility and functionality of opt-out links.
- Utilize software features to manage opt-out requests efficiently.

3. Data Protection and Privacy:

Your software should align with data protection laws, but configuration and management are key.

Actionable Tips:

- Configure software settings according to privacy laws.
- Stay updated on data protection regulations.

4. Ethical Marketing Practices:

Content compliance is a user responsibility. Ensure your content is ethical and truthful.

Actionable Tips:

- Perform regular content reviews.
- Educate yourself on marketing and advertising laws.

5. Staying Informed and Updated:

Laws and software change. Stay informed and conduct compliance audits.

Actionable Tips:

- Monitor legal developments.
- Schedule regular audits of your marketing practices.

6. Leveraging CRM and Email Software Responsibly:

Use these tools as part of a larger responsible marketing strategy.

Actionable Tips:

- Understand and manage the compliance features of your software.
- Combine software capabilities with legal and ethical knowledge.

7. Consulting Legal Professionals:

If you have any doubts about the legality of your marketing practices, consult with an attorney specializing in this area. Legal professionals can provide tailored advice and ensure your campaign aligns with current laws.

Disclaimer

This chapter is intended for informational purposes only and does not constitute legal advice. Laws and regulations can vary by jurisdiction and are subject to change. Always seek professional legal counsel for specific legal issues or concerns.

Conclusion

CRM and email marketing tools can be great assets in ensuring your real estate drip campaigns comply with legal and ethical standards. However, it's essential to actively manage these tools, stay informed, and seek professional advice when necessary. This approach will help you build campaigns that are not only effective but also legally sound and ethically responsible. From ensuring adherence to anti-spam laws like the CAN-SPAM Act to respecting client privacy and data security, this chapter provides actionable guidance to help you create campaigns to do just that. By prioritizing these aspects, you'll build trust with your audience and maintain a reputation of professionalism and integrity in your real estate practice.

33

CONCLUSION: POWER OF REAL ESTATE DRIP CAMPAIGNS

As we reflect on the transformative insights presented in this guide, it becomes clear that real estate drip campaigns are not just beneficial—they are essential. These campaigns represent the cutting edge of real estate marketing, a testament to the evolution and competitiveness of today's market. Here, we encapsulate the unparalleled advantages they offer.

- Unmatched Engagement and Efficiency: Real estate drip campaigns epitomize the pinnacle of client engagement. They enable realtors to maintain continuous, effective communication with clients and leads. This consistent engagement, automated yet personalized, ensures that realtors stay at the forefront of clients' minds, crucial in today's fast-paced market.
- Cost-Effectiveness Meets Market Reach: Drip campaigns redefine the cost-to-benefit equation in real estate marketing. By delivering impactful messages at a fraction of the cost of traditional marketing, they allow realtors to extend their reach exponentially, ensuring that no potential lead is left untouched.
- Unrivaled Personalization: The ability to tailor messages to the specific needs and interests of each client is where drip campaigns truly shine. This personalization fosters a deeper connection between realtors and their clients, paving the way for more meaningful interactions and enhanced client loyalty.
- Optimization of Time and Resources: Drip campaigns are a boon in terms of time management and resource allocation. By automating repetitive tasks, they free up valuable time for realtors,

DRIP, DRIP, SOLD

allowing them to concentrate on high-impact activities like closing deals and expanding their network.

- Superior Lead Nurturing and Conversion: The strategic nurturing of leads through tailored information and regular check-ins transforms prospects into clients. Drip campaigns serve as a powerful tool in converting leads, gently guiding potential clients through the buying or selling journey with consistent, relevant information.

The journey through the benefits of drip campaigns reaffirms their status as a cornerstone in the real estate industry. They are more than tools; they are catalysts for success, empowering real estate professionals to exceed in a highly competitive landscape. This book has laid out not just the 'how-to's' but the 'must-dos' for thriving in modern real estate through effective drip campaigns.

How to Use Real Estate Drip Campaigns to Build Relationships and Close More Deals

The power of drip campaigns in forging lasting relationships and closing deals cannot be overstated. As underscored throughout this guide, these campaigns are the heartbeat of successful real estate practices. They are the bridges that connect agents to clients, transforming prospects into successful closings. By truly understanding these campaigns' potential outlined below, realtors can create meaningful connections with clients, streamline their journey, and transform satisfaction into long-term success.

- Foundation of Trust and Credibility: Trust is the bedrock of successful real estate transactions. Drip campaigns help establish and cement this trust by positioning realtors as reliable sources of valuable information, thereby enhancing their credibility and reputation in the market.
- Deep Understanding and Client Satisfaction: By providing content that aligns with clients' specific needs and preferences, drip campaigns demonstrate a realtor's commitment to understanding and addressing individual client concerns, thereby elevating client satisfaction.

CONCLUSION: POWER OF REAL ESTATE DRIP CAMPAIGNS

- Enhancement of the Client Journey: From initial interest to final transaction, drip campaigns enrich the client's journey. They offer timely information, guidance, and reassurance, making the complex process of buying or selling property smoother and more enjoyable.
- Generation of Valuable Referrals: Satisfied clients are the best sources of new business. Through effective drip campaigns that keep past clients informed and engaged, realtors can encourage a steady stream of referrals, fueling business growth.

The effectiveness of drip campaigns in nurturing relationships and facilitating deal closures is an undeniable truth in today's real estate narrative. Each chapter in this guide has built upon this truth, illustrating drip campaigns as indispensable in cultivating a prosperous and enduring real estate career.

Importance of Selecting the Right Type of Drip Campaign for Your Business

In a market as dynamic and competitive as real estate, selecting the right type of drip campaign is not just a strategy—it's a necessity. This guide has illuminated the path to choosing campaigns that resonate deeply with your audience and align seamlessly with your business goals, ensuring you stay ahead in the game.

Incorporating the right drip campaign into your real estate marketing strategy can make the difference between blending in and standing out. By focusing on the key elements below, you can ensure your campaigns are not only effective but also tailored to meet your audience's needs and your business objectives.

- Strategic Audience Analysis: Understanding the demographics, preferences, and behaviors of your target audience is crucial. This knowledge enables realtors to select drip campaigns that resonate most strongly with their specific audience segments, ensuring maximum impact.
- Alignment with Business Ambitions: Aligning drip campaigns with your overarching business goals - whether it's brand building, lead generation, or client retention - is key to achieving desired outcomes and driving business growth.

- Ensuring Content Resonates: The content of drip campaigns must be carefully crafted to address the interests and needs of the audience. Whether it's market insights for investors or neighborhood guides for first-time buyers, the content should provide real value to recipients.
- Adaptability in a Fluid Market: The real estate market is ever-changing. Selecting drip campaigns that can be quickly adapted to shifting market conditions and trends ensures that realtors remain relevant and effective in their communication strategies.

The essence of this guide culminates in understanding the profound impact of selecting the appropriate drip campaign. It's a decision that shapes your business's future, positioning you not just as a participant in the real estate market but as a frontrunner. Drip campaigns, as we've seen, are not just parts of the real estate toolkit; they are the very lifelines of a thriving real estate practice in today's market.

Closing

In concluding this guide on real estate drip campaigns, it's clear that these tools are more than just a marketing strategy; they're an essential component for success in today's real estate market. This journey has equipped you with the knowledge and skills to effectively utilize drip campaigns, ensuring that your approach to real estate marketing is both modern and efficient.

Drip campaigns stand out as a key asset in the realtor's toolkit, offering a unique blend of consistent communication, client engagement, and market adaptability. They are essential for nurturing leads, building lasting client relationships, and staying competitive in an ever-evolving industry.

As you move forward, implementing the insights and tactics from this guide, remember the power of personalization, the importance of aligning campaigns with your specific business goals, and the need for ongoing adaptation to market changes and client feedback.

May this guide serve as a valuable resource in your journey to leverage drip campaigns for building a robust, responsive, and successful real estate practice. Here's to harnessing the potential of drip campaigns to achieve new heights in your real estate career.

GLOSSARY

A/B Testing: Comparing two versions of a webpage, email, or SMS message to determine the better performer.

Analytics: Computational analysis of data for evaluating marketing campaign effectiveness.

Automated Valuation Models (AVMs): AI-driven tools used for property valuations.

Call-to-Actions (CTAs): A prompt in an email or SMS message that encourages specific action.

Click-Through Rates (CTR): The ratio of users who click on a specific link to the number of total users who view an email or SMS message.

Client Engagement: Building relationships with potential or current clients through regular, targeted communication.

Client Journey: The complete experience a client goes through with a real estate business or agent.

Client Satisfaction Surveys: Measuring clients' satisfaction with services and experiences.

Content Generation: Creating material like text, images, and videos for marketing.

Conversion Rates: The percentage of recipients who complete a desired action after receiving a drip campaign message.

Customer Lifetime Value (CLV): The total revenue a business can expect to earn from a single customer throughout the entire duration of their relationship. In real estate, CLV reflects the value of repeat business, referrals, and long-term client relationships generated through exceptional service and strategic marketing efforts.

Customer Relationship Management (CRM): Technology for managing interactions with potential and current clients.

335

Data-Driven Insights: Conclusions from data analysis in marketing campaigns.

Drip Campaign: A set of marketing emails or SMS messages sent out automatically on a schedule.

Email Marketing Software: Software for managing email marketing campaigns.

Interactive Content: Content that encourages active participation, like polls or quizzes.

Lead: a potential client who has expressed interest in buying, selling, or renting a property and has provided contact information for follow-up.

Lead Conversion: Transforming potential leads into active clients in real estate.

Lead Nurturing: Developing relationships with buyers at every sales funnel stage.

Market Analysis: Examining the real estate market to understand trends and make decisions.

Market Foresight: Predicting future market trends, often facilitated by AI and data analysis.

Market Updates: Information about current trends in the real estate market.

Nurture: the process of building relationships with potential clients over time through personalized communication and valuable content to guide them toward a buying or selling decision and/or referral.

Open Rates: The percentage of email recipients who open an email.

Personalization: Customizing content in drip campaigns to address the specific needs and interests of the recipient.

Post-Transaction Campaigns: Maintaining relationships with clients after a sale.

Referral Generation: Encouraging clients to recommend services to others.

Response Rates: The number of responses received from marketing campaign recipients.

Return on Investment (ROI): A measure of the efficiency of an investment in marketing campaigns.

Segmentation: Dividing a target audience into subgroups based on criteria such as behavior or demographics.

SMS Engagement: Interaction and response rates to SMS messages in a drip campaign.

Target Audience: The intended group of people for a drip campaign.

Virtual Property Tours: Digital tours of a property using virtual reality or video technology.

DRIP, DRIP, SOLD

www.ingramcontent.com/pod-product-compliance
Lightning Source LLC
Chambersburg PA
CBHW070416230125

20710CB00012B/346